PARTITION OF INDIA AND ITS IMPACT ON THE SCHEDULED CASTES OF BENGAL

PARTITION OF INDIA AND ITS IMPACT ON THE SCHEDULED CASTES OF BENGAL

Rup Kumar Barman

ABHIJEET PUBLICATIONS
NEW DELHI 110002

ABHIJEET PUBLICATIONS
4658-A, 21 Ansari Road, New Delhi 110002
Phone: 011-22960492, 65698474
E-mail: abhijeetpublication@gmail.com

PARTITION OF INDIA AND ITS IMPACT ON THE SCHEDULED CASTES OF BENGAL

First Published 2012

ISBN 978-93-81136-58-4

PRINTED IN INDIA

Published by J.K. Singh for Abhijeet Publications, New Delhi-110002, Lasertypeset by Gaurav Graphics, Delhi and Printed at Himanshu Printers, Delhi.

Dedicated
To the victims of Partition of India

Preface

In the recent years 'development-induced displacement' and rehabilitation of the 'forced migrants' have become significant issues all across the world where India is no exception. But immediately after the partition (in 1947), India was not properly ready to deal with the flow of 'conflict-induced forced migrants' mainly as 'refugees' and 'asylum seekers' from erstwhile East Pakistan (East Bengal). Experience of the refugees from East Pakistan was thus full with misery, atrocities and ill-treatment in post-partitioned India. Again the Scheduled Castes of North Bengal, inspite of not being refugees (rather as hosts); have appeared as worst sufferers of the partition of 1947. These aspects of partition of India obviously require intensive researches. Keeping this historical necessity in mind I undertook a Major Research Project titled *Impact of Partition of India (1947) on the Scheduled Castes of Eastern India with Special References to West Bengal,* sponsored by the Indian Council of Social Science Research (ICSSR, New Delhi) in 2008. This work is the ultimate outcome of the said project.

In this work I dealt with some basic questions. First question is 'how far the Scheduled Castes of Bengal have been placed in the historical writings on Partition of India?' Secondly I reviewed the socioeconomic status of the Scheduled Castes of pre-partition Bengal in order to understand the impact of partition on them. Third question of this work is 'how the partition did generate the forces of 'forced migration' that strengthened the flow of migration of the minorities from East Pakistan to India?' Here I also dealt with the rehabilitation policy of the Government of West Bengal and the Union Government of India. Fourth question of the present study is 'how far did the refugee Scheduled Castes face severe troubles in their rehabilitation?' In this connection I have also examined the nature of treatment of the host government(s) and the society towards them. 'Did the migration from East Pakistan led to the growth of regional movement in North Bengal propelled by the Scheduled Castes?' is the fifth question of this study. However, I could not deal with the issues like impact of the partition on the cultural lives of the Scheduled Castes.

I am grateful to the ICSSR for its financial assistance. In this occasion I like to express my gratitude to the officers and staffs of the ICSSR for their active cooperation with me. I am also grateful to the officials and staffs of the Research Section, Office of the Registrar, Office of the Deputy Registrar (Academic) and Office of the Finance Officer of Jadavpur University, Kolkata; who took all official burdens to operate this project.

Printed source materials of the present study have been collected from different archives, libraries and institutions. I am grateful to several libraries and academic institutions and their staffs such as, Central Library, Jadavpur University; Library of the Department of International Relations, Jadavpur University; National Library, Kolkata; Cultural Research Institute, Kolkata; Center for Studies in Social Sciences, Kolkata, North Bengal State Library, Cooch Behar; West Bengal State Archives, Kolkata; Anthropological Survey of India, Eastern Region, Kolkata; West Bengal Secretariat Library, Kolkata; Sub-Divisional Library, Alipurduar; Bureau of Statistics, Government of West Bengal, Kolkata; and so on.

I have collected oral data from different districts of West Bengal and Assam. In order to generalize the whole issue I took interviews of the persons of East Bengal origin from some districts of West Bengal like Nadia, Murshidabad, North 24 Parganas, South 24 Parganas, Cooch Behar, West Midnapur and North Dinajpur. I have also conducted filed survey in different villages having huge concentration of the local (non-displaced) Scheduled Castes in order to understand the attitude of the hosts to the immigrants. Collection of data through fieldworks and interviews became easier to me due to the active participation of my students particularly Miss Channamma Mondal (Research Assistant of the Project), Shri Rajesh Biswas, Shri Bivas Haldar, Shri Ankan Ray, Shri Bimal Chandra Barman, Shri Mrityunjoy Pramanik, Shri Niren Barman, Shri Bholanath Mondal and Sonali Naskar.

I am also grateful to those persons who expressed their feelings about the partition of Bengal of 1947 and its impact on them. Here I like to express my gratitude to Mr. Niranjan Haldar, Mr. R.S. Barman, Late Susanta Haldar, Smt. Renuka Barma and Smt. Arati Barman, my mother; who clarified many points of my present research by telling some untold stories of condition of the Scheduled Castes of erstwhile East Pakistan.

I am also grateful to my colleagues of the Department of International Relations and the Department of History of Jadavpur University, Kolkata. Prof. Alok Kumar Ghosh, being a notable scholar on the present subject; has actively encouraged my study. Prof. Debi Chatterje, editor of the *Voice of Dalit* and Professor of the Department of International Relations, Jadavpur University; has provided me with an opportunity to publish some of the findings of the present study in the *Voice of Dalit*. Prof. Ranjan Chakraborty, Coordinator of the UGC- SAP of the Department of History, has invited me to present my ideas in a National Workshop on *Nature Transformed: Ecology, Environment and Conservation in Global and South Asian History*, Department of History, Jadavpur University, February 23-24, 2011. I have also shared my ideas on the present research with the participants of the *Annual International Seminar* of the Itihas Academy, Dhaka, 18th February 2011; and Annual National Seminar on *Colonial and Post-Colonial Eastern India: New Perspectives,* 2nd and 3rd March 2011, Department of History, Rabindra Bharati University,

Kolkata. I am indebted to all of them. Dr. Sudeshna Banerjee, Dr. Tridib Santapa Kundu, Dr. Chandrani Banerjee Mukherjee, Prof. Omprakash Misra and Prof. Juthika Barma have always encouraged me to complete the work in due time. I am indebted to them.

Last but not the least; I am grateful to my students of the Department of International Relations, Jadavpur University; for their active interactions with my studies on post-partition forced migration. For any queries, critical comments and suggestion the author is available at *rupkumarbarman@gmail.com*.

Rup Kumar Barman
Associate Professor,
Department of History
&
Coordinator,
Centre for Ambedkar Studies
Jadavpur University
Kolkata 700032

Contents

Glossary

Adhiar	= Sharecropper
Antaja	= Marginal people
Aratdar	= Commission agent
Arjal	= Lower caste Muslims who have been identified as Other Backward Castes.
Asprishya	= Untouchable
Asouch	= Ceremonial pollution
Baor	= Floodplain lake
Beel	= Floodplain lake
Bhadralok	= Gentlemen
Bideshi	= Foreigner
Bideshi kheda	= Expulsion of the foreigners
Bhatia khedao	= A slogan for expulsion of the East Bengali immigrants and refugees
Brahman	= Brahmin or the priestly caste having top position in the Hindu caste hierarchy
Chakladar	= A holder of *chakla* land or tenure holder

Chhilka	=	Proverb/Proverbial rhymes
Chukanidar	=	A intermediary between the *zamindar*/ state and the cultivator
Chunari	=	producer of lime
Deshi	=	Indigenous
Dewani/Dewnia/Giri	=	An independent peasant of Cooch Behar region who had the capacity of supplying cattle and seed to the tillers.
Direct Action	=	A Programme of the Muslim League for achieving Pakistan just before the partition of India.
Duilay/Duliya/Dule	=	Palanquin bearer
Gana Anasan	=	Mass hunger
Harijan	=	Untouchables of India who have been designated as *harijan* by Mahatma Gandhi
Islamization	=	Process of conversion of the Non-Islamic people into the faith of Islam
Izara	=	Lease
Izaradar	=	Lease holder
Jadu palang	=	A kind of wild grass
Jal jar jala tar	=	Fisheries for fishermen, a slogan raised by the fishermen of West Bengal
Jotedar	=	Holder of a *jote* land, an intermediary between the cultivator and *zamindar*/ chukanidar
Halua	=	Ploughman
Haat	=	Weekley market place
Kamla	=	Ordinary agricultural labourer
Khas	=	Vested
Kshatriya	=	Warrior caste having second position in the Hindu caste hierarchy

Kshatriyaization	=	Process of elevation of the non-Kshatriya people to the status of the Kshatriyas
Mouza	=	Revenue yielding village
Kuvachaka	=	Evil speaker
Nikari	=	Fish trader/commission agent/ intermediary between the fishermen and the fish retailers.
Paikar	=	Intermediary between the producer the retailer
Puja	=	Worship
Shastra	=	Religious Texts
Sraddha	=	An after death ceremony for breaking ceremonial pollution.
Sudra	=	Forth caste of the Hindu caste hierarchy having degraded social position.
Swadeshi	=	A popular movement developed in India as a protest against the partition of Bengal in 1905
Tal	=	palm tree
Talukdar	=	Holder of a *taluk* or tenure holder
Tari	=	Intoxicated juice of palm tree
Udvastu	=	Refugee
Vaishya	=	Cultivating or trading caste having third position in the Hindu caste hierarchy
Zamindar	=	Land holders

Abbreviations

AISCF	=	All India Scheduled Caste Federation
AKSU	=	All Kamtapur Student Union
AKRASU	=	All Koch Rajbanshi Student Union
APL	=	Above Poverty Line
ASI	=	Anthropological Survey of India
BKRKM	=	Bharatiya Koch Rajbongshi Kshatriya Mahashabha
BKRP	=	Bharatiya Kamta Rajjya Parishad
BPL	=	Below Poverty Line
CPI (M)	=	Communist Party of India (Marxist)
DDA	=	Dandakaranya Development Authority
FCS	=	Fishermen Cooperative Society
GCBPA	=	Greater Cooch Behar Peoples' Association
ICSSR	=	Indian Council of Social Science Research
ISCP	=	Independent Scheduled Caste Party.
ISI	=	Indian Statistical Institute

KLO	=	Kamtapur Liberation Organization
KPP	=	Kamtapur Peoples' Party
KRI	=	Koch Rajbongshi International
LF	=	Left Front
ML	=	Muslim League
MLA	=	Member of Legislative Assembly
MLC	=	Member of Legislative Council
MOBC	=	Most Other Backward Castes
OAU	=	Organization of African Unity
OBC	=	Other Backward Castes/Class
SC	=	Scheduled Castes
ST	=	Scheduled Tribe
UF	=	United Front
UKD	=	Uttar Khanda Dal
ULFA	=	United Liberation Front of Assam
UNDR	=	Universal Declaration of Human Rights
UNHCR	=	United Nations' High Commission for Refugees
UNESCO	=	United Nations Economic and Social Council
UTJAS	=	Uttarbanga Tapasili Jati O Adibashi Sanghathan
WBFC	=	West Bengal Fishermen Conference

Introduction

Decolonisation in the post-Secoond World War period although politically liberated many Afro-Asian countries but violence and disruption of multiple characters had generated a trend of forced migration in many newly born states. In this context birth of independent India and Pakistan in 1947 is a significant one where 'forced migration' became a general phenomenon. Post-partition migration was a two-way traffic i.e. from India to Pakistan and from Pakistan to India. From Pakistan the Hindus, Sikhs as well as other religious minority communities began to migrate to India since they thought India would be their safer destination. Like West Pakistan, the minorities of erstwhile East Pakistan (present Bangladesh) began to migrate to India either as 'forced migrants' primarily as 'refugees' or as 'voluntary migrants'.

Resettlement of the migrants was a complicated problem in India particularly for those people who did not have sufficient marketable assets. Their struggle for resettlement in the new land made them an 'oppressed social category.' In many cases their human rights have been seriously violated. In this context experience of the Scheduled Castes as 'refugee' or as 'asylum seeker' was more miserable because of their social and occupational background. So they could not properly resettle in India although both the Government of India and the Government of West Bengal had adopted certain schemes for their rehabilitation. While the upper caste Hindu refugees tried to settle mostly in the urban and suburban centers by establishing squatters' colonies, the Scheduled Castes refugees on the other hand were forced go to the rural and backward areas. They were also deported to the jungle and hilly tracts of Uttar Pradesh, Madhya Pradesh, Orissa and Andaman and Nicobar Islands in the name of rehabilitation. The way of rehabilitation and the assistance as given to them were proved as derogatory. So many of them left the rehabilitation sites in the 1960s and 1970s. In these states many Scheduled Caste migrants, on the other hand, have been deprived from the opportunity of the reservation policy, the tool of 'protective discrimination'. Although in West Bengal most of the Scheduled Caste communities of colonial period have retained their 'scheduled status' to enjoy the fruits of reservation but the reservation policy could not bring real progress in their lives. Their position is still vulnerable.

Migration of the East Bengalese in large scale, on the other hand; had created a different type of sociopolitical tension among the Scheduled Castes of North Bengal as hosts. The Rajbanshis (largest Scheduled Caste community of West Bengal), who were majority in certain districts of North Bengal in pre-partition days; lost their prominence because of domination of the new settlers in all aspects of society, politics, economy and culture of North Bengal. So the Rajbanshis of North Bengal have raised the question of their strangulated cultural identity and demanded a 'separate state'.

So the partition of Bengal in 1947 seems to be appeared as a serious challenge for the survival of the Scheduled Castes of Bengal. Although several scholars have already highlighted the causes and the process of partition of India and the process of rehabilitation of the East Bengali upper Caste Hindu refugees (existing literatures on this subject have been critically reviewed in the chapter one) but the 'Scheduled Caste refugees' as an 'excluded social category' has not received proper attention. In such a background in this work an attempt has been made to highlight the political, economic and social impact of the partition of Bengal of 1947 on the people of West Bengal in particular and Eastern India in general. Process of rehabilitation of the refugees with special references to the Scheduled Castes and their struggle for survival have also been carefully investigated. I have also critically examined the regionalism in North Bengal as the side effect of the partition and the process of professional mobility among the Scheduled Castes of Bengal as a whole.

Present work is divided into eight chapters including an introduction and a conclusion. In the 'introductory chapter I have presented the whole structure of the work. In the chapter one I have critically examined the historiography of the partition of India and the location of the scheduled castes on it. Socio-economic and cultural background of the Scheduled Castes of colonial Bengal has been analyzed in the chapter two. In the chapter three I dealt with the transition of the 'caste politics' of the Scheduled Castes of Bengal from 'bargaining power' to 'marginal location' along with the process of partition of Bengal in 1947. Fourth chapter is based on the migration of the minority communities from East Bengal or East Pakistan to India and the policy of rehabilitation of the Government of India and the Government of West Bengal. In the fifth chapter I have critically examined the experience of the Scheduled Caste refugees in West Bengal and other provinces of India. In the sixth chapter I have analysed the impact of the partition of Bengal on the Scheduled Castes of North Bengal particularly on the Rajbanshis. In this chapter I have also highlighted the transformation of feeling of deprivation of the indigenous Scheduled Caste communities to regional movement based on ethno-linguistic identity. In the last chapter I left my observations in the form of a conclusion.

1

Partition of India and the Scheduled Castes of Bengal in Historical Writings

Studies on the 'partition of India' of 1947, migration of the refugees and their rehabilitation, nation building processes in India, Pakistan and Bangladesh; and other issues related to partition are increasing day by day. Since postcolonial India, Pakistan and Bangladesh have engulfed with multiple interrelated problems such as communalism, terrorism, cross border migrations and ethnic conflicts which have colonial i.e. pre-partitioned historical background; historiography of partition is thus developing rapidly as these issues are being analyzed by the social scientists in multiple perspectives. Partition of India in the East i.e. Bengal; has also drawn wide attention of the scholars since the pre-partition days what has been increased considerably after 1947. We can broadly categorize the partition related historical works into few groups such as—(i) studies on political aspects of partition including provincial politics and communalism, (ii) historiography of forced migrations and rehabilitation of the refugees, (iii) studies on violence and gender related issues, (iv) partition memories, etc.

In these studies the marginal social groups like the Scheduled Castes, however, have been sadly neglected. Although in the recent years some scholars have paid little attention to the plights of the Scheduled Caste refugees but many aspects of impact of partition on the Scheduled Castes are yet to be properly reconstructed. It suggests a critical analysis of the 'partition historiography.' Thus in this chapter an attempt has been made to review the historical studies on the partition of India especially on the partition of Bengal in 1947. Here I would also highlight the location of the East Bengali Scheduled Caste refugees in the historiography of partition of Bengal.

1.1. India's Partition and Historical Studies

Let us start our review of the historiography with the studies on partition of India which are based on the last phase of colonial rule. The politics of last decade of colonial India specially the achievement of independence through the constitutional negotiation (generally called the phase of 'high politics') has been a common aspect of historical studies on India's partition. Here we notice that the administrative policy of the colonial rulers and their underlying purpose of communal politics or the 'Divide and Rule' strategy had created such a complex situation by which partition of India became inevitable. This view was popularized by several politicians-cum scholars since the 1940s. Studies like— *India Divided* of Rajendra Prasad,[1] *Muslim Politics 1906-1942* of Humayun Kabir,[2] *The Communal Triangle in India* of Asoka Mehata and Achhut Patwardhan[3] etc., have emphasized the point that the communal politics of the Muslims in India was the offshoot of the policy followed by the British for weakening the nationalist struggle.[4] In the post-partition period a large number of literature have been produced on the growth of communalism and its contribution to the origin of partition of India where the onus of partition was allocated to the British policy of patronage to the Muslim communalism. The British official argument of safeguarding the weaker section of the Indians such as the Muslims through the 'separate electorate' practically culminated into the development of two opposite communal identities based on religion. Stubbornness of the Muslim League for Pakistan in the 1940s by dividing India was ultimately accepted by the

Congress for which partition was inevitable in 1947. This traditional approach of the origin of partition was further echoed in many writings such as Lal Bahadur's *Struggle for Pakistan: Tragedy of the Triumph of Muslim Communalism in India,* [5] Sucheta Mahajan's *Independence and Partition: The Erosion of Colonial Power in India,*[6] etc.

Last decade of the colonial rule and the 'politics of difference' have been studied by many notable scholars in order to reconstruct the process and strategies of partition of the Indian subcontinent. Here *The Crisis of Indian Unity 1917-1940* of R.J.Moore[7], *Congress, Muslim League, and Partition of India* of S.R.Bakshi, [8] *Mountbatten and the Partition of India* of L.Collins and D. Lapierre[9], etc., are worth mentioning.

The generalized approach of origin of partition of India, however, has countered by many historical works produced by the pro-Pakistan scholars. To them, Muslim League's demand for 'separate homeland for the Muslims' was a natural corollary of the social and political development that took place in India since the beginning of Muslim rule. They argued that identity of the Indian Muslims was rooted on religion, not in language or ethnicity or any other marker of identity. This approach of historical consciousness was developed basically in the 1940s with the publication of some historical works such as *The Meaning of Pakistan* of F.K. Durani,[10] *Why Pakistan* of S. Rahman,[11] etc. This approach was further nourished by the Pakistani scholars in Pakistan or in the West. Here we may refer to the works like *The Muslim Community of Indo-Pakistan Subcontinent 610-1947* of Ishtiaq Hussain Qureshi,[12] *Moslem Nationalism in India and Pakistan* of Hafiz Mallik,[13] *Pakistan: The Formative Phase 1857 – 1948* of Khalid Bin Sayed,[14] etc. To these scholars Pakistan was the Muslim destiny.[15] This approach was supplemented by the publication of some documentary works on Pakistan such as—*Makers of Pakistan and Modern Muslim India* of A.H. Albiruni,[16] and *The Partition of India and Mountbatten* of Latif Ahmed Sherwani.[17]

In the 1980s we notice some notable works on the partition of India and birth of Pakistan with some new assumptions. Here Ayesha Jalal's *The Sole Spokesmen: Jinnah, The Muslim League and the Demand for Pakistan*[18] deserves special attention. Jalal has argued that from 1940 main political objective of M.A. Jinnah was to achieve an equal status in all India politics and Pakistan demand was basically a tool of bargaining. But Jinnah was compelled to accept the 'moth eaten Pakistan' offered by the 3rd June plan, the only alternative available to him.[19] Jalal was although criticized both in Pakistan and in India but her work has opened a new vista to revise may old perceptions regarding the political aspects of partition.

A group of scholars, on the other hand; preferred to emphasize on the international political development particularly in South Asia since the Second World War. To them origin of partition of India was rooted on the wartime political development[20] and the decline of administrative capability of the colonial power.[21] These obviously were supplementary factors for the decline of British rule in India which ultimately led to the partition. This approach was further enriched by some Oxford-based studies like—— *Churchill, Cripps and India 1939-1945* of R.J. Moore,[22] *Partition and Independence of India* of M.N.Das,[23] *The Origins of the Partition of India 1936-1947* of Anita Inder Singh,[24] etc.

To some scholars, international political development after Second World War led to the growth of the possibility of the decolonization in Asia. Thus as a major colonial country of South Asia, India's freedom was almost inevitable. The British authorities were thus looking for the transfer of power to the Indians with their due prestige. So partition here was a useful means of decolonization.[25] India's partition as the culmination of decolonization got attention from many scholars. Oxford-based studies like—*Linlithgow and India: A Study of British policy and the political impasse in India 1936-43* of Gowher Rizvi,[26] *Escape from Empire* of R.J. Moore,[27] etc., have significantly enriched this aspect of partition. In this connection Anita Inder Singh's work *The Origins of the Partition of India 1936-1947* is a significant one where she has emphasized that 'the long term strategic interest of the British counseled them against partition, but that their short term tactics contributed to its fruition.' According to her 'the transfer of power to India and Pakistan in August

1947 was the first major act of decolonization by the British, with far reaching consequences on their international status. Partition symbolized the successful culmination of the Muslim League's campaign for a sovereign Pakistan, while it was the anti-thesis of the Congress wish to achieve a secular, united, democratic and independent India.'[28]

In the 1990s we again notice the growth of literatures on India's partition. There are some edited volumes which have dealt with different general aspects of the partition of India like—*India's Partition: Process, Strategy, and Mobilization*[29] and *India Partitioned: The other face of freedom* [30] edited by Mushirul Hassan; *Towards Freedom: Documents on the Movement for Independence in India, 1942-1944*[31] edited by P.S.Gupta; etc. Here we find some individual contribution too such as—Avtar Singh Bhasin's *Some Called it Partition Some Freedom*;[32] and *Laws Relating to Partition* of *India* by Manindra Nath Das.[33] These works have highlighted the process, strategy and mobilization for partition through the creation of Pakistan and India.

The 1990s, however, is the witness of a new trend in historical writing on India's partition specially violence, atrocities, refugee rehabilitation and human cost of partition got more priority rather than the political causes of partition. Here the narratives of the individuals began to be emphasized as an alternative version of the cost of partition. The feminism and the subaltern studies had considerably influenced the partition historiography. Instead of political aspects and the official version of causes of partition the victims of partition particularly the women have become main subject of partition studies. Ritu Menon, Kamala Bhasin, Urbashi Butalia, Gyanendra Pandey and a host of other professional historians had opened this new vista.[34] Here Urvashi Butalia's *The Other Side of Silence* (1998)[35] and *Borders and Boundaries: Women in India's Partition* of Ritu Menon and Kamala Bhasin[36] are noteworthy. This trend in historical writings based on oral testimonials has added a human face in the reconstruction of the history of India's partition. In this direction Gyanendra Pandey's studies are very much relevant where he critically analyzed the historiography of partition and emphasized on reconciling history and memory with the official biographies of the state.[37] It is, however, is not beyond criticism.

With the beginning of the twenty-first century many new writings have enriched the historiography of India's partition. Here we notice the growth of studies on both the history of pre-partition politics and post-partition development including communal violence, displacement and forced migration, resettlement and state policies of both India and Pakistan.[38]

1.2. Studies on Partition in the East

After having a brief idea about the historical writings on the partition of India and the refugee issues in all India level we may now discuss about the historiography of partition of Bengal. Studies on the partition of Bengal and its impact were initiated immediately after the partition due to the influx of the Hindu refugees from East Bengal. Administrative requirements about the statistical data on the refugees and their proper rehabilitation had compelled the government to undertake systematic investigation about the refugees what actually initiated the studies on the partition of Bengal. Thus we possess several studies carried out by the individual scholars as well by the government departments what can be divided into some groups such as: (1) studies on pre-partition politics of Bengal including the growth of communalism, (2) studies on settlement of the East Bengali refugees, (3) studies on the partition memories and refugee women, etc., (4) studies on the partition of Bengal and the Scheduled Castes, etc.

1.2.1. Studies on Pre-Partition Politics of Bengal and Communalism

'High politics' of partition of India and the provincial level political development including the growth of communalism in the eastern side of undivided India have received considerable attention of the scholars since the last quarter of the twentieth century. Partha Chaterjee's seminal work *Bengal 1920-1947: The Land question* (1984) has categorically raised the point that the 'class power' instead of 'state power' had dominated the politics of Bengal since 1920. The interest of the feudal class (mostly represented by the Hindu zamindars, traders and the professionals) was demonstrated as organized Hindu politics in many occasions. Thus the peasant (comprising the Muslim cultivators and the lower caste Hindus) resistance to feudal domination and usurious exploitation in Eastern Bengal became communal.[39] Communal mobilization of the politics of Bengal later nourished in *Communal Riots in Bengal, 1905-47* (published in 1991) of Suranjan Das is a significant one.[40] Das has specially emphasized on the Calcutta riots of 1946 and reflected the changing pattern of the Hindu-Muslim relations in Bengal. Just in the next year i.e. 1992 Soumitra De has published his excellent work titled *Nationalism and Separatism in Bengal: A Study of India's Partition*.[41]

In this direction *Bengal divided: Hindu communalism and partitions 1932-1947* (1994) of Joya Chatterji[42] is more interesting. She undertakes a detailed study of causes of partition of Bengal. According to her 'partition of Bengal was actually rooted on the middle class interest of the Hindu landlords which ultimately translated into communalism.' She argued that the Hindus of Bengal had also evolved a parallel separatist trend along with the separatist politics of the Muslims.[43] 'This study suggests that not only was the Congress High Command ready to pay the price of the partition in order to strengthen its hold over an unitary India, but that the Bengal Congress campaigned successfully for the vivisection of its province on communal lines.'[44] In regards to the Muslim middle class of Bengal a similar position can be noticed in the article *'Misreading Partition Road Signs'* of Hamza Alavi (2002).[45] This article emphasizes on the interest of the Muslim *ashrafi* (upper classes) in the partition. According to him

> 'the Muslim feudal families had led the Bengal Muslim League since its inception. This was challenged by the rise of Fazlul Haq and the KPP, which had a base among the rich peasants. After the 1937 elections, the KPP and the Muslim League formed a coalition government. This was an 'alliance' of conflicting class interests. Fazlul Haq was soon isolated. By this time (in

> 1938), H.S. Suhrawardy, a minister in the government, had assumed the charge of the Muslim League organization. In 1943, Abul Hashim, a man who professed a confused mixture of socialism and Islam, was elected as the party's secretary..... During the 1945-46 elections, when Suhrawardy kept himself in Calcutta, Abul Hashim, organised an extraordinary campaign amongst the poor peasants of Bengal on economic issues. This resulted in a massive and unprecedented landslide victory for the Muslim League. The stage was now set for the partition'.[46]

It is, however, no way an alternative version of partition history.

Ideological aspects of communalism, communal politics of the 1940s and communal violence have received special attention in the recent years too.[47] Rakesh Batabyal's *Communalism in Bengal: From Famine to Noahkhali 1943-1947*[48] explores the ascent and trajectory of communal ideology in pre-partition Bengal particularly from the famine of 1943 to the outbreak of communal riots in Noahkhali in 1947. This work shows that after 1943 there were regular clashes between communalism and nationalism and communal ideology replaced to nationalism.

1.2.2. Studies on the Settlement of the East Bengali Refugees

Studies on the forced migration of the Hindus and other minority communities from East Bengal to West Bengal and other parts of India for resettlement and the history of their struggle in the new land actually started since 1950 although much attention paid by the historians on these issues only since the 1990s. Early studies on the East Bengali refugees were actually initiated by the government (both Union and West Bengal) for administrative requirement because immediately after the partition the state capital as well as its suburban areas of West Bengal together with border districts flooded with the influx of the refugees from East Bengal. 'Concentration of the displace persons were becoming more and more acute in those places which were comparatively easily approachable.'[49] So the Government of West Bengal as well as the Government of

India began to face numerous problems in these settlement areas. Under this circumstance the Government of India had instructed the Indian Statistical Institute (ISI) of Calcutta to 'collect valid information of these migrant victims in the state'.[50] Thus the ISI had conducted a survey during the period between May 25, 1948 and September 9, 1948 on the refugees of Calcutta and its suburban areas. On the basis of this survey, Kanti B. Pakrasi had produced an excellent work titled *The Uprooted: A Sociological Study on the Refugees of West Bengal* in 1971.[51] Pakrasi mainly dealt with the sociological problems of the migrants including relief, rehabilitation, and family structure of the refugees, caste influence on the resettlement, occupational mobilization of the immigrants and the process of social assimilation, etc.

Like the ISI, the Anthropological Survey of India (ASI) had also carried out an almost similar survey in the 1950s in two selected refugee settlements viz. Jirat in Hooghly, a Govt. sponsored rural refugee resettlement centre; and Azadgarh set up by the refugees themselves near Jadavpur. This study was the outcome of the project conceived by the Government of India along with the UNESCO to 'understand the underlying causes of social tension among the refugees who came to West Bengal from the then East Pakistan'. The survey report of the ASI was published in 1959 titled *Studies in Social Tension among the Refugees from Eastern Pakistan* edited by B. S. Guha.[52] This study reveals that the displaced Hindu population from erstwhile East Pakistan moved into India because of the frustration, insecurity of life and property.'[53]

A similar survey was also carried out by the State Statistical Bureau of Government of West Bengal on the non-camp migrants during the period between 20th December 1950 and 15th January 1951. This survey report titled *'Report on the Sample Survey for Estimating the Socio-Economic Characteristics of Displaced Persons Migrated from Eastern Pakistan to the State of West Bengal'* was finally submitted to the Government on 21st December 1951 by N. Chakravarti.[54] This survey had estimated the total migrants from East Pakistan during the period between 15th October 1946 and 15th January 1951. This report also estimated community, caste and sex wise distribution of the migrant families with their occupational mobility of the migrants. The reports of the Department of the Relief and Rehabilitation of Government of West Bengal as well as census office have also highlighted many aspects of the refugee history.

The official version of history of rehabilitation of the refugees from erstwhile East Pakistan became more sophisticated in the writings of Hiranmoy Bandyopadhyay. His well-known work *Udvastu* (1970)[55] is an excellent account of the post-partition refugee problems in West Bengal. Being a government officer of high profile and having practical experience of the Department of Refugee Rehabilitation of West Bengal, Mr. Bandyopadhyay has illustrated many aspects of refugee problem. He started his account with the identification of causative factors of influx of the refugees to West Bengal from the then East Pakistan. He also elaborated the process of their rehabilitation in different districts of West Bengal. This work of Hiranmoy Bandyopadhyay had received wide attention of the scholars as well as the general readers immediately after its publication.

But just in the next year, a huge number of people began to migrate from East Pakistan to India due to the outbreak of the Indo-Pak war and the beginning of liberation movement in East Pakistan. So India particularly West Bengal and other border states again received huge number of refugees as the cost of emergence of independent Bangladesh. But the post 1971 migrants began to be branded as illegal migrants or as foreigners in different parts of northeast India and West Bengal.[56] So we find further studies on the refugee problems both by the government and the researchers. In the 1980s, the Centre for Social Science Research of Calcutta had published some notable articles and occasional papers on the impacts of the partition of Bengal and the influx of the refugees to the urban and suburban areas of West Bengal particularly in the growth of urbanization.[57] However, historical writings on the refugee resettlement, government policy and the impact of the partition of Bengal began to flourish with various dimension since the 1990s particularly with the publication of *The Marginal Men* (1990) of Prafulla K. Chakraborti.[58]

According to Prafulla K. Chakraborti '*The Marginal Men* is a chronicle of the unrecorded history of the tragic migration of the East Pakistan refugees and of their near annihilation.' He also argued that the influx of the refugees and their struggle for survival had strengthened the position of the Communist and Marxist Left politics in West Bengal.[59] Whole argument of Chakraborti was elaborated by three major points. Firstly he depicted in detail the miserable condition of the millions of uprooted and displaced persons from East Pakistan who were compelled to leave their country of forefathers due to the communal violence and changing pattern of relationship between the majority and the minority communities. Secondly Chakraborti categorically reviewed the rehabilitation policy of the government what according to him was actually of 'non-performance.'[60] Thirdly the CPI(M) dominated Left Front reaped this fruits generated from the failure of the government. Prafulla K. Chakraborti, however, had avoided the impact of the influx of the refugees on the non-migrant marginal communities of West Bengal. Inspite of limitations, his writing has inspired many scholars to look after the issue of refugee resettlement with new perspectives. Here we can mention the writings of Nilanjana Chatterjee, Ganesh Kudaisya, Ross Mollik,[61] Joya Chatterji, and few others. Nilanjana Chatterjee mainly emphasised on the settlement of the East Bengali refugees in the urban and suburban areas and on the politics of their rehabilitation.[62] Like Nilanjana Chatterjee, Joya Chatterji's writings are also based on the settlement of the refugees in the urban centres.[63] Chatterji, however, has highlighted some points on the settlement of the refugees in the rural areas of West Bengal and migration of the Muslims from West Bengal to East Pakistan.[64]

Ranabir Samaddar's writings of the 1990s, on the other hand, have critically examined the continuity of migration from the then East Pakistan and present Bangladesh. His edited volume *Partition Experience of the East: the Second Partition of Bengal* (1997),[65] a product of the Calcutta Research Group; and his own book *Marginal Nation: Trans-border Migration from Bangladesh to West Bengal* (1999)[66] are worth mentioning. Calcutta Research Group again published a seminal work in 2000 on the partition of Bengal and refugee settlement titled *Refugees in West Bengal: Institutional Processes and Contested Identities*.[67] It is a very interesting collection of the articles edited by Pradip Kumar Bose on the processes of resettlement of the East Bengali refugees and the role of the state. Although main title of the book is *Refugees in West Bengal* but there are some articles which have dealt with the settlement of the East Bengali refugees in Central India and Andaman and Nicobar Islands. Alok Ghosh has highlighted the resettlement strategy at Dandakaranya while Sabyasachi Basu Ray Chowdhury has discussed about migration of the East Bengali refugees to Andaman.[68] Other articles of this book are mainly based on the settlement and survival strategies of the refugees those who took shelter in Southern Bengal truly speaking in Calcutta and its suburbs.[69] However, Samir Das, Sandip Bandyopadhyay and Sarbani Sen's articles dealt with the legal aspects as well as the role of the state[70] in handling the refugee rehabilitation. Rest of the articles of this book are on the memories of partition.

Among the academic institutions, the Centre for Refugee Studies, the Centre for Women Studies and the Centre for Ambedkar Studies of Jadavpur University have paid serious attention in the early years of the twenty first century towards the migration of the refugees from East Pakistan and their settlement. Three major publications like *The Trauma and the Triumph: Gender and Partition in Eastern India* (2003),[71] *Forced Migration in the South Asian Region* (2004)[72] and *Dalit Lives and Dalit Vision in Eastern India* (2007)[73] produced by these centers have highlighted different aspects of the partition of Bengal in 1947 and its impact.

In the recent years, studies on the demographic aspects of migration of the East Bengali refugees and their struggle for survival are increasing day by day. Here we may talk about '*Divided Landscapes, Fragmented Identities: East Bengal Refugees and their Rehabilitation in India 1947-79*' of Ganesh Kudaisya;[74] *Bengal before and after the Partition (1947): The Changing Profile of a Province* of Chittabrata Palit and Ujjal Roy;[75] '*The Big March: Migratory Flows after the Partition of India*' of Prasant Bharadwaj,

Asim Khwaja and Atif Mian;[76] etc. At the same time migration of the Muslims from West Bengal to East Pakistan has received attention of some scholars.[77]

1.2.3. Studies on the Memories of Partition and Vulnerable Sections

Bengali literatures on partition and post-partition life with romantic touch have increased significantly in both Bengals (West Bengal and Bangladesh). But historical studies on the memory of partition of Bengal and partition related violence are comparatively less in number than literary studies. However, following the studies on memories of partition in the western part (Punjab), historians have also paid adequate attention to reconstruct the memory of partition in historical perspective since the last decade of the twentieth century.

The East Bengalese, especially the worst victims of partition, could not forget their days in East Bengal. Their memories on East Bengal (both happy and bitter experiences) had haunted them to write something or to tell their stories to others. Their accounts, memoirs, the nature of remembering, and the experience in life due to the partition of Bengal have drawn attention of the historians for rewriting the history of partition. However, these accounts in many cases are full with exaggeration and biasness. Among such accounts *Chhere asha gram* (*The abandoned village* (1975)[78] has been widely referred and reviewed in connection with the reconstruction of history of post-partition atrocities committed against the Hindus in East Bengal. This volume actually is a collection of essays published in the *Jugantar*, a Bengali newspaper in 1950 onwards. It was ultimately published as a book in 1975 compiled and edited by Dakshinaranjan Basu. Dipesh Chakraborty has critically examined the nature of these memories particularly the structure of the sentiments expressed in these essays in his widely circulated article *Remembered villages: Representations of Hindu-Bengali memories in the aftermath of the partition' (1995)*.[79]

Hiranmoy Bandyopadhyay's *Udvastu* (1970) as referred earlier has also a part on the pre-partition experience in Eastern Bengal and on the causative factors of migration of the Hindus.

Bandyopadhyay has highlighted that the development of a kind of situation where the minorities received frequent threats from the majority Muslims for which uncounted number of people left East Bengal inspite of their strong attachment with the land of their forefathers. Stories and incidents of sexual harassment and degradation of prestige and honour of the women, forced eviction, physical torture and forcible conversion to the faith of the majority community, etc., were also occasionally discussed in the *Udvastu*. *Udvastu* was widely used as a source for the reconstruction of history of migration from East Pakistan. First two chapters of Prafulla Chakrabarti's *The Marginal Men* have widely used this work as historical source what has been followed by subsequent historians.

Memories and experience of the most vulnerable section of the society like the women got special attention of the historians since the 1990s. It has already been mentioned that the issue of 'women and partition of India' began to be highlighted with the publication of articles and later books by Urvashi Butalia, Ritu Menon and Kamala Bhasin on Punjab experience in the 1990s. In case of Bengal, memory and experience of partition of Bengali women (beyond literary image) got the touch of the trained historians only with the beginning of the twenty-first century. *Seminar*, a reputed journal published from New Delhi; in its one special issue titled *Porous Border, Divided Selves: A Symposium on Partition in the East"*,[80] (February 2002, No. 510) has raised the question of partition of Bengal in gender perspective. Later articles of this issue was published as an edited volume in 2003 titled *The Trauma and the Triumph: Gender and Partition in Eastern India*.[81] In this work partition of Bengal has been analysed with gender, class and community perspectives. 'Focussing on what women experienced, felt and witnessed, the editors (Josodhara Bagchi and Subhoranjan Dasgupta) have drawn upon interviews with women who were uprooted, on diaries, memoirs and creative literature.' This book thus has provided an invaluable discussion on displacement, rape, loss, and why women pay the price.[82]

We posses another notable work on the partition experience and the past memories of East Bengal in the collection of interviews titled *Dhvangsa O Nirman: Bangiya Udvastu Samajer Svakathitha Bibaran* published in 2007.[83] This work actually based on the interviews of the refugees or migrants from East Bengal those who took shelter in Vijaygarh colony, Saktigarh and Santoshpur adjacent to Jadavpur University of South 24 Parganas district; and Agarpara of North 24 Parganas district. However, there are four interviews of the persons those who were natives of the locality where the East Bengalese established their colonies. Regarding the settlement of the colony at Vijaygarh Debabratta Dutta has produced an excellent monograph titled *Vijayarh Ekti Udvastu Colony*[84] long before the publication of *Dhvangsa O Nirnan*. At the same time we also possess two other notable articles on the settlement of refugee colonies and their memories published in the *Refugees in West Bengal: Institutional Processes and Contested Identities* as mentioned earlier. Here '*Adjustment and Transition in a Bengali Refugee Settlement: 1950-1999*'[85] by Dipankar Sinha on Samargarh Refugee Colony and *Growing Up Refugee: On Memory and Locality* by Manas Ray on Netaji Nagar colony are noteworthy.[86]

In the recent years several books and articles have been produced by different reputed scholars on 'nostalgia of East Bengal',[87] refugee women,[88] forced migration in the old age as well as problems of the old age in the refugee colonies[89] and other vulnerable sections of the forced migrants, and impact of partition,[90] in multidisciplinary perspective.

1.2.4. Partition of Bengal and the Scheduled Castes

Studies on the impact partition of Bengal on the Scheduled Castes are comparatively less in number. However, social reforms and political participation of some Scheduled Caste communities of colonial Bengal have drawn attention of the professional historians. We also possess some notable works on the resettlement of the Scheduled Castes in Dandakaranya, Marichjhapi, Uttar Pradesh, Uttaranchal and Andaman and Nicobar Islands. But these works are no way suffiicient to understand the long term impact of the partition of India on them. It can be clarified from the following discussion.

Sekhar Bandyopadhyay has written extensively of the transformation of the Chandals into Namasudras and their political participation in colonial Bengal. Bandyopadhyay's writings have been supplemented by many others contemporary books and articles. Swaraj Basu, Sukhabilas Barma, Rup Kumar Barman and few other scholars have comprehensively written on the social formation of the Rajbanshis of colonial Bengal and their subordination in the post-partition period. Regarding partition, Sekhar Badyopadhyay's one article titled *'Changing Borders, Shifting Loyalties: Religion, Caste and the Partition of Bengal in 1947'* (1999) is notable one.[91] This work is nothing but a supplementary to his previous writings on the political participation of the Namasudras in the pre-partition days in Bengal.

However, these writings are less concerned about the impact of partition of Bengal on the Scheduled Castes or their migration to other places for resettlement. Regarding the rehabilitation of the Scheduled Caste refugees in Dandakaranya we have some significant studies. Saibal Dasgupta, a civil servant to the Government of India; as the Chairman of the Dandakaranya, Development Authority (DDA), had published some articles in the beginning of 1965 in the *Economic Weekly* describing the state of agriculture, an investigation about the industries and the urban and semi-urban employment of Dandakaranya. Later Alok Ghosh has compiled these articles as a book together with Mr.Gupta's resignation letter in the post of Chairman of the DDA and other related documents.[92] Rehabilitation of the East Bengali refugees at Dandakaranya had further received attention of the scholars of international repute with the publication of the K. Maudood Elahi's article *Refugees in Dandakaranya* in 1981.[93] Alok Ghosh editor of the Saibal Dasgupta's book had also studied the plights of the of the Scheduled Caste refugees at Dandakaranya in his articles *Bengali Refugees at Dandakaranya: A Tragedy of Rehabilitation*[94] and *The East Bengal Refugees: From Crisis to Identity*.[95]

Since Dandakaranya was not suitable for proper rehabilitation of the East Bengali refugees so return of the refugees from Dandakaranya was common trend since the beginning. It was further increased when the Left Front (LF) Government came into power in West Bengal in 1977. Around 15000 refugee families left Dandakaranya in order to resettle in West Bengal.[96] Attempts of the refugees for resettlement at Marichjhapi were countered by the LF Government with brutal forces. It led to the serious violation of human rights of the Scheduled Caste refugees.[97] So when failed to stop the efforts of resettlement of the Dandakaranya-returned refugees at Marichjhapi 'the West Bengal government started on January 26, 1979, an economic blockade of the settlement with thirty police launches. Thus supply of food, drinking water and other essential items were stopped. Their huts were razed, and fisheries and tube wells were destroyed.'[98] So the refuges who took shelter at Marichjhapi were mostly forced to return to their old place although 4128 families were perished in transit, died of starvation, exhaustion, and many were killed in Kashipur, Kumirmari, and Marichjhapi by police firings.[99] So the Marichjhapi incident is a significant chapter of studies on the refugees resettlement in West Bengal; particularly of the Scheduled Caste refugees. Here we find some notable articles and books like— *Refugee Resettlement in Forest Reserves: West Bengal Policy Reversal and the Marichjhapi Massacre* of Ross Mallick (1999),[100] *Marichjhapi: Naisabder Antarale* of Jagadish Chandra Manadal,[101] *Atrocities on the Dalits Since the Partition of Bengal* of Dilip Halder,[102] *Marichjhapi: Chinnadesh, Chhinna Itihas*,[103] etc. However, atrocities on the refugees at Marichjhapi and violation of their human rights still deserve careful historical investigation since these writings are not enough for complete understanding of the dalit refugee history.

Apart from Dandakaranya and Marichjhapi, resettlement of the East Bengali Scheduled Caste refugees in Uttaranchal, Uttar Pradesh and Andaman and Nicobar Islands deserve careful attention. In Uttar Pradesh the East Bengali Scheduled Castes refugees got the land for settlement in several districts like Bijnor, Bereilly, Pilbhit, Meerut, Badaun, Kanpur, Lakhimpur Kheri, Rampur, Bahraich, etc. Two districts of Uttaranchal (formerly under Uttar Pradesh) like Nainital, Udham Singh Nagar had also received a significant number of East Bengali refugees along with the Punjabi refugees. The East Bengali refugees were mostly from Cooper's Camp of Nadia and

Charbedia Camp of Orissa.[104] Sucheta Kriplani as Chief Minister of Uttar Pradesh (2 October 1963 – 14 March 1967) had brought around 1600 East Bengali refuge families from Mana Transit Camp of Dandakaranya.[105] But this episode of refugee settlement of the East Bengalese has received no attention of the professional historians. However, we have some narratives on this episode like *Nainitaler Pathe Pathe* of Nitish Biswas.[106]

Andaman and Nicobar Islands what once was infamous for imprisonment of the freedom fighters of Indian mainland, was also chosen as a land for resettlement of the East Bengali refugees where the agriculturists i.e. the Scheduled Caste (mostly the Namasudras) were deported. The refugee rehabilitation in Andaman, however, has been constructed by many scholars other than the government officials. First systematic study on the East Bengal refugee settlers of Andaman was carried out by Surajit Sinha in 1952.[107] Sinha highlighted the condition of the refugee settlers along the caste, sex and socio-cultural lines and reviewed the possibility of further settlement of the East Bengali refugees. Like Sinha, P.K. Sen's work on Andaman published in 1955 titled *Land and People of the Andaman* also indicated the possibility of the resettlement in other Islands of the region by clearing forest.[108] From the perspective of refugee history a notable work, published in 1990, titled *The Uprooted* (1990) has included one article on the ecological consequences of the refugee settlement in Andaman and Nicobar Islands.[109] We got three important studies on the settlement of the East Bengali refugees in Andaman with the beginning of new millennium like—*Exiled to the Andamans: The Refugees from East Pakistan* (2000),[110] *Migration in the Andaman and Nicobar Islands during 1951-1991 from East Bengal: Trend and Flow* (2007)[111] and *Colonization and Rehabilitations in Andaman and Nicobar Island.*[112]

The studies on the Scheduled Caste refugees in most cases are concentrated on the agriculturist. Scheduled Castes of other professions had been overlooked. However, Rup Kumar Barman has recently raised the points of impact of partition on the fishermen communities in his writings like—*Dalit Refugees or Refugee Dalits? Post-Partitioned Dalit Lives in Eastern India*,[113]

The Fisheries of Bengal: From Colonial Management to Sustainable Development,[114] *Caste and Class Awareness among the Fishermen of Bengal*,[115] and *Fisheries and Fishermen: A Socio-economic History of Fisheries and Fishermen of Colonial Bengal and Postcolonial West Bengal*.[116]

These studies, however, could not raise the point of impact of resettlement of the East Bengalese on the local people i.e. pre-settled communities. It is a fact that along with West Bengal, entire Northeast India mostly the border districts had received the East Bengali refugees and voluntary migrants in large scale. In some districts they outnumbered the locals and destabilized the entire socioeconomic and economic relations of the pre-partition days. Assam, Tripura and Meghalaya because of their geographical location and having social and economic relations with the people of East Bengal had received the East Bengalese very generously after the partition of Bengal. But this generosity very soon turned into repugnance against the East Bengalese when the local people of this region began to be subordinated in terms of economic, cultural and political prominence. So an anti-outsider feeling had developed in different states of Northeast India. Here the East Bengalese were clearly branded as outsiders or as *bideshi* (foreigner). So expulsion of the outsiders was a major causative factor of regional and sub-national movement in Northeast India. This trend has been critically examined by a large number of scholars in connection with the analysis on the growth of ethnic, regional and sub-national movement in Northeast India.

Like Northeast India, a trend of anti-East Bengali feeling had developed in northern part of West Bengal too. Here some local sociopolitical organization had strongly opposed the large scale migration from East Bengal. Rup Kumar Barman has highlighted some points of the impact of the partition on the pre-resettled Scheduled Castes of North Bengal in his writings like— *Contested Regionalism: A New Look on History, Cultural Change and Regionalism of North Bengal and Lower Assam*, [117] *Contested Ethnicity and Regional Assertion: A Study from Contemporary North Bengal*,[118] *Partition of Bengal And Struggle For Existence of The Scheduled Castes*.[119] This point of impact of partition had also been focused in some other writings.

1.3. Observation

Studies on the partition of Bengali of 1947 so far been carried out are mostly concentrated on the political and communal factors of partition and suffering of the East Bengali upper Caste Hindu migrants (both forced and voluntary migrants) and their struggle for resettlement. Foundation of colonies by the refugees particularly in southern West Bengal, their struggle for survival and gradual assimilation with the general population along with their political participation have been specifically analyzed by the historians what have also been supplemented by the literary works. Memories of 'partition related violence', gender issues and critical analysis of the literary works and films have also enriched the partition historiography on the eastern side of India. We have also noticed some historical studies related to the government policy of rehabilitation (both inside and outside West Bengal), rehabilitation related politics and tragedy of rehabilitation, etc.

The twentieth century historiography of partition of Bengal has not included the studies on the experience of the Scheduled Castes as refugee/forced migrants or as pre-settled communities i.e. as local. It is only with the beginning of the new millennium some scholars have attempted to highlight the plights of the Scheduled Castes refugees. These studies again are region centric or individual case centric such as Dandakaranya, Marichjhapi, Andaman, Nainital and North Bengal. Further research is thus essential in order to reconstruct a complete history of the partition of Bengal in 1947 and its impact on the Scheduled Castes.

NOTES AND REFERENCES

1. Rajendra Prasad, *India Divided* (Bombay: Hind Kitab Ltd, 1947).
2. Humayun Kabir, *Muslim Politics 1906-1942 and Other Essays* (Calcutta: Firma K.L. Mukhopadhyay, 1969).
3. Asoka Mehata and Achyut Patwardhan, *The Communal Triangle in India* (Allahabad: Kitabstan, 1942).
4. Ian Talbot and Gurhapal Singh, *The Partition of India* (New Delhi: Cambridge University Press, 2009), p. 9.

5. Lal Bahadur, *Struggle for Pakistan: Tragedy of the Triumph of the Muslim Communalism in India 1906-1947* (New Delhi: Sterling 1988).
6. Sucheta Mahajan,*Independence and Partition: The Erosion of Colonial Power in India* (New Delhi: Sage, 2000).
7. R. J. Moore, *The Crisis of Indian Unity 1917-1940* (Oxford: Clarendon Press, 1974).
8. S. R. Bakshi, *Congress, Muslim League, and Partition of India* (New Delhi: Deep & Deep Publications, 1990).
9. L. Collins and D. Lapierre, *Mountbatten and the Partition of India* (New Delhi: Atlantic, 1982).
10. F. K. Durani, *The Meaning of Pakistan* (Lahore: Muhammad Asraf, 1944).
11. S. Rahman, *Why Pakistan* (Lahore: Islamic Book Service, 1946).
12. Ishtiaq Hussain Qureshi, *The Muslim Community of Indo-Pakistan Subcontinent 610-1947* (Karachi: Ma'aref, 1977).
13. Hafiz Mallik, *Moslem Nationalism in India and Pakistan* (Washington DC: Public Affair Press, 1963).
14. Khalid Bin Sayeed, *Pakistan: The Formative Phase 1857–1948* (Karachi: Oxford University Press, 1968).
15. Talbot and Singh, *The Partition of India*, p. 10.
16. A. H. Albiruni, *Makers of Pakistan and Modern Muslim India* (Lahore: Muhammad Ashraf, 1950).
17. Latif Ahmed Sherwani, *The Partition of India and Mountbatten* (Karachi: Council for Pakistan Studies, 1986).
18. Ayesha Jalal, *The Sole spokesmen: Jinnah, The Muslim League and the Demand for Pakistan (*Cambridge University Press, 1985).
19. Ian Talbot and Gurhapal Singh: *The Partition of India.*, p. 12.
20. *Ibid.*, pp. 11-12. For more details see F.G.Hutchins, *India's Revolution, Gandhi and the Quit India Movement* (Cambridge M.A.: Havard University Press, 1973); Amit Kumar Gupta (ed.), *Myth and Reality: The Struggle for Freedom in India* (New Delhi: Manohar, 1987).
21. For this approach see D. C. Potter, Manpower shortage and the end of colonialism: The Case of Indian Civil Service, *(Modern Asian Studies 7(1973)* pp. 47-73, Simon Epstein: District Officers in Decline: The Erosion of British Authority in the Bombay Country side, *Modern Asian Studies 16(1982),* pp. 493-518.
22. R.J. Moore, *Churchill, Cripps and India 1939-1945* (Oxford: Clarendon Press, 1979).

23. M. N. Das, *Partition and Independence of India* (New Delhi: Vision Books, 1982).
24. Anita Inder Singh, *The Origins of the Partition of India, 1936-1947* (Delhi: Oxford University Press, 1987).
25. Partition as a useful means of decolonization was argued by many scholars. Here we can mention the theoretical works like—Radha Kumar: The Troubled History of Partition, *(Foreign Affairs* v. 76 (Jan. /Feb. 1997), p. 22; Nicholas Sambanis: Partition as a Solution to Ethnic War: An Empirical Critique of the Theoretical Literature, *World Politics* 52 (July 2000), p. 437.
26. Gowher Rizvi, *Linlithgow and India: A study of British policy and the political impasse in India 1936-43* (London: Royal Historical Society, 1978).
27. R.J. Moore: *Escape from Empire: The Attlee Government and the Indian Problem* (Oxford: Clarendon, 1983).
28. Anita Inder Singh, *The Origins of the Partition of India 1936-1947* (Delhi: Oxford University Press, 1987), quoted from jacket of the book.
29. Mushirul Hasan, *India's Partition: Process, Strategy, and Mobilization* (Delhi: Oxford University Press, 1993).
30. Mushirul Hasan, *India Partitioned: The Other Face of Freedom* (Delhi: New Lotus Collection, 1995).
31. P.S. Gupta, *Towards Freedom: Documents on the Movement for Independence in India, 1942-1944* (Delhi: Oxford University Press, 1997).
32. Avtar Singh Bhasin, *Some Called it Partition Some Freedom* (Delhi: Siba Exim Pvt. Ltd., 1998).
33. Manindra Nath Das, *Laws Relating to Partition* of *India*, 5th ed., (Calcutta: Eastern Law House, 1999).
34. See Gyanendra Pandey, The Prose of Otherness, in D. Arnold and D. Hardiman (eds.): *Subaltern Studies*, Vol. IV, (Delhi: Oxford University Press, 1994), pp. 188-221; Memories of Partition, *Seminar, vol. 420*, August 1994; Veena Das, *Critical Events: Moments in the Life of the Nation* (Delhi: Oxford University Press, 1994), Urvashi Butalia, "Community, State and Gender: On women Agency during partition" *(EPW,* 24th April 1993), Ritu Menon and Kamala Bhasin: "Recovery, Rapture, Resistance: Indian State and Abduction of Women during Partition", (*EPW,* 24th April 1993).
35. Urvashi Butalia, *The Other Side of Silence: Voices from the Partition of India* (New Delhi: Penguin Books, 1998).

36. Ritu Menon and Kamala Bhasin, *Borders and Boundaries: Women in India's Partition* (New Delhi: Kali for Women, 1998).
37. Gyanendra Pandey, *Remembering Partition, Violence, Nationalism and History in India* (Cambridge University Press, 2001); Gyanendra Pandey, "India and Pakistan, 1947-2002", *Economic and Political Weekly*, March 16(2002);——, 'Can a Muslim Be an Indian?' *Comparative Study of Society and History*, 608-629. Also see David Gilmartin: 'Partition, Pakistan, and South Asian History: In Search of a Narrative', *The Journal of Asian Studies*, 57, 4. (November 1998), 1068-1095.
38. For general history see Yasmin Khan, *The Great Partition: the Making of India and Pakistan* (Yale University Press, 2007); Vazira Fazila-Yacoobali Zamindar, *The Long Partition and the Making of Modern South Asia* (Columbia University Press, 2007). For post-partition violence and forced migration see, Sarah Ansari, *Life after Partition: Migration, Community and Strife in Sindh, 1947–1962* (Oxford: Oxford University Press, 2005); Papiya Ghosh: *Partition and the South Asian Diaspora: Extending the Subcontinent*, (New Delhi, Routledge, 2007); Omprakash Misra (ed.), *Forced Migration in the South Asian Regions: Displacement, Human Rights and Conflict Resolution* (New Delhi: Manak Publications Pvt. Ltd, 2004). Ian Talbot and Gurhapal Singh: *The Partition of India*, (Cambridge University Press, 2009).
39. Partha Chatterjee, *Bengal 1920-1947: The Land Question* (Calcutta: KP Bagchi and Company, 1984), p. 190.
40. Suranjan Das, *Communal Riots in Bengal, 1905-47* (Oxford University: South Asian Studies, 1991).
41. Soumitra De, *Nationalism and Separatism in Bengal: A Study of India's Partition*, (New Delhi: Vikas and Har Anand Publications, 1992).
42. Joya Chatterji, *Bengal Divided: Hindu Communalism and Partitions 1932-1947*, (Cambridge University Press, 1994), First paperback Indian edition, (New Delhi: Foundation Books, 1996).
43. *Ibid.*
44. *Ibid.*, p. 266.
45. Hamza Alavi, *Misreading Partition Road Signs*, (Economic and Political Weekly, November 2-9, 2002), pp. 4515-4523.
46. *Ibid.*, p. 4523.
47. For more details see A.J.Karma, *The Prolonged Partition and Its Progroms: Testimonies on Violence against Hindus in East Bengal 1946-64* (New Delhi: Voice of India, 2000); Suniti Kumar Ghosh, *The*

Tragic Partition of Bengal (Allahabad: Indian Academy of Social Sciences, 2002).

48. Rakesh Batabyal, *Communalism in Bengal: From Famine to Noahkhali 1943-1947* (New Delhi: Sage Publications, 2005).
49. Kant B. Pakrasi: *The Uprooted: a Sociological Study of the Refugees of West Bengal, India* (Calcutta: Editions Indians, 1971), p.42.
50. *Ibid.*, p. 43
51. *Ibid.*
52. B.S. Guha (ed.), *Studies in Social Tension among the Refugees from East Pakistan* (Delhi: Department of Anthropology, Government of India, 1959).
53. *Ibid.*
54. Government of West Bengal, *Report on the Sample Survey for Estimating the Socio-Economic Characteristics of displaces Persons Migrated from Eastern Pakistan to the State of West Bengal* (Calcutta: State Statistical Bureau, 1951).
55. Hiranmoy Bandyopadhyay, *Udvastu* (Calcutta: Sahitya Samsad, 1970).
56. For details see—Rup Kumar Barman, *Contested Regionalism: A New Look on History, Cultural Change and Regionalism of North Bengal and Lower Assam* (Delhi: Abhijeet Publications, 2007).
57. Pranati Chaudhury, *Refugees in West Bengal: A Study of the Growth and Distribution of Refugees Settlements within the CMD, OP55,* (Calcutta, CSSS, 1983); Asok Sen and Alok Banerjee, *Calcutta Metropolitan District in the Urban Context of West Bengal (1951-81)* (Calcutta: CSSS, 1983); etc.
58. Prafulla K. Chakraborti, *The Marginal Men: The Refugees and the Left Political Syndrome in West Bengal* (Kalyani: Lumiere Books, 1990).
59. *Ibid.*, p. xxiii.
60. *Ibid.*, p. xxiv.
61. Ross Mallick, Refugee Resettlement in Forest Reserves: West Bengal Policy Reversal and the Marichjhapi Massacre, *The Journal of Asian Studies*, Vol. 58, No. 1 (Feb., 1999),
62. Nilanjana Chatterjee, *Midnight's Unwanted Children: East Bengali Refugees and the Politics of Rehabilitation*. Unpublished Ph.D. dissertation (Brown University, 1992); Nilanjana Chatterjee, The East Bengal Refugees: A Lesson in Survival, in Sukanta Chaudhuri (ed.), *Calcutta: The Living City* (Calcutta: Oxford University Press, 1994).
63. Joya Chatterji, "The Fashioning of a Frontier: The Radcliffe Line

and the Bengal's Border Landscape, 1947-52", *Modern Asian Studies*, vol. 33, no 1 (1999), pp. 185-242; ———, "Right or Charity? The Debate over Relief and Rehabilitation in West Bengal", in Suvir Kaul (ed.), *The Partitions of Memories: The Afterlife of the Division of India* (Delhi: Permanent Black, 2001).

64. Joya Chatterji, *The Spoils of Partition: Bengal and India, 1947-1967* (Cambridge: Cambridge University Press, 2007).

65. Ranabir Samaddar (ed.), *Partition Experience of the East: the Second Partition of Bengal* (Calcutta: Research Group and New Delhi, Vikas Publication House, 1997).

66. Ranabir Samaddar, *Marginal Nation: Trans-border Migration from Bangladesh to West Bengal* (New Delhi: Thousand Oaks, London: Sage, 1999).

67. Pradip Kumar Bose(ed.), *Refugees in West Bengal: Institutional Processes and Contested Identities* (Kolkata: Mahanirban Calcutta Research Group, 2000)

68. Alok Ghosh, "Bengali Refugees at Dandakaranya: The Tragedy of Rehabilitation", in Pradip Kumar Bose (ed.), *Refugees in West Bengal: Institutional Processes and Contested Identities* (Kolkata: Mahanirban Calcutta Research Group, 2000), pp.106-129; Sabyasachi Basu Ray Chowdhury, "Exiled to the Andamans: The refugees from East Pakistan", in Pradip Kumar Bose(ed.), *Refugees in West Bengal: Institutional Processes and Contested Identities* (Kolkata: Mahanirban Calcutta Research Group, 2000), pp. 130-141.

69. Arun Deb, "The UCRC: Its role in establishing the Rights of Refugee Squatters in Calcutta", in Pradip Kumar Bose (ed.), *Refugees in West Bengal: Institutional Processes and Contested Identities*, (Kolkata: Mahanirban Calcutta Research Group, 2000), pp. 65-79; Dipankar Sinha, "Foundation of Refugee Market: A Study in Self Reliance initiative", in Pradip Kumar Bose(ed.), *Refugees in West Bengal: Institutional Processes and Contested Identities* (Kolkata: Mahanirban Calcutta Research Group, 2000), pp. 80-97; Bolan Gangopadhyay, "Reintegrating the Displaced, Refracturing The Domestic: A Report on the experience of Uday Villa", in Pradip Kumar Bose(ed.), *Refugees in West Bengal: Institutional Processes and Contested Identities* (Kolkata: Mahanirban Calcutta Research Group, 2000), pp. 99-107.

70. Samir Das, "Refugee Crisis : Responses of the government of West Bengal", in Pradip Kumar Bose(ed.), *Refugees in West Bengal: Institutional Processes and Contested Identities* (Kolkata: Mahanirban Calcutta Research Group, 2000); Sandip Bandyopadhyay, "Million Seeking Refuge: The Refugee Question in West Bengal 1971",

in Pradip Kumar Bose (ed.), *Refugees in West Bengal: Institutional Processes and Contested Identities* (Kolkata, Mahanirban Calcutta Research Group, 2000), pp. 32-48; Sarbani Sen, "The legal regime for refugee relief and rehabilitation in West Bengal 1946-58", in Pradip Kumar Bose(ed.), *Refugees in West Bengal: Institutional Processes and Contested Identities* (Kolkata, Mahanirban Calcutta Research Group, 2000), pp. 49-64.

71. Jasodhara Bagchi and Subhoranjan Dasgupta (eds.), *The Trauma and the Triumph Gender and Partition in Eastern India* (Kolkata, Stree, 2003).

72. Omprakash Misra (ed.), *Forced Migration in the South Asian Region: Displacement, Human Rights & Conflict Resolution* (New Delhi, Centre for Refugee Studies of Jadavpur University in Collaboration with Brookings Institution –SAIS Project Internal Displacement and Manak Publications Pvt. Ltd, 2004).

73. Biswajit Chatterjee and Debi Chatterjee (eds.), *Dalit Lives and Dalit Vision in Eastern India* (Kolkata, Centre for A Rural Resource on behalf of the Centre for Ambedkar Studies of Jadavpur University, 2007).

74. Ganesh Kudaisya, Divided Landscapes, Fragmented Identities: East Bengal Refugees and their Rehabilitation in India 1947-79, in *Singapore Journal of Tropical Geography, Vol.17, No 1(1996),* 24-49.

75. Chittabrata Palit and Ujjal Roy, *Bengal Before and After the Partition (1947): The Changing Profile of a Province* (Kolkata: Corpus Research Institute, 2004)

76. Prasant Bharadwaj, Asim Khwaja and Atif Mian, 'The Big March: Migratory Flows after the Petition of India', *EPW* (August 30) 2008, pp. 39-49.

77. For this approach see Joya Chatterji, *The Spoil of Partition: Bengal and India, 1947-1967* (Cambridge University Press, 2007); Papiya Ghosh, "Partition and South Asian Diaspora", in Omprakash Mishra (ed): *Forced Migration in the South Asian Region: Displacement, Human Rights & Conflict Resolution* (New Delhi: Centre for Refugee Studies of Jadavpur University in Collaboration with Brookings Institution –SAIS Project Internal Displacement and Manak Publications Pvt.Ltd, 2004), pp. 111-142; Papiya Ghosh, *Partition and South Asian Diaspora: Extending the Subcontinent* (New Delhi: Routledge, 2007), Papiya Ghosh, *Muhajirs and the Nation: Bihar in the 1940s* (New Delhi: Routledge, 2010).

78. Dakshinaranjan Basu (comp. and ed.), *Chhere Asha Gram* (Calcutta, 1975).

79. Dipesh Chakraborty, "Remembered villages: Representations of Hindu-Bengali memories in the aftermath of the partition", *South Asia: Journal of South Asian Studies*, 18:2, 109-129. Also published in D.A.Low and Howard Brasted (eds.), *Freedom, Trauma, Continuities: Northern India and Independence* (New Delhi: Sage, 1998).
80. *Seminar* (February 2002, no 51).
81. Jasodhara Bagchi and Subhoranjan Dasgupta (eds.), *The Trauma and the Triumph: Gender and Partition in Eastern India* (Kolkata: Stree, 2003).
82. *Ibid.*
83. Tridib Chakraborti, Nirupama Ray Mandal and Poulami Ghoshal (compiled and edited), *Dhvangsa O Nirnam: Bangiya Udvastu Samajer Svakathitha Bibaran* (Kolkata: Seriban, 2007).
84. Debabratta Dutta, *Vijagarh Ekti Udvastu Colony* (Kolkata: Progressive Publishers, 2001).
85. Dipankar Sinha, "Adjustment and Transition in a Bengali Refugee Settlement: 1950-1999", in Pradip Kumar Bose (ed.), *Refugees in West Bengal: Institutional Processes and Contested Identities* (Kolkata: Mahanirban Calcutta Research Group, 2000), pp.142-161.
86. Manas Ray, "Growing up refugee: On memory and locality", in Pradip Kumar Bose(ed.), *Refugees in West Bengal: Institutional Processes and Contested Identities* (Kolkata: Mahanirban Calcutta Research Group, 2000), pp.162-199.
87. Sandip Bandopadhyay, *Deshbhag Deshtyag* (Kolkata: Anustup, 1994); Sandip Bandopadhyay, *Smriti aar Sattwa* (Kolkata: Progressive Publishers, 1999); *See* Anasua Basu Raychaudhury, "Nostalgia of 'Desh', Memories of Partition", *Economic and Political Weekly*. December 25, 2004; Pablo Bose, "Dilemmas of Diaspora: Partition, Refugees, and the Politics of 'Home'", *Refugee*, Vol. 23, No.1, Issue *Dilemmas of Diaspora,* Internet edition.
88. Gargi Chakravartty, *Coming out of Partition: Refugee Women of Bengal*, (New Delhi: Bluejay Books, 2005); Tridip Santapa Kundu, Bangali, "nari jibane deshbhager prabhab" in Goutam Chattopadhyay (ed.): *Itihas Anusandhan*, Vol. 13, (Kolkata, Farma K.L.M. Pvt. Ltd., 1999), pp. 589-599.
89. *See,* Tridip Santapa Kundu, "Bardhakye Bastuchyuti: Bangalay desbhagjanita durbhoger ekti dik" in Goutam Chattopadhyay (ed.), *Itihas Anusandhan*, Vol. 15, (Kolkata: Farma K.L.M.Pvt. Ltd., 2001), pp.392-397; Tridip Santapa Kundu, "Chhinnamul Chhalebela: Bangalay deshbhagjanita paristhitir ekti dik", in Goutam Chattopadhyay (ed.), *Itihas Anusandhan*, Vol.14, (Kolkata: Farma

K.L.M.Pvt. Ltd., 2000), pp. 296-293; Sudeshna Banerjee: "Displacement within Displacement: The Crisis of Old Age in the Refugee Colonies of Calcutta", *Studies in History,*19,2, n.s. (2003).

90. Sudeshna Chakraborty, "Udvastu Srot o Paschim Banglar Janajiban", in Swapan Basu and Harsha Dutta (eds.), *Bish Sataker Bangali Jiban o Samskriti* (Kolkata: Pustak Bipani, 2000), pp.171-179; Kali Prasad Mukhopadhyay, *Partition, Bengal and After: The Great Tragedy of India*, (New Delhi: Reference Press, 2007).

91. Shekhar Bandyopadhyay, 'Changing Borders, Shifting Loyalties: Religion, Caste and the Partition of Bengal in 1947', *Asian Studies Institute (1999).*

92. Alok Kumar Ghosh (ed.), *Dandakaranya—A Survey of Rehabilitation: Essays of Sri Saibal Kumar Gupta* (Calcutta: Bibhasa, 1999).

93. K. Maudood Elahi, "Refugees in Dandakaranya", *International Migration Review,* Vol. 15, No. 1/2, *Refugees Today* (Spring - Summer, 1981), pp. 219-225

94. Alok Ghosh, *Bengali Refugees at Dandakaranya: A Tragedy of Rehabilitation*, in Pradip Kumar Bose(ed.), *Refugees in West Bengal: Institutional Processes and Contested Identities* (Kolkata: Mahanirban Calcutta Research Group, 2000), pp. 106-129.

95. Alok Kumar Ghosh,"The East Bengal Refugees: From Crisis to Identity", in Biswajit Chatterjee and Debi Chatterjee (eds.), *Dalit Lives and Dalit Vision in Eastern India* (Kolkata: Centre for Rural Resource on behalf of the Centre for Ambedkar Studies of Jadavpur University, 2007.

96. Ross Mallick, "Refugee Resettlement in Forest Reserves: West Bengal Policy Reversal and the Marichjhapi Massacre", *The Journal of Asian Studies*, Vol. 58, No. 1 (Feb., 1999), p. 107.

97. *Ibid.*

98. *Ibid.* p.108.

99. *Ibid.* p. 111.

100. Ross Mallick, "Refugee Resettlement in Forest Reserves: West Bengal Policy Reversal and the Marichjhapi Massacre," *The Journal of Asian Studies*, Vol. 58, No. 1 (Feb., 1999), pp. 104-125.

101. Jagadish Chandra Mandal, *Marichjhapi: Naisabder Antarale* (Kolkata: Sujan Publications, 2002).

102. Dilip Halder, *Atrocities on the Dalits since the Partition of Bengal* (New Delhi: India, Mittal Publications, 2008).

103. Madhumay Pal, *Marichjhapi: Chinnadesh, Chhinna Itihas* (Kolkata: Gangchil, 2009).
104. Nitish Biswas, *Nainitaler Pathe Pathe* (Kolkata: Aiktan Gabeshana Sanghsad, 2002), p. 30.
105. *Ibid.* p. 105.
106. *Ibid.*
107. Surajit Sinha, *Resettlement of the East Pakistan Refugees in Andaman Islands, Report on Survey of further possibility of Resettlement 1952*, (Calcutta: West Bengal Government Press, 1955).
108. P.K.Sen, *Land and People of the Andaman* (Calcutta: The Post-Graduate Book Mart, 1955).
109. D. Venkateswar, "Ecological consequences of rehabilitation programmes in Andaman", in V. Sudarsan (ed.) *The Uprooted* (New Delhi: Gian Publishing House, 1990).
110. Sabyasachi Basu Roy Chowdhury, "Exiled to the Andamans: The Refugees from East Pakistan", in Pradip Kumar Bose(ed.), *Refugees in West Bengal: Institutional Processes and Contested Identities* (Kolkata: Mahanirban Calcutta Research Group, 2000), pp.130-141.
111. Chhonda Bose, "Migration in the Andaman and Nicober Islands during 1951-1991 from East Bengal: Trend and Flow", in Biswajit Chatterjee and Debi Chatterjee (eds.) *Dalit Lives and Dalit Vision in Eastern India* (Kolkata: Centre for Rural Resource on behalf of the Centre for Ambedkar Studies of Jadavpur University, 2007), pp. 94-106
112. Swapan K. Biswas, *Colonization and Rehabilitations in Andaman and Nicober Island* (New Delhi: Abhijeet Publications, 2009)
113. Rup Kumar Barman, *Dalit Refugees or Refugee Dalits? Post-Partitioned Dalit Lives in Eastern India*, in Biswajit Chatterjee and Debi Chatterjee (eds.), *Dalit Lives and Dalit Vision in Eastern India*, (Kolkata: Centre for Rural Resource on behalf of the Centre for Ambedkar Studies of Jadavpur University, 2007), pp. 112-119.
114. Rup Kumar Barman, "The Fisheries of Bengal: From Colonial Management to Sustainable Development", in Mahua Sarkar (ed.), *Environmental History: Recent Dialogue* (New Delhi: Kalpaz, 2007).
115. Rup Kumar Barman, "Caste and Class Awareness among the Fishermen of Bengal", *Voice of Dalit,* Vol. 1, No. 1 (Jan-July), 2008, 67-90.

116. Rup Kumar Barman, *Fisheries and Fishermen: A Socio-economic History of Fisheries and Fishermen of Colonial Bengal and Postcolonial West Bengal* (Delhi: Abhijeet Publications, 2008).
117. Rup Kumar Barman, *Contested Regionalism: A New Look on History, Cultural Change and Regionalism of North Bengal and Lower Assam*, (Delhi: Abjiheet Publications, 2007).
118. Rup Kumar Barman, Contested Ethnicity and Regional Assertion: A Study from Contemporary North Bengal, *Journal of History,* Vols. 22&23 (2004-05/2005-06), pp. 99-119.
119. Rup Kumar Barman, Partition of Bengal And Struggle For Existence of The Scheduled Castes: Impact of The Partition (1947) on the Rajbanshis of North Bengal, *Voice of Dalit,* Volume 2 Issue 2 (July-Dec 2009), pp. 141-163.

2

The Scheduled Castes of Colonial Bengal

Caste has been an inseparable part of Indian society since the beginning of settled human civilization where Bengal was no exception. Like other parts of India, cretin caste communities of Bengal were assigned lower social status in the caste hierarchy who have been classified as Scheduled Castes since the 1930s. In the pre-colonial literatures they were branded in different names according to their social position such as *chandalas*, *antajas*, *asprishyas*, etc. As an inseparable part of India's social and political culture, caste did not loss its pre-colonial flavour under the colonial rule. Rather the caste, as a social phenomenon, began to receive wide attention from both the 'colonial rulers' and the Indian political leaders in the late colonial period. The colonial administrators in most cases had retained the pre-colonial trend when they came forward to stratify the Indians according their own perception. They used 'caste' as a tool of social stratification in order to classify the Indians in different social categories irrespective of their religious and social affiliations. So the lower caste communities were mainly categorized as 'Hinduised Castes', 'Semi Hinduised Caste', 'Depressed Castes' and as 'Depressed Class' in the colonial administrative records of the nineteenth and early twentieth century. They began to be classified as Scheduled Castes with the adoption of the *Government of India (Scheduled Castes) Order (1936)*. In the last two decades of colonial rule the Scheduled Castes were emerged as a significant political entity in Bengal from a social identity. This transition of the Scheduled Castes undoubtedly was a significant part of sociopolitical lives of colonial Bengal. But the political location of the Scheduled Castes in the whole colonial Bengali society would remain sketchy without having a proper look on their social and economic background. So it is desirable to have some idea about the social position of the Scheduled Castes in the caste hierarchy of Hindu Bengali society and their economic relation with the non-Scheduled Caste communities.

The Scheduled Caste communities had to face a lot of social injustice. Many unreasonable restrictions were imposed over them since the time immemorial. In the colonial period too, they had to bear with the social stigmas. Thus they were treated as outcaste or *antebashi* or almost untouchables. They were equally oppressed in the class hierarchy. The occupations followed by them did not have enough opportunity of surplus appropriation. Socially their occupations were considered very much derogatory followed by the men of inferior social rank. In terms of their possession over the capital goods they were very much poor. So they could not develop their skills other than their traditional occupations. Lack of education and awareness and social restrictions made them an oppressed social category. However, beginning of social reforms among some Scheduled Caste communities had generated a sense of self-respect and inspired them to acquire modern education. Inspite of this positive development, the Scheduled Castes of colonial Bengal were very much backward in terms of both economic and social location in the colonial society of Bengal. In this chapter I would briefly discuss about the Scheduled Caste communities of colonial Bengal together with their socioeconomic condition.

2.1. Origin and Evolution of Caste System

As a social institution 'caste' has existence in India since the very beginning of settled human civilization. But this term is not an Indian one. It derives from the Portuguese term *casta* meaning 'pure bread.' However, we possess various terms in Indian languages which denote the meaning that of caste. *Varna* is a widely used term to mean caste which according to the traditional concept based on the fourfold functional division of the society. There is another term called *jati* (or its local equivalents) what refers to the endogamous social group. So *jati* and *varna* and their local equivalents are being used both by the social scientists and the governments of South Asian countries as an alternative of Western social concept like caste. Or in other words we can say inspite of having western provenance caste is now a common usage in South Asian society. So before discussing the location of the Scheduled Castes in the colonial society of Bengal it is desirable to have some idea about the origin of *jati/varna* or caste system in South Asian society.

There are divergences of views regarding the origin and growth of caste system in the Indian subcontinent. Generally it has been accepted that the caste system began to flourish in India with the influx of the Aryans, a warrior-nomadic tribe having pastoral and agricultural economic features. Growth of the Aryan civilization and culture and their interactions with the pre-Aryans of India had created a very complex caste system. In order to understand the beginning and growth of caste system in India historians and the social scientists have propounded certain possibilities like —religious-mystical, biological and socio-historical theories.

The religious theory explains how four *varnas* or castes were originated. The earliest reference to caste is found in the *Rig Veda*, most significant component of the Vedic literature, composed by the Aryans roughly between the 1500 BC and 1200 BC. In the subsequent period the Aryans have also produced *Samveda*, *Yajurveda* and *Atharvaveda*. These were basically the collection of hymns, prayers and formulae of life styles of the Aryans. These were supplemented by the composition of the *Brahmans*, *Upanishadas*, *Sutras* and *Shastras* in subsequent period. So gradually an elaborate philosophical system had developed in India particularly in the regions where the Aryans had spread their culture.

In the initial stage, caste as a social system did not have well-established character. Only the *Purushasukta* hymn of the *Rigveda* had referred about the origin of caste system. According to this hymn four castes, viz. Brahmin, Kshatriya, Vaishya and Sudra; were originated from the Brahma, the Supreme Being (the creator or *prakriti purusha*). It described that the Brahmins came from the mouth of the creator, the Kshatriyas from his arm, the Vaishyas from his thighs and the Sudras from his feet. This account is somewhat allegorical. It means that the Brahmins are the instructors of mankind, the Kshatriyas are the warriors and the Vaishyas and Sudras are the agriculturists and servant respectively.[1]

The *Bhagavat Gita*, however, has given an alternative version of origin of caste system. According to it four *varnas* are based on *guna* (quality) and *karma* (profession). The *Manava Dharma Shastra (Manusmriti)* and some other *shastras* have also attempted to classify the caste system as fourfold functional division of society. Thus the teachers and priests were classified as Brahmins, warriors and the kings were as the Kshatriyas, the traders were as Vaishyas and the artisans and servants were as Sudras. But unfortunately qualitative classification was turned into a hereditary classification since the Later Vedic period. Thus the *Manusmriti* had provided top position to the priestly class with some prerogatives. In the *Manusmriti* the priests were instructed to make a living by means of teaching the *Vedas*, reciting the *Vedas*, sacrificing for themselves, sacrificing for others, giving and receiving, etc.[2] Sudras on the contrary were asked to serve the priests. The *Manusmriti* had empowered the king to maintain the 'right' order. Manu had also recommended differential treatment for the members of different castes.[3] So the priestly caste was allowed to enjoy exemption from severe punishment in certain cases. Although the *Manusmriti* and other religious literature of the Aryans were accepted seriously by the Mainstream Hindus for centuries but they did not explain how the *jats* in each *varna* or sub-castes among the lower castes and the untouchables were born.

The biological theory claims that the qualities of an individual determine his position in the society. According to this theory there are three qualities of mankind viz.,— *satva*, *raja* and *tama*. *Satva* signifies the qualities like wisdom, intelligence, honesty, goodness and other positive qualities. *Rajas* include qualities like pride, velour and other passionate qualities. *Tama* qualities include dullness, stupidity, lack of creativity and other negative attitudes. These qualities have their significant impact in the time of adoption of one's profession. Thus teaching and profession of priests generally adopted by the Brahmins who said to have *satva* qualities. Accordingly Kshatriyas and Vaishyas adopt their respective jobs who possess *raja* quality. And the Sudras inherent *tama* qualities for which their professions are unclean and inferior.[4] Apparently the biological theory has some rationality but practically it is very difficult to classify all people of a particular caste into a particular group. Neither all Brahmins possess *satva* quality nor do all Sudras have *tama* quality. We may also find the *raja* quality among the Brahmins and *savta* quality among the Kshatriyas.

The socio-historical analysis is more acceptable as a theory of origin and development of caste system in India. It explains the creation of the *varnas, jats* and the *asprishyas* (untouchables). According to this approach the caste system began to develop with the arrival of the fair skinned Aryans from South Europe and North Asia in India (around 1500 BC). Before the Aryans there were different racial communities in India like Negritos, Mongoloids, Austroloids and Dravidians. The Aryans ignored the local cultures. They began conquering and taking control over local people. They organized among themselves into three groups. The first group was of the warriors and they were called Rajanya, later they changed their name Rajanya to Kshatriya. The second was of the priest, and they were called Brahmanas. The third group was of the farmers and craftsmen, and they were called Vaishyas. Besides, the three Aryan *varnas* there was Sudra *varna* whose members were simple workers of the society. Most of the pre-Aryan communities were integrated into the Sudra *Varna* or were made outcaste depending on their profession.[5]

In the beginning of Vedic period caste system was less important. Even there was no prohibition against the Sudras to listen the Vedas or to participate to any religious sacrament.[6] But from the Later Vedic period caste system began to spread in different places of India with the growth of Aryan civilization. At the same time certain restrictions were imposed on the lower castes and even on the upper caste women with the composition of the *smritis*, *samhitas* and *upanishads*.[7] As a result Brahmanical domination began to face challenges from the non-Brahmin castes particularly from the Kshatriyas and the Vaishyas. Rise of the Buddhism and Jainism in the sixth century BC was the most significant protest of this kind. Incidentally both these religions were propagated by the persons hailed from the Kshatriya ruling families i.e. Gautam Buddha (c.563 BC to 483 BC) and Vardhaman Mahavir (c 599BC – 527 BC) respectively. We notice religious reformation in the Brahmanical religious order too. With the coming of the Central Asian tribal ruling communities, beginning from the pre-Christian era, caste system had undergone certain changes because the Central Asians were assimilated with the Indian civilizations as the followers of Indian religious orders. Again we notice the growth of hierarchical caste system among the Buddhists too. In the early medieval period inter-caste marriages and growth of several new professions had further changed the pristine caste system. During this period we find the growth of numerous mixed communities (*jatis*) who have been assigned caste status according to the quality of their profession(s). We can get some idea about these new mixed castes from the *Brihatdharma Purana* and the *Brahmabaibartya Purana*. These two *Puranas* had classified the mixed castes into some categories like *Uttam Sankara*, *Madhyam Sankara* and *Adham Sankara* or as *Satsudra* and *Asatsudra*.[8]

Table: 2.1. Origin of Some Mixed Castes of Bengal and their Caste-Based Occupation(s)

Caste	*Father*	*Mother*	*Occupation(s)*
Andhra	Vaidehik	Nishada	Collecting forest products and hunting
Ambastha	Brahmin	Vaishya	Medical practice
Ashuri	Karan	Rajput	Agricultural work

Abhir	Brahmin	Ambastha	Cattle rearing
Kangshakar	Viswakarma	Sudra	Making and trading on bell metal
Karan	Vaishya	Sudra	Writer
Karmakar	Gopal	Tantubay	Iron work
Kalu	Kumbhakar	Kotkastra	Oil making
Kan	Jola	Hadi/Hari	Making musical instrument
Karabar	Nishada (Charmakar)	Vaidehik	Lather work
Kumbhakar	Malakar/	Karmakar/ Pattikar	Making earthen pot Tailik
Kudar	Rhishi	Brahmin	Making musical instrument
Krishirajak	Sadgop	Rajak	Agricultural work
Kaibartya	Nishad/ Kshatriya/ Swarnakar	Vaishya/ Kuber	Boat work/agricultural work/ menial job
Gangaputra	Let	Tiyar	Bearer of dead body
Gandhabanik	Ambashtha/	Rajput/ Brahmin	Seller of cosmetic products Vaishya
Gopa	Tantubay	Manibandh	Milkmen
Chandal	Sudra	Brahmin	Unclean profession
Charmakar	Tiyar	Chandal	Lather work
Chitrakar	Viswakarma	Sudra	Script writer
Churnakar	Var (Chunari)	Nat	Lime making
Dom	Let	Chandal	Making implements and furniture by the bamboo or bamboo works
Tantubay	Manibandha	Manikar	Weaving
Tambalik	Vaishya (Tamuli)	Sudra	Trade and commerce
Tiyar	Kshatriya	Rajput	Fishing
Tailik(Teli)	Baruni	Gopa	Making edible oil
Doyla(Duley)	Tailakar	Vaishya	Palanquin bearing
Dhibar	Gopa	Sudra	Fishing
Nat	Rajak	Soundink	Dancing and musical performance
Napit	Brahmin/	Sudra Kshatriya	Barber
Nishada	Brahmin	Sudra	Hunting
Pattikar	Chitrakar	Gopa	Making the images of deities
Poundra (Pod)	Vaishya	Sundi	Fishing/Agricultural work

Manikar	Tamrakutta	Sankhakar	Traders of Pearls
Malla, Matab	Let	Tiyar	Wrestler
Malakar	Karmakar	Tailik	Making and selling garland and flower
Mahishya	Kshatriya	Vaishya	Agricultural works and musical and dancing performance
Mlechha	Kshatriya	Sudra	Inferior works
Modak	Kshatriya	Sudra	Sweet making
Jugi	Veshdhari	Gangaputra	Bahurupi
Rajak	Dhibar	Tiyar	Washermen
Rajput	Kshatriya	Karan/ Ambastha	Ambassador
Let	Tiyar	Tailakar	Hunting
Bagtit(Bagdi)	Kshatriya	Vaishya	Fishing
Baruni(Barui)	Gopa	Tantubay	Betel leaf selling
Ben	Vaidehik	Ambastha	Drum beating
Baidya	Brahmin	Vaishya	Medical treatment
Byadha	Kshatriya	Swarbashi	Hunting
Shoundik (Sunri)	Vaishya	Tiyor	Making and selling country liquor
Swapach	Sudra	Brahmin	Hangman
Sankhakar	Gandha-banik/ Brahmin	Rajput/ Vaishya	Business on conch cell
Sadgop	Kshatriya	Sudra	Agricultural work
Swarnakar	Ambashtha/ Viswakarma	Vaishya/ Sudra	Goldsmith
Sutra(Suta)	Kshatriya	Brahmin	Horseman/ Chariot driver
Sutradhar	Viswakarma/ Karan	Sudra/ Vaishya	Carpenter
Sopak	Chandal	Pukkash	Butcher
Haddi	Let (Hadi/Hari)	Chandal	Pig farming

Source: Gurudash Chattopadhyay, *Jati Nirnay* (Calcutta: Bengal Medical Library, 1918), pp. 49.

In the medieval and the early modern period we notice further changes in the caste system. Although the lower caste communities had embraced the new egalitarian faiths like the Islam and Christianity but they could not develop their status. Thus the *arjal* and *atrap* section (*ajlaf*) of the Muslim society had been treated as the *Sudras* and *asprishayas* (untouchables) of the traditional Hindu society. Similarly the lower caste converted Christians were failed to remove the name of the 'dalit Christian'. Untouchables of traditional India are now popularly called the dalits.

The term dalit implies a condition of being under privileged and refers to people who are deprived of basic human rights and are suppressed on account of their lowly birth. Thus they are downtrodden and oppressed people who used to be identified by virtue of hereditary occupation(s) what are considered to be impure. The common notion about the dalit is that the dalit and the Scheduled Castes are synonymous. But the fact is that there are many people outside the Scheduled Castes who can also be termed as dalit. In a broader sense of the term by dalit here we mean all the lower classes in the Hindu caste hierarchy, the Scheduled Tribes, lower caste converted Muslims and Christians. However, in case of our present study we are mainly concerned about the Scheduled Castes of Bengal.

2.2. The Scheduled Castes of Colonial Bengal

In case of Bengal a total 76 communities were identified as Scheduled Castes in 1936 according to the *Government of India (Scheduled Castes) Order*. In postcolonial period some castes of 1936's list have been assigned Scheduled Tribe status in West Bengal. We can get some idea about the Scheduled Caste communities of colonial Bengal from the comparative analysis of the table 2.2 and 2.3 as given below.

Table 2.2: List of the Scheduled Castes of Bengal at per the Government of India (Scheduled Castes) Order 1936.

Sl. No Caste	*Sl. No Caste*	*Sl. No Caste*	*Sl. No Caste*	*Sl No. Caste*
1. Agariya	16. Dhenuar	31. Kadar	46. Kotal	61. Namasudra
2. Bagdi	17. Dhoba	32. Kan	47. Lalbegi	62. Nat
3. Bahelia	18. Doai	33. Kandh	48. Lodha	63. Nuniya
4. Baiti	19. Dom	34. Kandra	49. Lohar	64. Oraon
5. Bauri	20. Dosadh	35. Kaora	50. Mahar	65. Paliya

6. Bedia	21. Garo	36. Kapuria	51. Mahali	66. Pan
7. Beldar	22. Ghasi	37. Karenga	52. Mal	67. Pasi
8. Berua	23. Gonrhi	38. Kastha	53. Mallah	68. Patni
9. Bhati	24. Hadi	39. Kaur	54. Malpaharia.	69. Pod
10. Bhuinmali	25. Hajang	40. Kharia	55. Mech	70. Rabha
11. Bhuiya	26. Halalkhor	41. Khatik	56. Mehtor	71. Rajbanshi
12. Bhumij	27. Hari	42. Koch	57. Muchi	72. Rajwar
13. Bind	28. Ho	43. Konai	58. Munda	73. Santal
14. Binjhia	29. Jalia Kaibartya	44. Konwar	59. Musahar	74. Sunri
15. Chamar	30. Jhalo Malo or Malo	45. Kora	60. Nagesia	75.Tiyar and
				76.Turi.

Source: *The Government of India (Scheduled Castes) Order 1936.*

Table 2.3: Scheduled Castes of West Bengal, 2001

Sl. No Caste	*Sl. No Caste*	*Sl. No Caste*	*Sl. No Caste*
1. Bagdi, Duley,	16. Doai,	31. Kaur,	46. Namasudra
2. Bahelia,	17. Dom (Dhangad),	32. Keot (Keyot),	47. Nat,
3. Baiti,	18. Dosadh (Dusadh, Dhari, Dharbi)	33. Khaira,	48. Nuniya,
4. Batnar,	19. Ghasi,	34. Khatik,	49. Paliya,
5. Bauri,	20. Gonrhi,	35. Koch,	50. Pan (Sawasi),
6. Beldar,	21. Halakhor,	36. Konai,	51. Pasi,
7. Bhogta,	22. Hari (Mehtor, Methor, Bhangi, Balmiki)	37. Konwar,	52. Patni,
8. Bhuimali,	23. Jelia Kaibartya,	38. Kotal,	53. Pod (Poundra)
9. Bhuiya	24. Jhalo Malo or Malo,	39. Kurariar,	54. Rajbanshi,
10. Bind,	25. Kadar,	40. Lalbegi,	55. Rajwar,
11. Chamar (Charmakar, Mochi, Muchi, Rabidas, Rishi, Ruidas),	26. Kami (Nepali),	41. Lohar,	56. Sarki (Nepali)

12. Chaupal	27. Kandra,	42. Mal,	57. Sunri (Excluding Saha),
13. Dabgar,	28. Kanjar,	43. Mahar,	58. Tiyar,
14. Damai,	29. Kaora,	44. Malla,	59. Turi
15. Dhoba (Dhobi),	30. Karenga (Koranga),	45. Musahar,	60. Chai.

Source: Government of West Bengal, *Short Note on Scheduled Castes of West Bengal*, (Kolkata: Cultural Research Institute, Backward Classes Welfare Department, 2005).

From the historical point of view the Scheduled Caste communities had established their settlements in the Bengal region in distant past. Although we have some literary evidences about the existences of these castes but we cannot estimate their population strength in pre-colonial period. However, the population figures of these communities are available to us since the beginning of decennial census in 1871-72. The Rajbanshis (Koch and Rajbanshi), Namasudras (Chandals), Bagdis, Poundras (Pods), Bauris, Mochis, etc. were numerically most prominent Scheduled Caste communities of colonial Bengal. The Dhobas, Doms, Haris, Jelia Kaibartyas, Malos (Jhalo Malo), Lohars, Mals, Muchis (Rabidas), Paliyas, Sunris and Tiyors had average population figures in colonial days. The Bhuinmalis, Dushads, Kandras, Keots, Mallahs, Rajwars, Kadars, Kaoras, Karengas, Kotals, Mahars, Pashis, Patnis and Turis were comparatively smaller Scheduled Caste communities in terms of their population. The Behelas, Belders, Bhoktas, Binds, Chaupals, Doais, Ghashis, Gonrhis, Khatiks, Musahars, Nuniyas, Pans, etc. were minor Scheduled Caste communities of colonial Bengal. Let us have some general idea about these communities.

The Bagdis

One of the numerically prominent Scheduled Caste communities of colonial Bengal was the Bagdi. The Bagdis had major concentration in southwestern Bengal particularly in Bankura, Purulia, Birbhum, Burdwan, Midnapur and 24 Paraganas districts. They were also distributed in large scale in Nadia, Murshidabad, Howrah and Hooghly districts. Etymologically the word Bagdi has been derived from two terms *bag* (tiger) and *ti* (water).[9]

The myths of their origin also prove their attachment with water since very ancient time. One story as recorded in the colonial period tells that in order to test the fidelity of Shiva to her; goddess Parvati disguised herself as a fisherwoman. But Lord Shiva being tempted to that fisherwoman, made an intercourse with her. But when Parvati revealed her identity Shiva cursed her that the child to be born for their intercourse would be a Bagdi who would adopt fishing for livelihood.[10] Origin of the Bagdis is also linked with the origin of the Malla kingdom of Bankura. So the Bagdis had a tradition to place them as Kshatriya caste.

The Bagdis were divided into several sub-groups such as Tentulia, Kasikulia, Dulia, Ujha, Machhua, Gulimanjhi, Dandamanjhi, Kushmatia and Matial what actually originated from various occupations of the Bagdis. Traditional occupation of the Tentulias was making lime from the *tentul* (tamarind) tree. The Dulia Bagdis were basically palanquin (*duli*) bearer while the Machhua Bagdis were traditional fishermen. The Kushmatia and Matial were close to the earthwork (*mati*) and agricultural work. So it has been found that the Bagdis of Bengal, besides the palanquin bearing and agriculture works; were also engaged in catching and selling fish, making lime and earthworks. In agricultural sector they were mainly engaged as 'landless day labourer.'[11] So H.H.Risley had recorded in 1891 that 'in Western Bengal we find large number of them working as landless day labourers, paid in cash or kind, or as nomadic cultivators, tilling other men's lands on the *bhag-jot* system (sharecropping), under which they were remunerated by a definite share of the produce—sometime one half, sometimes less, as may be arranged with their landlord. I can recall no instance of a Bagdi holding a zemindari, or even a superior tenure such as patni or *mukarari*, of an importance.'[12]

This observation can give us an idea about the economic location of the Bagdis what together with their degraded social status had made them a very marginal community.

The Bahelias

The Bahelias in colonial Bengal were the members of a very

small Scheduled Caste community. In Bengal they mainly migrated from Bihar, Uttar Pradesh and Rajputana. They were mainly employed as soldiers in the army of king Krishna Chandra Roy (1710-1783) of Nadia.[13] So they were predominantly concentrated in Nadia district. The Bahelias in Bengal were also called Baheliya, Biola, Bayla, Bailia and Bahila. In Bengal they were engaged as hunter, landless agricultural labourer or as policemen or *Hazaras*.[14] They considered themselves as the offshoots of the Kshatriya communities of Western India such as Chhetri and Rajput but their neighbours used to treat them as Sudras. Their brethrens in Uttar Pradesh were known as Ahulia[15] who considered them as Rajputs. Here their traditional occupations were bird catching and making fans with peacock feathers.

The Baitis

The Baitis had constituted a small Scheduled Caste community in colonial Bengal. They were distributed in entire Bengal but in some districts they had major concentration such as Mymensingh, Dacca, Faridpur, Rangpur, Pabna, Malda, Murshidabad, Nadia, Jessore, 24 Parganas, Howrah, Hooghly, Burdwan and Midnapur. Traditionally they were the manufacturer of lime (*chun*) from shells. So they were also called Chunari or Chunia. They were also engaged in mat-making and weaving.[16] For procuring lime, the Baitis used to purchase shells from the Bediyas and the fishermen. Lime making, however, was not a monopoly of the Scheduled Caste Baitis. They had to share this occupation with the Muslim Baitis, Kathuria Sutas (wood cutters) and a section of the Bagdis.[17] Social status of the Baitis was very low in the Hindu caste hierarchy and often treated as *jalachal* group (from whom water can not be drunked). However, their product (lime) was very much touchable and had use among all people. So H. H. Risley observed in 1891 that 'although the Baiti is one of the most impure of Bengali castes, their water vessels defiling any pure Hindu, no one will refuse to chew lime moistened with water from these very same vessels.'[18]

The Bauris

The Bauris were socially one of the downtrodden castes of Western Bengal. They were divided into some sub-castes according to the place of their origin and regions of their concentration or their occupation such as—Mallabhumia, Mola, Malua, Dhulia, Sikharia, Panchakoti, Jhatia and Kathuria. Mallabhumia, Mola and Malua seem to be concentrated in the Mallabhum (Bankura) region while Dhalua indicates to Dhalbhum. Similarly Panchakotias were concentrated to Panchakote region (Purulia) and the Sikhrias were dominated in Sikharbhum i.e. in the tract lies between the Kansai and Barakar rivers.[19]

Cultivation, earth-working and palanquin-bearing were their traditional occupations. In the feudal polities of pre-colonial Western Bengal particularly in the Mallabhum and Manbhum regions the Bauris were also engaged as *paik* (ordinary solder) and caretakers of horses.[20] Like the Bagdis, the Bauris were also engaged in the agricultural work as day labourer. So they could not develop their economic status above the rank of day labour or under-raiyats. Socially they had very much inferior rank in terms of their location in the Hindu caste hierarchy.

The Beldars

The term Beldar has derived from *bel*, i.e. hoe. It indicate to their traditional occupation i.e. earthwork. They developed their expertise in digging earth and removing it in baskets carried on the head.[21] The Beldars were mainly concentrated in Bihar. Because of the expertise in digging the Beldars were extensively engaged in the coalfields of Western Bengal and Bihar. In Bengal they had very less population figure. However, some Beldars from Bhagalpur had settled themselves in Dinajpur and Malda districts.[22]

The Bhuinmalis

The Term *bhuinmali* has derived from two other common terms like *bhui* or *bhumi* (earth or land) and *mali* (gardener or caretaker). They were also called Bhuisundar in Bengal. They were divided into two sub-groups like Barabhagiya and Chhotabhagia. The

Barabhagia Bhuinmalis were basically cultivators, palanquin bearers and musicians. The Chhotabhagias were engaged in scavenging and other unclean menial works.[23] The Bhuinmali scavengers or sweepers were considered untouchable since they were not allowed to enter into the Hindu house[24] although service of the Barabhagiya Bhuinmalis particularly in the marriage, *shradha* (purification ritual after the death of a person) and *vastu puja* (worshiping the place for building house) was almost essential.[25]

In the colonial period the Bhuinmalis were mainly concentrated in Eastern Bengal particularity in Dacca, Faridpur, Bakharganj, Mymensingh, Tipperah, Rangpur, Dinajpur, Pabna and Rajshahi districts.

The Binds

Among the Scheduled Caste communities of colonial Bengal, the Binds had a very small population figure. They were mainly concentrated in Bihar and Uttar Pradesh. Only in Malda district of Bengal they had and still have little concentration. In Pabna, Nadia and Murshidabad districts the Binds had some scattered villages. Fishing, well sinking, building mud wall, mat and basket making, preparing saltpetre and doing earth works on roads and tanks were their traditional occupations.[26] In colonial Bengal the Binds were engaged in different occupation like fishing in the river system, earth and agricultural works, cutting tamarisk (*jhau*) on the sandbanks for selling them as firewood, making mud brasiers (*chullas*) generally used the country boat for cooking. The Binds were also cunning sportsman. The Binds were also seasonal collectors of rice from the rice field after harvest. They used to dig up the store of rice accumulated by the mud rates.[26]

The Chamars

Tanners and shoe makers popularly called Chamars were mainly concentrated in Northern, Central and Western India. They are also known as Charmakar, Rabidas, Chambhar and Ramdasia. In the colonial period they had significant presence in almost all districts of Bengal. According to the *Puranas* the Chamars were originated from a boatman and a Chandal (offspring of

Sudra father and a Brahmin mother) woman.[27] Manu, however, indicated that they were the offspring of a Nishada (offspring of a Brahmin father and Sudra mother) father and a Vaideha (offspring of a Vaishya father and a Brahmin mother) mother. In this connection it is to be remembered that both the Nishadas and the Vaideha's had marginal social base. So it seems that the Chamars had very much deplorable social status since the origin of this caste or the growth of traditional occupations. The Chamars were also engaged in some other subsidiary occupations particularly as musicians, landless day labourer and cobbler and as Tanti or weavers.[28]

The Chamars, because of their traditional occupations; were regarded impure and had very fated social rank. Some Chamars had no restriction to have flesh of dead cattle for which they were considered unclean. A late ninetieth century colonial observer, James Wise; had also recorded that 'the Chamar is inconceivably dirty in his habits, and offends others besides the Hindu by his neglect of all sanitary laws. Large droves of pigs are bred by them, and it is no uncommon sight to witness children and pigs wallowing together in the mire.'[29]

The Dhobas

The Dhobas were found in all parts of Bengal equally. This caste was regarded as unclean by the Hindu system as they used to wash the puerperal garments. This occupation, according to the Hindu ideas was reserved for out-caste and abandoned races.[30] The Brahmins did not take water touched by them. A section of the Dhobas had given up their traditional profession of washing cloths and taken to agriculture. They called themselves as 'Chasa Dhobas', and were regarded as of superior status to the ordinary Dhobas.[31]

The Doais

The Doai (called spelled as Doi) was a low caste community mostly concentrated in the northern part of Eastern Bengal particularly in Rangpur, Dinajpur, Cooch Behar, Mymensingh and Dacca districts. In the late nineteenth century they were found in large number especially along the banks of the Lakhya

River in Dacca.[32] The Doais were engaged in different professions such as ——palanquin bearing, load bearing, fishing and piggery. Many of them were found engaged in agriculture. The Doais were also engaged in mat (*pati*) making for which they were also called 'Patia Das.'[33] Socially the Doais had comparatively better position. They placed themselves in the Vaishya category of the *varna* system and did not accept food and water from Mehthor, Muchi and such others. All Varna-Hindus except the Brahmins and Kshatriyas accepted food and water from the Doais.[34]

The Doms

The Dom of colonial period was perhaps one of the most marginal Scheduled Caste communities in terms of social prestige. They were also called Dhangod. They believed that their original ancestor was Kalobir and their caste occupations were basket making, mat making and house thatching. Apart from these works, the Doms were also engaged as musicians and as 'day labourer'. They were divided into some social groups such as Chhachni Dom, Ankure or Ankuri Dom, Bajuni Dom and Magaya Dom.[35]

In the colonial period the Doms were mainly distributed in the Western Bengal districts such as Midnapur, Birbhum, Burdwan, Bankura, etc. In Eastern Bengal the Doms did not have significant concentration. Only in Mymensingh, the Doms had little concentration.

The Gonrhis

The Gonrhis believed to be the descendents of mythical Nishada boatmen who ferried Ram Chandra across the Ganges at Allahabad.[36] They were basically fish sellers although some of them were engaged in 'captured fishing'. We can get some idea about the occupations of the Gonrhis from their social divisions. They were divided into Kurvin, Manjhi, Chotaha and Chobi groups. The Kurvins were engaged in business and service. The Manjhi Gonrhis were basically boatmen. The Chotahas were traditional fishermen while the Chobis were fishermen of low category.[37] In the colonial period they were largely concentrated in Bihar but they had also concentration in Burdwan, 24 Parganas and Murshidabad districts of Bengal. Their social status varied from place to place.

The Halalkhors

The Halalkhors (also known as Halal-Khore, Bhangi, Bhangia, Mehtor, etc) of colonial Bengal were traditionally sweepers and scavengers. Hence their occupations were considered most unclean. Many of them had embraced Islam but could not elevate their social status.

The Haris/Hadis

One of the menial and scavenger castes of Bengal was 'Hari' (also called Mehtor, Mehtar, Bhangi and Balmiki). They were divided into nine sub-castes. Their traditional occupations were tapping date-trees, making bamboo combs, playing musical instruments at weddings and festivals, carrying palanquin, and scavenging. They were very lowly placed in the society. No one ate with 'Hari' or take water from their hands. Members of this caste were not allowed to enter the premises of great temples.[38] They were distributed in all districts of Bengal in the colonial period.

The Jelia Kaibartyas

The Jelia Kaibartyas were primary fishermen of Eastern and Northeastern India. The etymological sources of the term *kaibartya* are *ka* or water and *brata* or livelihood.[39] So meaning of the *kaibartya* is 'the people who earn livelihood from water' i.e. fishing and boating. The Kaibartyas were occasionally referred in the Indian classical literature particularly in the *Mahabharata* (*Anusashan, Chapters 50 and 51*), *Manu Smriti* and *Brahmabaibartya Purana*. Early Buddhist literature (*Dighanikaya, Brahmajalsuta*) and Asoka's inscription have also maintained the term *kaibartya*.[40] King Asoka gave them full right of catching fish from the internal water resources like the rivers, ponds, lakes, etc.[41] According to Manu, the Kaibartyas are the descendents of a

Nishad (*Das* or Non-Aryan) father who live by boating.[42] The Kaibartyas had large-scale settlements in Bengal since very ancient period. Legends and myths prevailed among the Kaibartyas prove that they had prominent position in Bengal in different historical period particularly during the Pala and the Sena rule (eighth to twelfth century AD).

The Kaibartyas had two distinct divisions according to their occupations. The Kaibartyas, engaged in agricultural works, were called Chashi Kaibartyas while fishing was primary occupation of the Jelia Kaibartyas. Although the Chashi Kaibartyas claimed the Mahishya status (equivalent to almost Vaishya Caste status) and had given up their attachment with the fishing[43] but Buchanan Hamilton in his survey on the districts of Eastern India found the Kaibartyas as one of the primary fishermen castes in the early nineteenth century.[44] The Jelia Kaibartyas had large concentration in Midnapur, 24 Parganas, Hooghly, Howrah, Burdwan, Nadia and Murshidabad districts in the colonial period. They were also noticed in large scale in Eastern Bengal and in the Brahmaputra valley (Lower Assam).[45] The Jelia Kaibartyas were also engaged in retailing of fish (as *paikar*) and as intermediaries in the fish market called *nikari* besides fishing in the water bodies.[46]

The Jhalo Malos or Malos

The Jhalo Malo or Malos were also primary fishermen of Bengal. They established their settlement in Bengal in the pre-historic period. In the early nineteenth century, Buchanan Hamilton found that the Malos were engaged in fishing throughout Bengal although majority of them were concentrated in Eastern Bengal[47] particularly in Mymensingh, Coomilla, Pabna, Jessore, Nadia and Murshidabad districts.

The colonial ethnographers had identified the Malos as Dravidian by race[48] but culturally they had their affinities with Patnis and Doms.[49] The educated section of the Malos of the early twentieth century, however, had created a notion that they are the descendents of the Kshatriya rulers of Western India who were compelled to conceal their Kshatriya identity and to migrate to Bengal due to the policy of persecution of the Kshatriyas followed by Parsuram in the prehistoric period.[50] Whatever the origin of the Malos it is true that fishing was their primary occupation during the pre-colonial and colonial period although some of them were also engaged in agricultural works. They had developed their own techniques and technologies of fishing including the art of making nets of different verities and other implements and processing fishes.[51]

The Koches

The Koches in colonial period had been classified by the colonial administrators in different names. They were often identified as Rajbanshis or compared with the Rabhas, Garos, Pani Koches and Paliyas. The Koches again were associated with the foundation of a kingdom in northern Bengal having its branches in Northeast India. By the end of the nineteenth century the Koch ruling families were deteriorated to the status of big zamindars or the rulers of native states.

Origin of the term Koch is a debatable one. Pre-colonial literatures have left some impression about the nomenclature of the Koch tribe. The Sanskrit texts compiled in Kamarupa have described the Koches as *Kuvacha* or as *Kubachaka* (evil speaker).[52] But the *Tabakat-i-Nasiri* of Minhasuddin Shiraz had illustrated this tribe as 'Koch.'[53] According to Suniti Kumar Chatterji the term *'koch'* has been originally derived from the Indo-Aryan source *kawamca*, written as *kamoca* which was *sanskritized* as *kamboja*.[54] The *kamboja* has been further elevated to the status of *kubachaka* through *Komc–Koch–Kubacha* continuum. On the contrary, there is equal possibility of tribalisation of the term *Kuvachaka* to Koch. So the term 'koch' is either tribalized form of the Sanskrit term *kuvacha* or koch was sanskritised as *kuvachaka*.

Whatever the etymological debate on the Koches, with the beginning of colonial ethnography and decennial censuses, social identity of the Koches became almost inseparable from that of the Rajbanshis. Buchanan Hamilton, who visited Rangpur and other parts of North Bengal in the early nineteenth century.

(1807-14) had observed that 'the Koches were designated as Rajbanshi although all Rajbanshis are not Koch'.[55] It means the term 'Rajbanshi' is a greater connotation where the Koches entered after abandoning their tribal customs and accepting Hindu traditions and rituals. Hamilton was endorsed by B.H. Hodgson (1847) who expressed that the Koches, Meches and the Kacharis originated from the great Mongolian race and Koches or Rajbanshis are merely the most *hinduized* form of the common stock.[56] So it appears that Koches were *rajbanshized* after their hinduization. So it is likely that the Koches were begun to be designated as *Rajbanshi* since the early nineteenth century.

Inspite of *kshatriyaization* of the Koches *Rajbanshi* was not a preferred title. But the colonial censuses in the beginning gave them equal caste status to both the Rajbanshis and Koches i.e. *Bhanga Kshatriya* or *Bratya Kshatriya*.[57] But it was challenged by the educated and landed elite of the Rajbanshi community. The Rajbanshi elites, fortified with modern education by codifying the common believes prevailed among them argued that they are the descendents of Raja Vardhana who being persecuted by Mahapadma Nanda fled to North Bengal.[58] Thus they are not identical with the Koches who had their ancestry with tribal folk. The Rajbanshi intellectuals of Rangpur founded a caste organization to differentiate the Rajbanshis from the Koches. The educated section of this community began to publish several works to prove the Rajbanshis as Kshatriyas (Poundra).[59] The Rajbanshi Kshatriya Samity, founded in 1910 at Rangpur, had the basic objectives to establish a distinct social identity of the Rajbanshis, de-linked from the Koches.[60] The census of 1911 recorded the Rajbanshi as Kshatriya. But in the census of 1921, the Koches were also recorded as Kshatriya. However, *kshatriyaization* of the Rajbanshis since 1913 had rapidly increased the figure of the Rajbanshi population while the figure of the Koches was declined. The figures of the Rajbanshis in 1921 was 1727111 which increased to 1806390 in 1931 while the figure of the Koches was decreased from 131273 in 1921 to 81299 in 1931.[61] It was due to the classification of the Koches as Rajbanshi.

The Lohars

The Lohars of Bengal were basically blacksmiths of Bihar. In respect of social status they were considered to be very low in Bengal, and were associated in matters of food and water with 'Bauris', 'Bagdis' and 'Malos'.

The Mals

In the colonial period the Mals were mainly concentrated in Southwestern Bengal. They were basically agriculturist although many members of this community had adopted other professions. Socially the Mals were very inferior.

The Mallahs

The Mallahs were basically boatmen although a section of them was also engaged in fishing and fish related business. The term was often applied to indicate all fishermen castes of Bengal such as the Binds, Chais, Gonrhis, Jelia Kaibartyas, Malos, Keyots and Tiyors.[62]

The Namasudras

Among the Scheduled Castes of colonial Bengal, the Namasudras were second largest in population strength. But the term 'Namasudra' is comparatively a new one. In the pre-colonial even in the early colonial period they were mainly known as Chandal and used to be called *Chanral* in colloquial language. It is only since the later half of the nineteenth century the Chandals of Bengal began to identify themselves as Namasudras. Demand of the Chandals for Namasudra caste identity culminated into a social movement in the early years of the twentieth century. From 1911 the Chandals began to be classified as Namasudras in the official records. So regarding the identity of the Namasudras of colonial Bengal we have to face a critical problem unlike other lower caste communities.

We find several contradictory traditions of origin of the Namasudras. The early colonial ethnographers and official surveyors have left some observations according to their own perception on Indian society and social stratification of Indian caste communities. In the early nineteen century, Buchanan Hamilton had recorded that the Chandals of Bengal were identical with the Dosadh tribe of eastern and northern India.[63] Again James Wise, in his *Notes on the Races, Castes, and Trades of Eastern Bengal* (1883), had classified the Chandals as Dravidian tribe.[64] James Wise was followed by Mr.Baverly who opined that the term Chandal is a generic title and the Chandal tribe is identical with the Mals of Rajmahal Hill.[65] H. H. Risley had also followed the same method of classification. He recorded in 1891 that 'the Chandals of Bengal invariably call themselves as Namasudra, and with characteristic jealousy higher division of the caste apply the name Chandal to the lower, who in their turn pass it to the Dom.'[66] So it appears that the Namasudras have been classified differentially in the colonial records.

There are different opinions regarding the possible origin of the Namasudras. First one is the Chandal origin of the Namasudras. Here we may focus light on the traditional views of origin of the Chandals. The Chandals, since the ancient period; have been considered one of the most degraded social castes who according to the tradition originated from the illicit intercourse of a Sudra man and a Brahmin woman. In the Sanskrit literature they had been depicted as lowest of mankind, as an outcaste, performing menial duties for the Brahmins, and living on the outskirts of cities. Iron ornaments, dogs and monkeys were their wealth. Gradually the term Chandal became a term of abuse and no caste community was agreed to identify itself as Chandal. But there is a significant problem regarding the Chandal origin of the Namasudras of Bengal. How far the huge concentration of the Chandals in a particular tract of Bengal was possible due to the union of the Sudra men and Brahmin women?

Second possibility is the tribal origin of the Chandals. It was basically popularized by the colonial ethnographers. The colonial ethnographers held the view that the tribal Chandals were gradually absorbed to non-tribal Hindu social system through the process of adoption of the Hindu culture and social traditions what has been conceptualized by the social scientists as 'Hindu method of tribal absorption', *sanaskritization* or detribalization. The colonial ethnographers had also popularized a view that the social transformation of the Chandals was stimulated by the emergence of the Chandals as a ruling community. In order to prove the formation of Chandal chiefdom, the example of "Chandal Raja" of Pala time was raised by them. During the Pala rule (eighth to twelfth century), the Chandal chief of Bhowal embraced the Buddhism whose successors gradually identified as Chandals after the decline of the Buddhism in Bengal.[67] But this argument does not get support from the modern knowledge of cultural or social anthropology. Most of the tribal communities of Eastern and Northeastern India, after the formation of their chiefdoms (and later on kingdoms) tried their best to legitimize them as a ruling caste through patronizing the non-tribal culture. By doing so, they were successful to place them as caste community of lower social status but not as untouchables.[68] Why the Chandals were branded as untouchable or social stigmas were imposed on them if they were the rulers?

Another possibility of origin of the Namasudras, as recorded by the colonial scholars; was the Brahmin origin. James Wise and H.H. Risley had recorded that the Chandals of Dacca claimed that they were Brahmins who degraded to Chandals by eating with the Sudras. Another story retained in the tradition that the ancestor of the Chandals of the Eastern Bengal was a Brahmin named Bamdev who's father (Vashistha) had cursed him to be degraded as Chandal for committing a ceremonial mistake.[70] This tradition is corroborating with another myth that the Namasudras of Bengal originated from a Brahmin scholars or sage named 'Lamasa Muni'. This Lamasa gradually got the form of *namasa* what (according to some Namasudras) was the origin of the term Namasudra.

Whatever the debate among the scholars about the origin, it is a fact that the term Namasudras is a new one. It is the composition of two term *nama* and *sudra*. In the colonial period the Namasudras were mainly concentrated in Eastern Bengal. They had significant concentration in Dacca, Mymensingh, Faridpur, Bakharganj, Tippera, Jessore, Khulna, Noakhali, Rangpur, Pabna, and Rajshahi districts of Eastern Bengal. In the Western

Bengal districts they had little bid concentration particularly in Midnapur, Burdwan, 24 Parganas, Murshidabad and Nadia.

From the occupational point of view the Namasudras were mainly engaged in the primary sector of economy what can be estimated from their social groups such as Halwah (cultivators), Ghashi (Grass-cutters), Kandho (palanquin-bearers), Karral (fishermen), Bari(carpenters), Berua (fishermen), Baqqal or traders and hucksters.

The Nats (Nar)

One of the dancing and musician castes of Eastern Bengal was the Nat. According to James Wise, the Nats of Eastern Bengal were identical with the 'Kathaks' of Northern India those who migrated to Bengal during the Muslim rule in Bengal.[71] The Hindu-Nats had a position corresponding to that of the Muslim Bajunia. It is also believed that many of the Nats had embraced Islam.[72]

The Nunias (Nuniyas)

The Nunias, a small Scheduled Caste community of Bengal, believed that extraction of salt and saltpeter from saline earth to be their traditional occupation.[73] So in colonial Bengal, they were found to be engaged in cultivation, saltpeter-making and various type of earthwork. The Nunias were largely distributed in Bihar and Orissa but they had significant concentration in the coastal belt of Midnapur as well as in Mymensingh of Eastern Bengal.

The Paliyas

One of the cultivator castes of Northern Bengal in colonial period was Paliya. Their identity and social status are closely linked with the Koches as discussed earlier.

The Pans (Sawasi)

The Pans were principally basket-makers and weavers in colonial India. They were mainly distributed in Bihar and northern India.

They had very less concentration in Bengal. However, they had been counted in Midnapur district in large scale in the late nineteenth century.

The Pasis

The Pasis were traditionally toddy tapers of North India. They used to extract juice from different palm (like *tal* and *khejur* or date palm) trees. The juice of date palm popularly called *tari* had use in manufacturing bread. Intoxicated *tari* was also a popular drink among the drunkard. The juice of palm was also a principal material for making sugar and molasses.

In case of Bengal, the Pasis had less concentration since extraction of juice from palm trees was not developed as a profession of any particular community. Here the owners of date palms either extract the juice themselves, or employ ordinary labourer to do so and shops for the sale of spirituous liquors were usually owned by the Sunris, another lower caste community.[74] Thus the toddy taping as a profession of the Pasis did not properly develop in Eastern Bengal. Socially the Pasis had inferior rank what can be compared with the Binds and Chains. The Brahmins and the upper caste Hindus did not take water from their hands. Although many Pasis had adopted agricultural work as their profession but they could not develop their social status.[75]

The Patnis

In Eastern Bengal the Patnis were found to be engaged in boating, fishing, basket-making, trading and cultivation. In social ranking they were more or less equal to, 'Malos' and Jelia Kaibartyas. The upper caste Hindus had restrictions to take water from their hands. The Patnis had their own barber and washer men of their own caste.[76]

The Poundras

The Poundras were engaged in different occupation of primary sectors such as agriculture, fishing and trading. They had large scale distribution in Midnapur, 24 Parganas, Khulna and Nadia.

The Poundras were also classified as Pod or as Padmaraj. They believed that they were originated from the ancient Pundras as mentioned in the *Mahabharata*. They claimed Poundra Kshatriya status in the early twentieth century. But practically they were regarded impure by the upper caste Hindus of Bengal.[77]

The Rajbanshis

The Rajbanshis were numerically largest Scheduled Caste community of Bengal. They were scattered all over Bengal along with some neighbouring provinces. They had significant concentration in Rangpur, Jalpaiguri, Dinajpur, Maldah and Darjeeling districts. They had highest concentration in Cooch Behar State. The Rajbanshis were also distributed in Lower Assam. The Rajbanshis of Southern Bengal, however, were different than their North Bengal brethrens in terms of occupation and social affiliation. In Northern Bengal, the Rajbanshis were/are a 'linguistic-cum-caste community' whereas in Southern Bengal they were basically a caste community of heterogeneous character.

From occupational point of view, the Rajbanshis of undivided Bengal were mainly dependent on the agricultural works. The Southern Rajbanshis particularly of Nadia, Murshidabad, 24 Parganas and Midnapur were engaged in fishing along with agricultural works. The Rajbanshis of Northern Bengal, however, were agriculturists. Fishing was no way their occupation although they had developed their own techniques and technologies of fishing.

The Rajbanshis of Northern Bengal were engaged in agricultural works both as land proprietor and as sharecroppers or as ordinary labourer. There were wide variations in the 'cultivators-landowners relationship' in northern Bengal and Cooch Behar State beginning from *zamindar* in the top to the agricultural labourers (*halua/kamla*) in the bottom. The *zamindars* used to get land directly from the government subject to the payment of fixed amount of revenue. The *jotedars* stood second in that hierarchy who were intermediary between the *zamindars* and the *chukanidars*. *Chukanidars* could sublet their lands to the *dar-chukanidars*. The *dar-chukanidars* could cultivate their land by their own initiative with the help of *halua* (agricultural labourer/agriculturists) or through their tenants called *adhiars* (sharecroppers). The suppliers of land to the *haluas* or *adhiars* were called *giri* in rural areas of that region. So the agricultural labourers or the *haluas* stood in the bottom of the 'landownership-production relations' hierarchy.[78]

There were again wide variations in the social position of landholders and actual cultivators in the rural areas of sub-Himalayan Bengal. While a big landholder in a village often designated as *dewani* (also called *dewnia* or *giri*) had prominent position, the *adhiars* or *haluas* were inferior in the village society. Again the *zamindars/jotedars/dewanis* had contact with upper castes what the ordinary *haluas* or *adhiars* had not. However, the relationship between the cultivators and the landowners in Sub-Himalayan Bengal particularly between the Rajbanshi cultivators and the *jotedars* was quite congenial because of common caste origin.

From the point of class, most of the Rajbanshis were *adhiars* (sharecroppers) who had good terms with the *zamindars* or *jotedars*. A few Rajbanshis of Rangpur, Jalpaiguri, Darjeeling, Cooch Behar State and Dinajpur districts were *zamindars* and *jotedars* particularly in the permanently settled areas. A very small section of the total population of this community had been stratified as middle class in the census of 1931. The educated section and the landed elites had formed the core section of the Rajbanshis in the late colonial period.

In undivided Bengal, the Rajbanshis had developed a kind of social integrity through the social reform movement popularly conceptualized as *kshatriyaization* which led to the growth of self consciousness and formation of a social identity. *Kshatriyaization* movement of the Rajbanshis was started in 1891 from the question of their social status in the decennial census what eventually placed the Rajbanshis as a distinct Scheduled Caste community in the late colonial rule.

The Rajwars

The Rajwars were classified by the colonial ethnographers as

Dravidian. They were concentrated in southwestern Bengal. They had seven sub-castes. Their traditional occupation was 'preparing and selling' flattened rice. There soocial rank was very low. The Brahmins did not take water from them.[79]

The Sunris

Manufacturing and sale of spirituous liquors were the traditional occupations of the Sunris of Bengal. They were distributed almost all districts of Bengal. Socially the Sunris had very much deplorable status although economically they had sound position. It is because of the social status, a Brahmin could not dare to utter the name of the Sunri caste before mid-day.[80] The term *Sunri* thus became an abuse in the Bengali language.

The Tiyors

The Tiyors were and occupationally still are the members of the primary fishermen caste of Bengal and Bihar. They were also found as boatmen, shopkeeper and agriculturists where fishes were not available. James Wise had identified the Tiyors as the pre-historic dwellers of the Gangetic delta.[81] Although the Tiyors were mostly concentrated in Western Bengal, they were also noticed in Eastern Bengal during the colonial period.[82]

2.3. Distribution and Occupational Background of the Scheduled Castes

Since the term 'Scheduled Caste' got legal shape only in 1936, we don't have figure of the Scheduled Caste communities of Bengal before 1941. However, the colonial government had started the census operation since 1870s on the basis of caste and religion for which we can get the figures of the castes who got Scheduled Caste status in later period. The census data of 1872 and 1881 show that the caste communities of present study had wide variation in terms of their population figures and distribution. Because in the initial stage of social stratification, the Indian caste communities were less concerned about the significance of social position in the official records. However, from the census data of 1881 we may clearly indicate about the regional concentration of certain communities. Here we find that the Chandals (later Namasudra), Jelia Kaibartyas, Sunris, Koches, Dhobis were largely concentrated in Eastern Bengal districts while the Bagdis, Bauris, Chamars, Doms and Haris had large concentration in Western Bengal.

Table 2.4: Distribution of Some Major East Bengali Scheduled Caste Communities (1881)

Division and Dist.	*Chandal*	*Jalia*	*Kaibartya*	*Pod*	*Sunri*	*Dhobi*
Burdwan	16887	5374	31592	42	1005	20
Bankura	1326	3310	25250	196	224	4412
Birbhum	2099	4059	9129	30	4861	3210
Midnapur	27826	20179	753435	13660	2523	41607
Hooghly	11845	10369	142526	1958	5	7988
Howrah	9282	6467	155653	14138	95	9324
Total in Burdwan Division	*69265*	*49758*	*1117585*	*30024*	*8713*	*66564*
24Pgs	21277	11424	14596	217187	1757	13973
Suburbs	1458	1060	17482	2000		4644
Calcutta	830	3021	16780	139		4070
Nadia	43780	19052	126063	4518	15335	10495
Jessore	160755	32775	32505	3551	4758	6205
Khulna	148802	20964	25895	66790	2012	2276
Murshidabad	17972	2867	100355	147	17582	7048
Total in Presidency Division	*394874*	*91163*	*464576*	*294332*	*41444*	*48711*
Dinajpur	7180	13560	37785	68	407923	2002
Rajshahi	29792	13774	63134	39	10459	1697
Rangpur	36795	8387	30612	8	432498	898
Bogra	9892	5220	15566	50	19055	552
Pabna	35319	39279	23306		4875	2225
Darjeeling	308	13	219		30801	330
Jalpaiguri	1875	3870	5838		208332	990
Total in Rajshahi (Jalpaiguri) Division	*139181*	*84103*	*176460*	*165*	*1113933*	*8684*
Dacca	202510	39274	40422		13498	11028
Faridpur	244923	28607	24010	1	1886	9827
Bakharganj	260771	13298	18080		924	21628
Mymensingh	148380	32011	94217	13	31997	17419

Total in Dacca Division	856584	113190	176729	14	48305	59902
Cittagong	2418	15312	4542		180	11446
Noakhali	18644	8602	16151		210	15151
Tippera	83023	12516	50290	33	2495	16555
Cittagong Hill Track	11	11	7		41	38
Total in Chittagong Division	*104096*	*36441*	*70990*	*33*	*2926*	*43190*
Total for Bengal Proper	1564000	374655	2006340	19788	1215321	227048

Source: Census, 1881

Table 2.5: Distribution of Some Major West Bengali Scheduled Caste Communities (1881)

Division and Dist	*Bagdi*	*Bauri*	*Chamar*	*Dom*	*Hari*
Burdwan	148788	82254	49229	39030	22121
Bankura	47146	117548	4495	17581	6251
Birbhum	42032	27258	30975	35316	23286
Midnapur	74497	12746	13387	16549	25573
Hooghly	134115	1861	21869	10825	13030
Howrah	54943	4	5815	3209	2150
Total in Burdwan Division	*501521*	*241671*	*130770*	*122510*	*92411*
24 pgs	78654	519	36586	3015	3441
Suburbs	8926	1	12911	1642	319
Calcutta	5407	4	8590	1705	657
Nadia	42946	2018	61058	3335	6415
Jessore	7859	717	37382	1044	487
Khulna	4437	1	26154	49	407
Murshidabad	30568	4411	22550	7505	7753
Total in Presidency Division	*117897*	*7671*	*205231*	*18295*	*19479*
Dinajpur	1536	1099	4043	2138	31934
Rajshahi	2002	162	5709	504	4045
Rangpur	242	146	3660	1806	5658
Bogra	1476	65	1909	331	6999
Pabna	2325	265	5792	1340	2216
Darjeeling	46	1	778	162	1237
Jalpaiguri	24527	30	2163	935	6625
Total in Rajshahi (Jalpaiguri) Division	*32154*	*1758*	*24054*	*7216*	*58714*
Dacca	2442	808	24988	538	1076

Faridpur	2232	300	4735	293	981
Bakharganj	864	87	2580	852	68
Mymensingh	2781	76	11289	1210	1855
Total in Dacca Division	*8319*	*1271*	*43592*	*2893*	*3980*
Cittagong	306	38	1092	9117	4972
Noakhali	39		571	380	148
Tippera	66	9	4353	804	1268
CHT					
Total in Chittagong Division	*411*	*47*	*6015*	*10301*	*6388*
Total for Bengal Proper	720302	252418	409662	161215	180972

Source: Computed from Census, 1881.

In the subsequent years many change had taken place in regards to the nomenclature of the lower caste communities since many of them returned as higher castes. However, regarding the distribution, the census data had no exceptional figure. Regional concentration of the major caste communities was a general feature. From the census figures of 1931 and 1941 it appears that the Rajbanshis and the Koches were mainly concentrated in the districts of Northern Bengal (Rajshahi Division and Cooch Behar State) and the Namasudras had large concentration in Southeastern Bengal (Dacca Division). The Poundras had large concentration in Southern Bengal particularly in the Presidency Division. The Bagdis and Bauris were mainly distributed in the districts of Southwestern Bengal especially in the Burdwan Division. Some Scheduled Caste communities like the Bhuinmalis, Doais, Jelia Kaibartyas, Malos, Patnis, etc. had more concentration in the districts of Eastern Bengal while the Behelas, Belders, Bhoktas, Ghashis, Gonrhis, Kadars, Keyots, Khatiks, Kandras, Nuniyas, Pans and Tiyors were largely distributed in Western Bengal districts. Regional concentrations of some large size Scheduled Caste communities (such as Namasudras, Rajbanshis and the Poundras) was a positive factor for their social and political identity formation in the late colonial period. But small population sizes of dispersed characters were detrimental for the smaller and minor Scheduled Caste communities in the process of their social unification.

Table 2.6: Population Figures of Some Scheduled Caste Communities of Colonial Bengal (Excluding Cooch Behar and Tripura States) in 1931 and 1941.

Sl.No.	*Name of the Caste*	*1931*	*1941*
1.	Bagdi	987333	662483
2	Bahelia	4449	1808
3	Baiti	8873	6541
4	Bauri	330993	331457
5	Bedia	7363	6229
6	Beldar	3139	5258
7	Bhuinmali	89802	61615
8	Bhuiya	33614	40258
9	Bind	19160	15057
10	Chamar	148661	127183
11	Dhobi	228666	187495
12	Doais	1073	3742
13	Dom	138926	118800
14	Doshad	35928	23033
15	Ghashi	5222	5326
16	Gonrhi	5159	2146
17	Hari	131852	92729
18	Jelia Kaibartya	349859	277861
19	Jhalo Malo	197789	163067
20	Kadar	1078	1613
21	Kandra	4670	11643
22	Kaora	170867	92926
23	Karenga	9855	8403
24	Khatik	1157	1268
25	Koch	80002	42806
26	Konai	41058	41486
27	Konwar	133	1977
28	Kora	46617	39240
29	Kotal	7651	6597
30	Lalbegi	4956	1659
31	Lohar	49968	67440

32	Mahar	1791	6917
33	Mal	111409	114359
34	Mallah	25903	18604
35	Mehtor	22911	23599
36	Muchi	411821	321600
37	Musahar	11585	10809
38	Namasudra	2086213	2150760
39	Paliya	43163	
40	Pan	791	1735
41	Pasi	18628	12990
42	Patni	39290	11686
43	Pod	667731	564993
44	Rajwar	21315	32338
45	Rajbanshi	1487469	
46	Sunri	76779	65654
47	Tiyor	96375	41403
48	Turi	17362	15784

Source: Census, 1931 & 1941.

The Scheduled Castes of colonial Bengal were not homogenous in terms of their class status. They were mainly identified according to their traditional occupation(s). Among the agriculturists, the Rajbanshis, Poundras, Namasudras, Bhuiyans, Kaoras, Palias, etc, were numerically prominent. The Bagdis, Bhuinmalis, Bahelias, Bauris, Belders, Bhogtas, Konais, Kotals, etc. were also engaged in agriculture. But these castes were basically landless agricultural labourer. The Doais, Gonrhis, Jelia Kaibartyas, Malos, Kandras, Khairas, Mallahs, Tiyors, Patnis, Ghashis and the Binds (including Chais) were traditionally fishermen castes. The Muchis (Charmakars) and Dabgars were engaged in leatherworks. The Pans and Chaupals were traditionally weavers while washing cloths was the occupation of the Dhobas. Basket making was the traditional profession of the Batnars and Doms. Halakhors, Haris, Mehtors and Lalbegis were scavengers and sweepers. The Lohars were traditionally blacksmiths while the Mals, Sapurias and Mushahars were snake-charmers. Selling of fruits was the traditional occupation of the Khatiks. Extraction of honey from the forests was traditional occupation of the

Kurariars. Making and selling country liquor was the traditional occupations of the Pashis and the Sunris. The Scheduled castes were also engaged in other menial works.

Table 2.7: Occupational Classification of Some Scheduled Caste of Bengal.

Sl. No	*Caste*	*Traditional Occupation(s)/Status*
1	Bagdi, Duley	Agricultural works, fishing, palanquin bearing, making fishing implements and other menial jobs.
2	Bauri	Cultivation, earth works, agricultural labour.
3	Bhuiya	Cultivation, agricultural labour.
4	Charmakar /Muchi/	Tanners, shoe makers, suppliers of lathers for making drums.
5	Dhoba	Washing cloths.
6	Dom/ Dhangar	Basket making, punkha pulling, house thatching.
7	Hari, Mehtor	Scavenging and sweeping, basketry, wage labour.
8	Jelia Kaibartya	Fishing, selling fish and making fishing implements.
9	Malo	Fishing, selling fish and making fishing implements.
10	Kaora	Agricultural works, fgishing, palanquin bearing.
11	Lohar	Iron works.
12	Mal	Snake-charming.
13	Namasudra	Agricultural works, fishing, Fishing, selling fish.
14	Paliya	Agricultural works.
15	Pod/Poundra	Agricultural works.
16	Rajbanshi	Agricultural works, fishing, selling fish.
17	Rajwar	Preparing and selling flattened rice.
18	Sunri (Excluding	Making and selling country liquor. Saha)
19	Tiyor	Fishing, selling fish and boating.

Sources: Compiled by self from H. H. Risley/ Tribes and Caste of Bengal, 2 vols., reprint edn. (Calcutta, Firma Mukhopadhyaya, 1981); Government of West Bengal, Short Note on Scheduled Castes of West Bengal, (Kolkata:Cultural Research Institute, 2005) and the field survey data.

It is a noticeable fact that most of the Scheduled Castes were underprivileged and belonged to the lower class. There were very few big tenure holders among the agriculturist

Scheduled Castes. Among the Rajbanshis and Palias of North Bengal, Namasudras of Eastern Bengal and the Poundras of Southern Bengal some people had placed them as landlords, otedars and as talukdars. Among other agriculturist Scheduled Castes, there was hardly any big land holders. In 1891, H.H. Risley had categorically mentioned that there was not 'a single Bagdi holding a zamindari, or even a superior tenure, such as patni or mukarari. Large number of them working as landless day labourer, paid in cash or kind, or as nomadic cultivators, tilling other men's land on the bhag-jot system.'[83] Position of the Bahelias and Bhuinmalis was no way better than the Bagdis. Similarly regarding the Bauris, H.H. recorded that 'few Bauris are rayats with occupancy rights but the majority probably be put down as under-*rayats* or landless day labourer'.[84] Other agriculturist Scheduled Castes had also similar position in the class hierarchy.

Class position of the fishermen Scheduled Castes (Doais, Gonrhis, Jelia Kaibartyas, Malos, Kandras, Khairas, Mallahs, Tiyors, Patnis, Ghasis and the Binds) was perhaps more miserable than the agriculturists because they were basically 'captured fishers' and had no possession over the artificial fisheries for pisciculture. Traditionally the zamindars were the owner of the fisheries who mostly were upper caste Hindus. They controlled the fisheries by leasing out them to the *izaradars* who always were not fishermen. The *izaradars* on the other hand used to sublet the fisheries to the primary fishermen. The fishermen had to pay a minimum rent to the owner of the fisheries. The traditional fishermen also used to take lease (*izara*) of the fisheries collectively under the leadership of their chief called *Sardar* or *Matabbar*. Besides paying the legal rents of the fisheries, very often they had to meet the extra demands of the *zamindars* and their officials.[85] The fishermen were often charged with extra levies called *pani charai* by the government officials.[86] The fishermen, however, had customary rights of fishing in the big rivers without charge.

There were different categories of fishermen in terms of their possession to the capital goods of fishing. They can be classified into three categories. Fishermen having boats, nets and other implements of fishing belonged to the first category. They used to employ the fellow fishermen as share-fishers. They could enjoy the major portion of the profit of fishing as the owner of the boats and nets or capital goods. The *aratdars* (commission agent) and the *nikaris* (fish mongers) were also the fishermen of the first category who often were the people of the non-fishermen castes. The *aratdars* not merely act as commission agent but also as lender of money and capital goods to the fishermen as advance for fishing in the big rivers and estuaries for a long period. In return the indebted fishermen were compelled to sell the fishes they catch to the *aratdars* at lower than market price fixed by the aratdars. The *aratdars* and the *nikaris* had also significant role in the marketing of the dried fish. So the fishermen of the first category of both capture fishers and the traders had better position in the class hierarchy.

The primary fishers, who did not have nets and boats of their own and generally work as share-fishers in the boats of the fishermen of first category; had constitute the second category of the fishermen in colonial Bengal. We can designate them as 'water labourer'. The primary fishermen could directly sell out the fishes they catch. Their womenfolk were the chief sellers of the fishes in the market.[87] But they did not have any control over the fish market. They were exploited both by the fishermen of the first category and the owners of the fisheries.

The third category comprised with the fish retailers generally called *paikar*. The *paikars* are the middlemen between the primary fishermen and the consumers or between the *aratdars* and the consumers. Like the primary fishermen, the *paikars* were also very poor. About the condition of the 'fish *paikars*' of the early nineteenth century Buchanan Hamilton wrote (1807) 'none of these have a capital of above 100 Rs. and any are so poor that they purchase the fish on trust and after having sold their fish in the market, go next morning to the actual fishermen, pay him for what fish they received, and take a fresh load on credit'.[88]

The bulk of the traditional fishermen as a whole, were very poor in terms of their position in the class society. The primary fishermen did neither have possession over the fisheries nor had real control over the fish distribution. They were depended to the whims of the nature. They were thus floaters having no assured mode of living.

Halalkhors, Haris, Mehtors and Lalbegis as scavengers and sweepers did neither have enough capital goods nor had the opportunity of surplus appropriation. Basket making, house thatching and earth working as the means of livelihood, were no way sufficient for upward class mobility. Although the handicrafts and weaving industries of Bengal had earned fame in India as well as non-Indian world but the Pans and Chaupal weavers were nothing but the ordinary weaving labourers. However, the Muchis, Sunris and the Dhobas had the possibility to develop them as entrepreneurs and as big businessmen but their social status had disqualified them.

From the occupational classification it appears that the Scheduled Castes were largely engaged in the primary sector of economy. They were the main suppliers of foodstuffs, fruits, fishes and other favourite manus of the Bengali dishes. All services for cleanliness (as claimed by the upper castes) were generally offered by the Scheduled Caste communities. But economically they did not have in good position in the class hierarchy.

2.4. Social Status and Reforms

Economically downtrodden Scheduled Castes were more oppressed in the social live. They were treated as out-caste in the Bengali Hindu Society. Their professions were looked down as derogatory works. So all the castes mentioned above were assigned lower status in the traditional caste hierarchy. Ancient law books (*shastras* and *smritis*) had treated them as Sudra or as *antaja* (people of inferior rank or marginal men) and often almost as *asprishya* (untouchables). *Brihaddharma Purana* had treated them as *madhyam sankara* (mixed caste of average social rank) and *antaja*. Similarly the *Brahmabaibartya Purana* classified them as *satasudra* (sudra caste of respectable rank), *asatsudra* (inferior sudra) and the *antaja*. Table 2.7 based on the *Brihatdharmma* and *Brahmabaibartya Purana* shows that the Scheduled Castes of Bengal were treated as *antaja* or as *asatsudra*.[89] So throughout the ancient period they were considered as almost untouchables and had an inferior rank in the caste society. In the medieval period too, they could not uplift their social status. The Bengali literatures particularly the *mangala literature*[90] and the *charitas* (biographies) of the Vaishnava[91] saints composed in the late medieval period have retained their degraded social status.

Table 2.8: Social Status of Some Scheduled Caste Communities of Bengal

Caste	*Classifications in Brihaddharma Purana*	*Classifications in Brahmabaibartya Purana*
Bagdi	*Antaja*	*Antaja*
Jelia Kaibartya	*Madhyam Sankara*	*Asat Sudra*
Keot	*Madhyam Sankara*	*Asat Sudra*
Malo	*Antaja*	----------
Namasudra	*Antaja*	*Antaja*
Poundra	----------	*Asat Sudra*

Source: Brihaddharma Purana and *Brahmabaibartya Purana.*

Whatever the social status of the Scheduled Castes in pre-colonial period, available colonial literatures have illustrated their marginalized socioeconomic condition. Although agriculture was the backbone of the economic life of Bengal but the agriculturist Scheduled Castes (such as the Bhuiyans, Kaoras, Namasudras, Palias, Poundras, Rajbanshis, etc.) did not have social respect as 'caste group'. The Namasudras in the nineteenth century were considered as Chandals who were not allowed to enter even into the outer circles of the 'Aryan system.'[92] The Namasudra students in the educational institutes and constable in the barracks were considered to be untouchables by the upper castes.[93]

The Rajbanshis, inspite of being agriculturist and even after being educated and competent enough; used to be humiliated by the upper caste Hindus solely for their lower social status. Panchanan Barma (1872-1935), a Rajbanshi thinker and social reformer; was abused publicly by his upper caste lawyer colleague in Rangpur only that he was a Rajbanshi.[94] The Rajbanshi students in the hostel, constable in the barracks, peasants in the *haats* (weekly markets) and villages had to bear with social injustice because of their lower caste origin.[95] The Poundras had also similar experiences.

The Brahmins and other upper castes of Bengal (such as the Kayasthas and Baidyas) did not accept water and food from like the Bagdis, Chandals, Dhobas, Kaibartyas, Malos, Rajbanshis Sunris, Tiyors and other lower castes of Bengal as they were considered polluted and *ajalchal* (from whom water is not acceptable)[96] social groups although most of them were the followers of the Hinduism. So in 1891 H.H. Risley found that the Malos were Vaishnavas and got service from the *napits* (barber) and *dhoba* (washermen) and the *patit Brahmins* (Brahmins of lower rank) but 'upper caste Hindus' had restrictions to take water from their hands.[97] Similarly the Bagdis were considered as outcaste and had no right to dine with other castes except the Bouris, Muchis and Manjhis. Contemporary and near contemporary Bengali novels have also vividly illustrated the miserable social status of these communities.[98] So it appears that the Scheduled Castes of Bengal were treated as 'almost untouchables' by the upper caste Hindus in pre-colonial and colonial Bengal what was a sheer unjust social practice.

The inhuman practice and traditions prevailed in the Bengali society for social differentiation began to get 'silent' attacks from the colonial society itself particularly with the beginning of decennial census in 1871-72. The method of social stratification of the colonial government on the basis of caste, race and religion have instigated the Indian castes, both lower caste and twice-born; to determine their caste status in the official records.[99] They now come forward with prayers to the census superintendents for assigning more respectable status in the official records. In most cases the lower caste communities of Bengal demanded Kshatriya caste status (such as the Rajbanshi, Malo, Poundra, Bagdis, etc.) while some caste claimed the Vaishya identity (such as Dhobas, Sunri, Bhuinmalis, Jelia Kaibartyas). Claim of Brahmin status was very rare. These demands were not confined in the official papers only. They also initiated social reforms in their own society for materializing the dreams of achieving respectable caste status. This social reform was stimulated by some new developments in Bengal under the colonial rule. By opening up English education and creating some new opportunities in public employment and profession the colonial rule made the social mobility wide spread.[100]

2.4.1 'Assertion of the Self' and 'Denunciation of Imposed' Identities: The Kshatriya Movements

Demand for Kshatriya (ruling or warrior) caste-status of the non-Kshatriyas and the tribal communities was not a new phenomenon in Bengal. The 'ruling section' of the pre-colonial kingdoms, emerged from tribal or lower social strata; had often claimed Kshatriya status in order to legitimize their rule over the multi-caste regional society. For kshatriyaization, they adopted suitable title and constructed fictitious genealogies by patronizing the Brahmin scholars.[101] This type of social mobility was obviously a social formation for achieving a political status. But the demand for a Kshatriya rank in the late nineteenth and the early twentieth centuries was something different. These demands came from the lowers castes of Bengal who did not have social respect in the traditional caste hierarchy. So it was an assertion for 'legitimacy of respectable social status.' These demands were strongly supported by the colonial state.[102]

Table 2.9: Demands of Kshatriya Status of Certain Castes of Colonial Bengal.

Caste	*Caste Organization*	*Demand(s)*
Rajbanshi	Bratya Kshatriya Unnati Bidhayani Sabha , Rajbanshi Kshatriya Samity	Kshatriya, Bratya Kshatriya, Barua Kshatriya
Jhalo Malo or Malo	Jhal Mal Bandhav, Bangiya Malla Kshatriya Samity	Malla or Bratya Kshatriya
Pod or Paundra	Sarva Banga Paundra Kshatriya Samity	Paundra or Bratya Kshatriya
Sadgop and Goalas		Yadav Kshatriya
Bagdi		Byagra Kshatriya
Koch		Koch Kshatriya

Most significant case of kshatriyaization in colonial Bengal was the Rajbanshi Kshatriya movement which was started in 1891 with the question of social status of the Koches and the

Rajbanshis in the census. The colonial ethnographers and the administrative historians had created a lot of confusion about the social status of the Rajbanshis in their observations what they started since the beginning of the nineteenth century. Although the Rajbanshis were silent about the social identity 'constructed' and 'imposed' by the colonial rulers till the late nineteenth century but their caste feelings got a sudden stimulus in 1891 when Mr.F.A. Skyne, District Magistrate and the census superintendent of Rangpur, issued an order to classify the Rajbanshis as 'Koch', another community of North Bengal and Lower Assam.[103] The Rajbanshis were not agreed to accept this order. Even they began to organise under the banner of their caste organization called 'Rangpur Bratya Kshatriya Unnati Bidhayani Sabha' founded by Hara Mohan Khajanchi; a Rajbanshi zamindar of Shyampur (Rangpur) in 1891 for the establishment of a distinct Kshatriya caste identity of the Rajbanshis.[104]

The Rajbanshis got a significant achievement in their social movement when they founded a centrally organized caste association called Kshatriya Samity in 1910 in Rangpur under the leadership of Panchanan Barma (Sarkar), a lawyer by profession.[105] Main purposes of this Samity were to (i) establish a Kshatriya identity of the Rajbanshis, (ii) inform the government that the Koches and the Rajbanshis are different castes, (iii) publications and circulations of the newspapers and periodical about the Rajbanshis and their cultural heritage, and (iv) foundation of hostels for the Rajbanshi students and of financial organization for the benefits of the Rajbanshis.[106]

In order to popularize their Kshatriya identity the educated Rajbanshis came forward to popularise the view that *Rajbanshis* are the descendents of a Kshatriya ruler called Bardhan. *Rajbanshi Kulapradip* (1907) of Hara Kishore Adhikary, *Rajbanshi Kulakarika* and *Kuladipana* of Avay Narayan Barma, *Rajbanshi Kula Kaumudi* of Jagamohan Singha (1913) and a few other writings published in the early twentieth century had constructed a fictitious kshatriya lineage of the Rajbanshis of North Bengal.[107] Writings and circulation of this kind of history stimulated the kshatriya feelings of the Rajbanshis. Their demand for Kshatriya caste identity status was ultimately recognized by the colonial government in 1911. The Census Officer of Purnia district ordered the assistants of the census operation on 11 January 1911, to stratify the Koches and the Rajbanshis separately. The Deputy Commissioner of Goalpara had also allowed the Rajbanshis to classify them as Kshatriya. Mr.E.W. Denith, Superintendent of Cooch Behar State, issued a similar order.[108] So O Mally, the Census Superintendent; wrote in 1911 that 'the former request (of kshatriya status) was granted without hesitation as there is no doubt that at the present day irrespective of any question of origin the Rajbanshis and the Koch are separate castes.'[109] So the assertion for a Kshatriya status of the Rajbanshis was a by-product of the decennial census introduced by the colonial state.

Since, mere official recognition could not establish a respectable social status of the Rajbanshis, they approached the Brahmins/who had (even still have) the sole right of determining the caste status of any community of traditional Indian society! Under the leadership of Panchanan Barma, the Rajbanshis acquired the support of the Brahmins of different centers of 'Brahmanical Sanskrit culture' such as Mithila, Kamarup, Navadwip and Cooch Behar. Pandit Jadaveswar Tarkaratna of Rangpur, Sri Kamakshya Nath Sharma Tarkavagis, Professor of Sanskrit College of Calcutta, and the Kamrupi Brahmins of Cooch Behar; had recognized the Rajbanshis as Kshatriya. These scholars had also prescribed the necessary process of elevation of their social status to the Kshatriya by performing certain religious rituals.[110] Under the banner of the Kshatriya Samity, 400 delegates of the Rajbanshis of different districts of Bengal and Assam gathered at Deviganj of Jalpaiguri district in 1913 and they publicly declared them as Kshatriya. They now began to hold *paita* or sacred thread like the Brahmins, Kshatriyas and other upper castes.[111] Within a year the Rajbanshis organized 292 such gathering in different towns and villages of North Bengal and Assam. More than one *lakh* Rajbanshis hold sacred threads (*paita*). They had also adopted some rituals and customs from the upper castes. Even they assumed caste Kshatriya surnames like Barma, Barman, Ray, Singha, etc., as prescribed in the *Brihaddharma Purana* instead of *Das.*[112]

In the meantime the Rajbanshis got a chance from the colonial state to prove their Kshatriya identity due to the outbreak of the First World War in 1914. Since military service was the traditional (monopoly?) occupation of the Kshatriyas in pre-colonial India, the Kshatriya Samity tried to employ the Rajbanshi youths in the British Indian Army.[113] Mr. F.J. Monahan, Commissioner of the Presidency Division, assured the Kshatriya Samity to constitute a separate company for the Rajbanshi youths.[114] Around four hundred Rajbanshis from Jalpaiguri, Dinajpur and Rangpur and around eight hundreds from Dhubri district of Assam had joined the First World War.[115] Formation of a separate kshatriya regiment, however, was not materialized due to the end of the war in 1918. But experience and feelings of war of the Rajbanshis had stimulated their kshatriya feelings. Panchanan Barma, as the charismatic leader of the Rajbanshi Kshatriya Samity and for his active support to the British Indian Government was accorded the prestigious Roy Saheb and MBE awards by the British Government in 1919.[116]

Like the *kshatriyaization* of the Rajbanshis, the Malos and Poundras of Bengal had also attempted to construct their Kshatriya identity by composing self-history in the 1920s. The Poundras began to identify themselves as Pundarika, Padmaraja, Punro and Poundra or as Pundari. The Sarba Banga Poundra Kshatriya Samity (All Bengal Poundra Kshatriya Samity), founded in 1917 under the leadership of Anukul Chandra Naskar, Jay Krishna Mandal, Mahendra Nath Karan and few other *bhadralokas* of the this community; played a significant role in the caste awareness among the Poundras. Anukul Chandra Naskar, being the secretary of the organization, had placed a demand to W. H. Thomson, the Superintendent of Census; to declare them as Kshatriyas. Thomson wrote (on 17th January, 1921) that 'I have no objection to the use of the word Poundra in place of Pod.'

Similarly the caste organization of the Malos called 'Jhal Mal Bandhav' or Bratya Kshatriya Samity was founded under the leadership of Brajanath Das, Ananta Chandra Das, Kripanath Das, Uddhav Chandra Malla Barman (Pabna), Jatindra Mohun Das (Mymensingh), Sashi Bhusan Das Ray, Suresh Chandra Barman and Dinanath Talukdar. This organization attempted to prove that the Malos are the descendents of the Kshatriyas of Northwestern India who lost Kshatriya identity after their migration to Bengal. *Dwitiya Varna Kshatriya* (Mymensingh, 1923) and *Sanschipta Kshatriya Tatta* (Dacca, 1923) of Mahendra Nath Malla Barman, *Jalla Malla Kshatriya Itihas* of Brajanath Das (Bagura), Jyoti of Shashi Bhusan Das Ray (Dacca) and *Sanschipta Jalla Malla Kshatriya Tatta* (Dacca) of Dharma Chand Malla Barman are some important contributions of the Malos which stressed on their Kshatriya status. The British Government in the census of 1931 also recognized the Malla Kshatriya status demanded by the Malos. Similarly the Bagdis and the Goalas also demanded the Byagra Kshatriya and the Yadav Kshatriya status respectively. Even the Koches (who merged them with the Rajbanshis) had asserted themselves as Koch Kshatriya.

These Kshatriya aspirants of Bengal (like the Rajbanshis) had also acquired the prescription of the Brahmins to achieve their goal of respectable social status within the caste structure. With the help of Brahmanical prescription they held sacred thread (*paita*) what was considered as a symbol of standardization of their caste status. The Malos after holding *paita* began to adopt the titles like Malla Barman, Jhalla Barman and Das Barman in the 1920's. And instead of observation of thirty days *ashouch* (ritual pollution after death) now they introduced the customs of thirteen days.[117] The Paundras also introduced similar custom in their caste society.[118] Similary the Ahirs, Kurmis and the Koeris of Bihar began to sanskritise their caste rituals by holding *paita* and performing other rituals for *kshatriyaization*.[119] So adoption of *paita*, a symbol of caste Hindu society became an issue for all lower castes of Bengal who wanted to place them as a Kshatriya in the caste hierarchy. But they did not challenge the social superiority of the Brahmins and the upper castes. So the Kshatriya movement did not have any anti-upper caste feeling.

However, there was a positive aspect of the Kshatriya movement of the lower castes of Bengal. They not merely kept them busy with the adoption of upper caste ritual practices, they realized that the adoption of educational practice (of the upper castes) is essential for real progress of their caste status.

So Panchanan Barma, father of the Rajbanshi Kshatriya movement, wrote in 1910 that 'there is the need of reformation among the Rajbanshis who always considered them as Kshatriya. Adoption of good traditions and abolition of evil customs from the society is social reform.... Social reform is impossible without education. Education is vital for cultivating good spirits and exchanging views among the caste fellows.... So there is the need of newspaper for cultural exchanges.'[120]

Thus the Rajbanshis of North Bengal had founded a hostel for their students at Rangpur in 1914[121] along with the Kshatriya Chhatra Samity, a student organization; to mobilize the Rajbanshi students. At the same time the Rajbanshi Kshatriya Samity began to publish a monthly magazine titled *Kshatriya Patrika* since 1920. Consolidation of fellow feelings among the Rajbanshis of North Bengal, Assam and other places of Northeast India through the publication of news of achievements of the Rajbanshis and their present condition was its main purpose. Although its publication was stopped after few years but the Kshatriya Samity continued to publish law books of Hindu rituals and rules and regulation of the Samity in order to spread the Kshatriya feeling among the Rajbanshis. Publication of such kinds are *Kshatriya Byabastha* (rules of kshatriyaization), *Upanayan Byabastha, Sandhya Paddhati, Kshatriya Samitir Niyamabali, Mandali Sthapaner Niyamabali, Upanayan Grahan Niyamabali,* etc.[122] These publications had direct impact on the educated section of the Rajbanshis while the rest of the caste fellows were induced by them.

There are few more literary pieces produced by the Rajbanshi middle class intellectuals of the early twentieth century particularly in the local languages/dialect of Rangpur. Panchanan Barma, editor of the *Sahitya Parishat Patrika* of Uttar Banga Sahitya Parishat; had interest on the literary activities. In order to revive the folk literature prevailed among the Rajbanshis, he collected the proverbs and phrases (called *chhilka*) of the local people. His *Dangdhari Mao* and *Beta Chaoar Prati Dangdhari Mao* poetries, Jagannathi Bilai (a short story), *Kamata Bihari Sahitya* (an article) and few other works were published in the local language of Rangpur, which according to Panchanan Barma is 'Kamata-

Bihari' language. These works of Panchanan Barma had not only revived the folk literature of North Bengal but also contributed to the development of a 'restricted code' like the Rajbanshi.[123] This 'restricted code' had been observed as Rajbanshi dialect by G.A. Grierson in 1927.

Other Kshatriya aspirants had also adopted such steps such as publication of periodicals, magazines and spread of education for their social development. The Malos began to publish their own magazine called *'Jhal Mal Badhav'* where their socioeconomic problems and way of their solution were regular items. This magazine tried to enhance the fellow-feelings among the Malos. It had wide circulation in the Eastern Bengal districts like Mymensingh, Dacca, Sylhet, Comilla and Pabna. Regarding the education, achievement of the Malos was not satisfactory. The *Titas Ekti Nadir Naam*, a Bengali novel written by Adwaita Malla Barman, a Malo novelist; shows negative attitudes of the ordinary Malos about the need of education. However, the educated section tried to spread the education among the Malos under their own initiative.[124] The Poundras were more enthusiastic regarding education than the Malos.

The caste movements of the Kshatriya aspirants of Bengal had also paid attention to the economic grievances of the poor fellows. Thus the Rajbanshi Kshatriya Samity established a bank called Kshatriya Bank in 1921 in Rangpur under the initiative of Kshetra Nath Singha.[125] Similarly the fishermen such as the Malos and the Jelia Kaibartyas of Bengal and Assam had keen interest on the economic aspects of their profession. So they founded a provincial level organization called All Bengal and Assam Provincial Fishermen Conference (Nikhil Bangiya O Assam Pradeshiya Matsyajibi Sammilani). It was organized under the leadership of Ramani Mohun Biswas, Hemanta Kumar Sarkar, Basanta Kumar Majumder and Hemaprabha Majumder. In its third Conference held at Madaripur of Faridpur district on 11-12 March 1926, Kazi Najrul Islam (1899-1976), famous poet of Bengal; encouraged the fishermen for their collective action to organize themselves for the development of their economic status.[126] The fishermen also started the cooperative movement since the 1920s.

The Captain Bheri Fishermen's Cooperative Society marked the beginning of corporative movement among the fishermen. The Bidyadhari Fishermen Cooperative Society had induced it. The Captain Bhery was registered on 24th April 1927 only with a membership of 16. Initially this society had to face critical problems regarding the ownership of the water bodies. But finally this society got the possession of the *bhery*. *Annual Report of the Cooperative Societies of 1930* recorded that, in the Presidency Division, the Captain Bhery Society has now succeeded in obtaining undisputed possession of the fishery of that name after a protracted litigation with the zaminder'.[127]

The Captain Bhery Society had also adopted the policy of spreading education among the fishermen particularly among the members of this society. It had an Educational Fund too. This society further encouraged other fishermen to organize similar cooperative society. So in the 1930s number of the fishermen cooperatives of Bengal increased to 7. It was obviously a significant feature of the cooperative movement of India.

But the leadership of the caste organizations of the Kshatriya aspirants of Bengal had been remained under the elite class comprising the lawyers and zamindars. Panchanan Barma and other Rajbanshi *bhadralokas* were aware about the limitations of class character of leadership of their caste movement.[128] The Malla Kshatriya and Poundra Kshatriya movement had no exceptional features in the leadership. So the social movements for the formation of a standard Kshatriya caste identity cannot be classified as mobility for 'economic consolidation.' But with a caste organization, performance of upper caste rituals and fellow feelings, the Rajbanshi, Poundra and the Malos had structurally integrated their castes. Thus caste, a parameter of social stratification, after misused disgracefully in social oppression, had secured a more solid ground instead of its dissolution.

2.4.2. From Chandals to Namasudras: Caste Protest, Social Reforms and Alternative Cultural Practices

Investigation on the social reforms of the lower castes of colonial Bengal would remain incomplete without having a look on the caste identity formation among the Chandals. The Chandals had very measurable condition in the caste society of Bengal although most of them were the follower of different popular sects of the Hinduism. The question of social reforms was raised among the Chandals in 1872 when the Kayasthyas (an upper caste Hindu community) refused to dine in a house of the Chandal headman of Faridpur who invited them in a *sraddha* (after death ritual purification) ceremony. Even they instigated other upper castes of the locality for refuting that invitation.[129] This humiliation had instigated the Chandal headmen of that region to take some immediate steps for their social elevation and consolidation of the caste feelings. In a meeting of the Chandals held in 1872 they took the following resolutions: (i) women must in future not visit *haats*, (ii) service of no kind whatever be taken from other castes, (iii) food prepared by all other Hindu castes, other than the Brahmins, was not to be partaken of.[130] These resolutions were not confined in the papers. They materialized these into practice. They refused to work in the fields of upper castes or to serve the upper caste Hindus. It eventually got the form of an organized strike as a protest against the inhuman social practices of the upper caste Hindus of Faridpur-Bakharganj region of Eastern Bengal. So the District Magistrate of Faridpur, found that the '.....fields untilled, the houses unthatched, and not a Chandal in the service of Hindu or Mahamedan or, a Chandal woman in any market.'[131] It shows the structural integrity of the Chandals which was reinforced by the charismatic leadership of Harichand Thakur (1812-1878), the founder of the Matua sect.

Mukhe naam hate kaam (work and worship) was the motto of the Matuas. Harichand, instead of any formal religious culture, had stressed on hard work, spread of education, earning wealth and government jobs, formation of organizations and off course to achieve social unity. After Harichand's death his son Guruchand Thakur took the leadership of the Matua sect. He founded the Matua Mahasangha in 1881. The Matua gradually developed as a popular sect guided by Guruchand and later by his successors which still is in existence in West Bengal and Bangladesh.

Most significant feature of the social reforms of Harichand

and Guruchand was the spread of education although they themselves had no chance to get western education. Guruchand stated that "I will not be worried whether you eat or fast, but I want your children to be educated first." He was of firm belief that—without education lower castes could not get any chance to become a part of administration. Guruchand was so passionate that he founded around 1800 schools.[132]

In the meantime, the Chandals had declared themselves as Namasudra. So in 1891 H.H.Risley wrote that 'in the Pirozpur thana of Bhakharganj the Chandals have recently started a combined movement to call themselves Namas, to wear shoes, and not to take rice from Kayasth or Sudras.'[133] The mouthpiece of the Chandals called '*Namasudra Surhid*' had spread the messages of the caste feelings. Ultimately the Chandals were recognized by the British Government as Namasudras in 1911. The Namasudras further desired the Brahmin status. So in 1931 the Namasudras of Khulna and Mymensingh had claimed to be Namabrahman.[134]

The social movement of the Namasudras had added a significant chapter in the politics of Bengal in the pre-partition days. During the '*swadeshi era*', (1905-1911) the nationalist leaders sought the support of the Namasudras against the partition of Bengal of 1905. But Guruchand expressed that the upper castes of Bengal are habituated to use the foreign cloths and consumer goods hence the concept of *swadeshi* and the boycott of foreign goods would be relevant to them only. Guruchand again refused to cooperate with the Swarajists during the period of the diarchy (1920-1936). The Namasudras themselves were interested to enter into the Legislative Council. As a whole the Namasudras as a largest Scheduled Caste community of Bengal had emerged as significant sociopolitical power by the first quarter of the twentieth century with an alternative cultural practice i.e. Matua sect.

The Haris, another Scheduled Caste community of Bengal had come forward with an alternative social practice under the Balahari or Balarami sect. The Balahari sect was founded by Balaram Hadi in the late early nineteenth century in Nadia district. The Balahadis opposed the orthodox Brahmanical Hinduism as well as the superstitious practice of other popular sects. By the 1870 the Balahari sect had around 20000 followers of different untouchable castes including Hadis, Doms, Bagdis, Muchis, (Badia) Bedes, Malos, Namasudras.[135] The Balaharis, however, had less attention to the positive aspects of social development like spread of education.

2.4.2. Occupational Mobility, Identity formation and Social Differentiation

Upward social mobility in colonial Bengal in many cases was closely linked with the occupational mobility. Although occupational mobility of entire caste was impossible but it has been noticed that a section of any particular community had changed its traditional occupation(s). This type of mobility instead of social integration had created self-contradiction. Here we may mention the caste reforms among the Sunris, Dhobas, Patnis, Jelia Kaibartyas, Bhuimalis, etc.

It has already been indicated that higher grade Brahmins of Bengal did not take water from the hands of the Sunri-Sahas.[136] The term Saha is of Sanskrit origin. It derives from Sanskrit *sadhu*, meaning a moneylender and a trader. So Saha was a common title of the mercantile Hindu castes of Bengal including Gandhabanik, Sankhabanik, Tilli, Tanti and Sunri. Again the Saha is a separate caste community of Bengal who use different surnames including Saha, Pramanik, Poddar, Das, Ray, etc. They were inferior in social status than the Gandhabanik, Sankhabanik, i.e. the Nabashakhs. Condition of the Sunris was more deplorable because of their traditional profession i.e. making and selling country liquor. Thus they claimed Saha or Vaishya caste status which was more respectable to them. The Sahas on the other hand tried to improve their social status by detaching them from the Sunris.[137]

Vaisya caste status other than the Sunris was also coveted by the Bhuinmalis, Dhobas and Jelia Kaibartyas. The Bhuinmalis of Mymensingh had undertaken social reforms for the establishment of Vaishya status. They also claimed to be descended from Mallas of Mallabhum (Bankura).

The Dhobas were regarded as unclean Sudras by the upper castes because of their caste profession i.e. washing cloths. Hence some Dhobas had given up their traditional profession and adopted agriculture. The agriculturist Dhobas called themselves Chasa-Dhobas which according to them was more superior social status than the ordinary Dhobas.[138] So occupational mobility was appeared as a means of 'caste identity formation' what is equally linked with the social reforms.

Strategy of occupational mobility like the Dhobas was also adopted by the Kaibartyas, both Chashi (Halia or Halika or agriculturists) and the Jelia (Jalika or fishermen). While the Chashi Kaibartyas claimed the Mahishya (caste Hindu) status, the Jelia Kaibartyas asserted themselves as Chashi Kaibartya. In order to elevate the caste status, many Jelia Kaibartyas had discarded their traditional profession i.e. fishing; and adopted agricultural works. At the same time they also changed their traditional customs and even surnames.[139] In some cases the Jelia Kaibartyas demanded the Kshatriya (Kshatra Kaibartya) status in the 1920s.[140] So the caste mobility among the Kaibartyas had multiple directions what can be compared with the Patnis of Bengal.

The Patnis traditionally were boatmen. They were also seasonal agriculturist and fishermen. In 1891 H.H. Risley had recorded them as 'a low boating, fishing, basket-making, trading and cultivating caste of Eastern Bengal.'[141] It indicates diverse professional identity of the Patnis for which the Patnis considered them as equivalent to the agriculturist Hindu castes of Bengal like the Mahisyas. In the 1880s they claimed that that 'they have raised themselves in the social scale by prohibiting the remarriage of widows, and in various small matters they ape the prejudice of the higher castes.'[142] Subsequently they declared themselves as Lupta-Mahisya caste what according them was respectable one.[143] Such claim, however, had contained the seeds of self-contradictions because the non-agriculturist section (such as fishermen and boatmen) were not qualified enough for upgradating their caste status.

2.5. Observations

Social reforms among the so-called lower castes of Bengal for upward social mobility as we have discussed in the foregoing section of this chapter had manifold directions. Firstly it was a by-product of the colonial rule. Spread of education (what was restricted to them in the pre-colonial Hindu society) had inspired them to raise voice against the social injustice prevailed in the society. Again classification of the Indians and their enumeration had provoked these caste communities to achieve a respectable status in the official records. It has been noticed that the census officials were frequently approached by the different caste organizations for elevation of their caste status. In some cases researches and observations of the colonial administrators had stimulated the caste feelings of theses communities (as in the case of the Rajbanshis).

Secondly the social reforms among the lower castes had two specific strategies –(i)eliminations of cultural practices of their own including social customs, rituals, food habits, etc.; considered unclean by the upper castes; and (ii) adoption from the upper castes including social practice, customs, holding scared thread, etc. But the adoption of cultural practices of the upper castes was often proved derogatory for the lower castes. Here we may discuss about the widow remarriage. In the traditional society of the lower castes, remarriage of the widows and the divorcee women was a common trend what was restricted among the upper castes. While the upper caste Hindus had started social movements for widow remarriage in the mid-nineteenth century, the lower castes of Bengal had imposed restrictions on the widows of their own society (as in the case of the Patnis and Malos). Again the free movements of the womenfolk of the lower castes in the public space became restricted (as in case of the Namasudras). It indicates the elimination of certain good practices from the lower caste society in the name of caste identity formation. However, adoption of educational practice was a positive aspect of the lower caste social reforms which had most significant contribution in their social development.

Thirdly leadership of these social movements in most cases remained under the control of the educated and landed elites (such as the Kshatriya movements of Rajbanshi, Malo, Pundra) except the Namasudra and Balahari movements. The Namasudra movement till 1937 was controlled from the rural base while in other cases urban areas such as Calcutta, Dacca, Mymensingh, Rangpur, etc, were the centers of these social movements.

Fourthly social reforms to some extent had reinforced the occupational mobility. Western education no doubt was the major factor for the emergence of a 'lower caste middle class' comprising members of different castes. Agriculture and trade were taken up by the non-educated section instead of the traditional (so-called unclean) occupations as a marker of social prestige. Such occupational mobility, however, generated a force of social disintegration because occupational mobility of entire caste was a utopian dream. Hence, the people remained with the traditional caste occupation were considered unclean by their own caste fellow who were successful to change their profession.

Table 2.10: Educational Scenario of Scheduled Castes Bengal in 1921

Caste	*Total Population*	*Literate*	*Illiterate*
Bagdi	886,821	18,920	867,901
Bauri	303,013	1,778	301,235
Chamar	147,654	4,596	143,058
Dhoba	227,295	17,691	209,604
Dom	147,859	2,662	145,197
Hari	143,593	2,692	140,901
Koch	131,272	4,293	126,979
Lohar	65,092	1,640	63,447
Mal	117,271	2,657	114,614
Malo	221,192	9,829	211,363
Muchi	417,225	8,006	409,219
Pod (Poundra)	575,994	70,109	505,885
Rajbanshi	1,663,948	96,140	1,567,808
Bhuimali	81,796	3,722	78,074

Namasudra	2,004,911	150,548	1,854,363
Dosadh	39,529	1,791	37,738
Jalia Kaibartya	383,225	22,946	360,279
Kaora	110,141	3,803	106,338
Patni	43,784	2,723	41,061
Sunri	92,246	15,334	76,912

*Source: Census of India 1921,*V.5 *(Bengal), Part II,* p. 240.

One of the significant positive sides of the social reforms was the realization of the need of primary education. In the pre-colonial and early colonial days the Schedule Caste communities of Bengal were educationally extremely backward. Due to the nature of their profession they did not have any chance to get education. In those days most of the members of Scheduled Caste communities thought that the education was a matter of concern for the upper castes only. So, they had nothing to do with school-education. But now the social reformers of the Rajbanshis, Namasudra, Poundras, Malos, etc. had taken positive step for the spread of primary and higher education. So in the census of 1921 we find that some Scheduled Caste communities particularly the Namasudras, Sunris, Rajbanshis, Malos, Dhobas, Jelia Kaibartyas, Patnis and the Poundras had achieved little progress in the primary education. However, some Scheduled Caste communities like the Bagdis, Bauris, Doms, Haris, Lohars, Mals, Muchis, etc, could not do well.

Whatever the shortcomings of the social movements of the lower castes of colonial Bengal, it is a fact that the social reforms under the banner of caste organization had structurally integrated them. They felt that were successful to establish a respectable (!) caste identity as announced by them (and in some case with an alternative cultural practice). So the caste, as a social institution, had secured a more solid ground.

Notes and References

1. Ekta Singh, *Caste System in India: A Historical Perspective* (Delhi: Kalpaz Publications, 2005), pp. 20-23, 99-101.
2. Debi Chatterjee, *Ideas and Movements against Caste in India: Ancient to Modern Time* (Calcutta: Print O Graph Publishing, 1998), p.12
3. *Ibid.*

4. Ekta Singh, *Caste System in India,* pp. 33-34.
5. *Ibid.*, pp. 34-36, 100.
6. *Ibid*, pp. 20-22.
7. Chino Rao Yagati, *Dalit Studies: A Bibliographical Handbook* (New Delhi: Kanishka Publishers and Distributors, 2003), p. 3.
8. *Brihaddharma Purana*, edited by Panchanan Tarkaratna, 2nd ed., (Calcutta: Bangabasi Electro-Machine Press, 1314 B.S.), *Part III, Chapter 13.*
9. G.K.Ghosh and Sukla Ghosh, *Legends of Origin of the Castes and Tribes of Eastern India* (Calcutta: Firma KLM, Pvt. Ltd., 2000), p 66.
10. H.H. Risley, *The Tribes and Castes of Bengal*, Vol.1, reprint edn., (Calcutta: Firma Mukhopadhyay, 1981), p. 37.
11. *Ibid.*, 42.
12. *Ibid.*. 42.
13. K.S.Singh, *The Scheduled Castes,* revised edn. (Calcutta: Oxford University Press and Anthropological Survey of India, 1999), p. 72.
14. H.H. Risley, *The Tribes and Castes. vol. I,* p. 45.
15. K.S. Singh, *The Scheduled Castes,* p. 73.
16. H.H. Risley, *The Tribes and Castes of Bengal*, vol. I, p. 52; also see K. S. Singh, *op. cit.,* p. 82.
17. H.H. Risley, *Ibid.*
18. *Ibid.,* p. 53; James Wise, *Notes on the Races, Castes, and Trades of Eastern Bengal*, Not Published (London, Harrisson and Sons, 1883), p.209
19. H. H. Risley, *The Tribes and Castes of Bengal*, vol. I, p. 78.
20. K.S. Singh, *The Scheduled Castes* p.176.
21. H.H. Risley, *The Tribes and Castes of Bengal*, vol. I, p. 86.
22. Government of West Bengal, *Short Note on Scheduled Castes of West Bengal* (Kolkata: Cultural Research Institute, Backward Classes Welfare Department, 2005), p. 6.
23. James Wise, *Note on the Races,* p. 223; H.H. Risley, *The Tribes and Castes of Bengal*, vol.I, p. 106.
24. H.H. Risley, *Ibid.,* p. 106
25. James Wise, *Note on the Races,* p. 224.
26. H.H. Risley, *The Tribes and Castes of Bengal*, vol. I, p. 133.

27. *Ibid.* p. 175.
28. *Ibid.*, p. 181.
29. James Wise, *Note on the Races,* p. 252.
30. H.H. Risley, *The Tribes and Castes of Bengal, vol.I,* pp. 229-232.
31. Nripendra Kumar Dutta, *Origin and Growth of Caste in India* (combined volume) (Calcutta: Firma KLM Mukhopadhyay Pvt. Ltd., 1969), p. 124.
32. H.H. Risley, *The Tribes and Castes of Bengal*, vol.I., p. 238.
33. James Wise, *Notes on the Races, Castes and Trades of Eastern Bengal,* p. 264.
34. Government of West Bengal, *Note on the Scheduled Castes*, p. 16.
35. K.S.Singh, *The Scheduled Castes,* p. 485.
36. H.H. Risley, *The Tribes and Castes of Bengal*, vol. I, p. 294.
37. Government of West Bengal, *Note on the Scheduled Castes,* p. 20.
38. H.H. Risley, *The Tribes and Castes of Bengal,*, vol.I., pp. 314-316.
39. Nripendra Kumar Dutta, *Origin and Growth of Caste in India*, p. 300.
40. *Ibid.*
41. G.K.Ghosh and Sukla Ghosh, *Legends and Origin of Castes*, p. 53.
42. *Ibid.*, p. 299.
43. *Ibid.*, p. 303.
44. Montgomery Martin, *The History, Antiquities, Topography and Statistics of Eastern India*, 5 vols. (1838), reprint edn. (Delhi: Cosmo Publications, 1976), vol. V, p. 531.
45. Haliram Dhekial Phukan, *Assam Buranji,* edited by Jatindra Mahun Bhattacharjee (Guwahati: Mokshada Pustakalay, 1369 B.S), p. 88.
46. H.H. Risley, *The Tribes and Castes of Bengal*, vol. I, p. 382.
47. Buchanan Hamilton had noticed the Gangrars in the Brahmaputra Valley and Dacca. He also recorded the techniques and technologies of fishing of the Gangrars. For details see-- Montgomery Martin, *Eastern India,* vol. V, p. 531.
48. H.H. Risley, *The Tribes and Castes of Bengal*, vol. II, p. 65.
49. Montgomery Martin, *Eastern India*, vol. III, p. 531.
50. Rup Kumar Barman, "Malo Samajer Atmachetana O Adwaita Malla Barman", in Susanta Haldar (ed.), *Bhasaman*-8, (Kolkata: Adwaita Malla Barman Educational and Cultural Society, 2006), p. 35. The argument of persecution policy of Parsuram had been utilized by the lower caste intellectuals of Bengal particularly those who led their caste fellows for Kshatriya caste status in colonial Bengal in the early twentieth century. The Jhalo Malos

claimed that they were the descedents of Jhallas and Mallas of Northern India. Hence they are Kshatriyas and in order to prove the Kshatriyas status the educated Malos had produced several monographs. Writings of such kinds are ---Mahim Chandra Malla Barman, *Jhalla Malla Parichaya* (Mymensingh: 1331 B.S.); Mahendra Nath Malla Barman, *Dwitiya Varna Kshatriya* (Mymensingh: 1914); Mahendra Nath Malla Barman, *Sanchipta Kshatriya Tatta* (Dacca: 1923); Brajanath Das, *Jhalla Malla Kshatriya Itihas* (Bagura), Sashi Bhusan Das Ray, *Jyoty* (Dacca), Dharmachand Malla Barman, *Sancshipta Jhalla Malla Kshatriya Tatta* (Dacca, 1923); etc.

51. *Titas Ekti Nadir Nam (A River Called Titas)*, a Bengali novel of Adwaita Malla Barman; shows that the Malo fishermen were numerous in Eastern Bengal. This novel was first published in the *Muhammdai,* a Bengali monthly journal; in the 1940s. Later it was published as a complete novel in 1956 (Calcutta, Puthighar, 1956). In the subsequent years, it has been translated into several languages including English and French. See *Adwaita Malla Barman Rachana Sangraha* edited by Achintya Biswas (Kolkata, Deys Publishing, 2000), p. xiii; or *A River Called Titas,* an English translation by Kalpana Bardhan (New York: Penguin Books, 1992).

52. *Yogini Tantra,* edited by Swami Sarveswarananda Saraswati (Calcutta: Naba Bharata Publishers, 1385, B.S.), pt. 1, ch. 12; N.N. Vasu, *Social History of Kamarupa* (3 vols.), reprint ed., (New Delhi: Northern Book Center, 1972), vol.1, p. 71.

53. Minhas-ud-din Shiraj, *Tabakat-i-Nasiri, translated into English* by H.G.Raverty, reprint ed., (New Delhi: Orient Books, 1970), p. 560.

54. Sunity Kumar Chatterji, *Kirata Jana Kriti: The Indo-Mongoloids: Their Contribution to the History and Culture of India,* reprint ed. (Calcutta: The Asiatic Society, 1998), p.113; Sunity Kumar Chatterji, *The Place of Assam in the History and Civilisation of India* (Gauhati: Gauhati University, 1970), p.20.

55. Montgomery Martin, *Eastern India,* vol. 5, Rangpur and Assam, p. 545.

56. B.H. Hodgson, *Essay the first on the Koch, Bodo and Dhimal Tribes,* (Calcutta: Baptist Mission Press, 1847).

57. H.H. Risley, *The Tribes and Castes of Bengal,*, vol.1, p. 492.

58. Upendra Nath Barman, *Rajbanshi Kshatriya Jatir Itihas* (Bengali), 4th ed. (Jalpaiguri, 1401 B.S), pp. 1-25.

59. Hari Kishore Adhikari, *Rajbanshi Kulapradip,* (1314 B.S.), Maniram Kavya Bhusan, *Rajvanshi Kshatriya Dipak* (1318 B.S.); Hari Kishore

Adhikari, *Paundra Kshatriya Kula Dipana* (1319 B.S.); Jaganmohon Singha, *Kshatriya Rajbanshi Kulakoumudi,* etc.

60. Kshetra Nath Singha, *Roy Saheb Panchanan Barmar Jibani Ba Rangpur Kshatriya Samitir Itihas* (Rangpur, 1940), p.13. For more details about the Rajbanshi Kshatriya movement see, Rup Kumar Barman: "Contested Ethnicity and Regional Assertion: A Study from Contemporary North Bengal", in *Journal of History,* Vols. 22&23 (2004-05/2005-06), pp. 99-119; Rup Kumar Barman, "Caste Identity Formation: Mobility and Elite Leadership", in B.K. Shaha (ed.), *Wealth and Welfare* (Kolkata: Academic Enterprise, 2005), pp.53-64;
61. N.K. Dutta, *Origin and Growth of Caste*, p. 139.
62. H.H. Risley, *The Tribes and Castes of Bengal,* vol. II, p. 64.
63. Montgomery Martin, *The History, Antiquities, Topography and Statistics of Eastern India,* 5 vols. (1838), reprint edn. (Delhi: Cosmo Publications, 1976).
64. James Wise, *Notes and the Races*, pp. 257-61.
65. H.H. Risley, *The Tribes and Castes,* vol. I, p. 185.
66. *Ibid.*, p. 184.
67. Sekhar Bandyopadhyay, *Caste, Protest and Identity in Colonial India: The Namasudras of Bengal 1872-1947* (Surrey: Curzon Press, 1997), p. 12.
68. For more details about the formation of tribal chiefdoms in Eastern and Northeastern India in the pre-colonial period *see* Surajit Sinha (ed.), *Tribal Polities and State Systems in Pre-Colonial Eastern and North Eastern India* (Calcutta: CSSSR, 1987); Rup Kumar Barman, *From Tribalism to State : Reflections on the Emergence of Koch Kingdom: Early Fifteenth Century to 1773* (Delhi: Abhijeet Publications, 2007).
69. H.H. Risley, *The Tribes and Castes of Bengal*, vol.I, p.184.
70. *Ibid.*
71. James Wise, *Notes on the Races,* p. 351.
72. H.H.Risley, *The Tribes and Castes of Bengal*, vol. II, pp. 129-30.
73. *Ibid.,* p.136
74. James Wise, *Notes on the Races,* p. 356
75. H.H.Risley, *The Tribes and Castes of Bengal*, vol. II, p 167
76. *Ibid.*, pp. 170-171.
77. *Ibid.*, pp. 176-177.
78. The *zamindars* were the backbone of politics and culture of

Bengal. They occupied a significant place in the Bengali society since the pre-colonial days. The *jotedars* were comparatively smaller in terms of their possession over land their social domination than the *zamindars.* In northern Bengal, the *jotedars* were often treated as *zamindars*. For more details about the land revenue settlement of Cooch Behar State and the Duras areas see – Harendra Narayn Choudhuri, *The Cooch Behar State and its Land Revenue Settlements* (Cooch Behar: The Cooch Behar State Press, 1903); D. Sunder, *Survey and Settlement of the Western Duars in the District of Jalpaiguri 1889-95* (Calcutta: Bengal Secretariat Press, 1895); Charu Chandra Sanyal, *The Rajbanshis of North Bengal* (Calcutta: Asiatic Society, 1965).

79. H.H. Risley, *The Tribes and Castes of Bengal*, vol. II, pp. 192-194.
80. *Ibid.*, pp. 275-280.
81. *Ibid.* 328.
82. W.W. Hunter, *Statistical Account of Bengal, vol. V, Districts of Dacca, Bakarganj, Faridpur and Mymensingh,* reprint edn., (New Delhi, D.K. Publishing House, 1974), p. 329.
83. H.H. Risley, *The Tribes and Castes of Bengal,*, vol. I, p. 42.
84. *Ibid.,* vol. I, p. 81.
85. W.W. Hunter, *Statistical Accounts of Bengal,* vol. 6, p. 367.
86. *Ibid*, vol. 7, p.29.
87. *Ibid.*, vol. 5, p. 593; H.H.Risley, *The Tribes and Castes of Bengal*, vol. 2, p. 66.
88. Martin, *Eastern India*, vol. 5, p, 593.
89. *Brihaddharma Purana,* edited by Panchanan Tarkaratna, 2nd ed., (Calcutta: Bangabasi Electro-machine Press, 1314 B.S.), Part 3, Chapter 13, vs. 29-56, pp. 339-40.
90. The *mangala* literature particularly *Manasa Mangala, Annada Mangala, Chandi Mangala* and *Gosani Mangala* composed in the late medieval Bengal although eulogized the worshiping of certain folk female deities by the then trading and the ruing communities of Bengal but also highlighted the socioeconomic condition of the traditional fishermen communities of the region.
91. The *charitas* or biographies of the Vaishnava saints of the late medieval period particularly the biographies of Sankardeva and his disciples have vividly illustrated the lives of the lowers castes of Bengal and Lower Assam including the fishermen. Mention may be made of the followings — Bhusan Dvija, *Mahapurusha Sankardeva,* edited by Durgabar Barkakati, (Jorhat, 1925); Ramananda

Dvija, *Guru Charita,* edited by M. Neog, (Nalbari, 1957); Upendra Chandra Lekharu, *Katha Guru Charita*, edited by H.N.Dutta Barua, 4th ed., (Guwahati: Dutta Barua Publishing Pvt. Ltd., 2002); Haliram Mahanta, *Sankar Charita,* (Sualkuchi, 1925); Daityari Thakur, *Mahapurusha Sri Sankardeva aru Sri Madhav Devar Jiban Charita*, edited by H. N. Datta Barua (Nalbari, 1978); Ramcharan Thakur, *Guru Charita,* edited by H.N. Dutta Barua, 18th edn. (Guwahati: Dutta Barua Publishing Pvt. Ltd., 2001).

92. H.H. Risley, *Tribes and Castes of Bengal,* vol. 1. p. 183.

93. Rup Kumar Barman, *Caste and Class awareness among the fishermen of Bengal, Voice of Dalit*, Vol.1, No. (Jan.-June 2008), p. 71.

94. Upendra Nath Barman, *Rajbanshi Kshatriya Jatir Itihas* (Bengali), (Jalpaiguri, 1400 B.S.), p. 60; Kshetra Nath Singha, *Ray Saheb Panchanan Barmar Jibani Ba Rangpur Kshatriya Samitir Itihas*, (Rangpur, 1940), p. 13.

95. Upendra Nath Barman, *Sekaler Uttar Bangla O Amar Jiban Smriti,* (Jalpaiguri, 1985), pp. 43-46.

96. Hites Ranjan Sanyal, *Social Mobility in Bengal* (Calcutta: Papyrus, 1981), p. 38.

97. H.H. Risley, *The Tribes and Castes of Bengal*, vol. II, p. 65.

98. For details about the social status of the fishermen lower castes *see* Rup Kumar Barman, *Malo Samajer Atmachetana O Adwaita, Malla Barman; idem,* Adwaita Katha Sahitye Samajchitra: Bahu Kaunik Dristite, in Susanta Haldar (ed.), *Bhasaman-5*, (Kolkata: Adwaita Malla Barman Educational and Cultural Society, 2003), pp.104-115; *idem*, Water Pollution and the Fishermen, in Susanta Haldar (ed): *Bhasaman-6*, (Kolkata: Adwaita Malla Barman Educational and Cultural Society, 2006), pp. 22-28.

99. Nicholas B. Dirks, *Castes of Mind: Colonialism and the Making of Modern India* (Delhi: Permanent Black, 2001), pp. 198-227.

100. Sekhar Bandyopadhyay, *Caste, Culture and Hegemony: Social Domination in Colonial Bengal* (New Delhi: Sage Publications, 2004), p. 25.

101. For details *see* Rup Kumar Barman: *Contested Regionalism*, (Delhi: Abhijeet Publications, 2007).

102. Christophe Jaffrelot, *India's Silent Revolution: Rise of the Low Castes in North India Politics* (Delhi: Permanent Black, 2003), p. 146.

103. They Koches were the ruling community of Cooch Behar State. They had established a kingdom in the beginning of the sixteenth century. For more details see Rup Kumar Barman, *From Tribalism*

to State: Reflection on the emergence of the Koch Kingdom (Delhi: Abhijeet Publications, 2007).

104. Kshetra Nath Singha, *Roy Saheb Panchanan*, p. 8.

105. Gobinda Mohan Sarkar, Organizing Secretary of the Samity, Sri Madhusudhan Ray, a Lawyer of Jalpaiguri and the first president of the Samity, Sri Kamini Kumar Singha Ray, zamindar of Dimla, Sri Harikishor Barma, zamindar of Simulbari and many other Rajbanshi zamindars and intellectuals had actively co-operate with Panchanan Barma in the foundation of the Rajbanshi Kshatriya Samity.

106. Upendra Nath Barman, *Thakur Panchanan Barmar Jibancharit,* fourth edn., (Jalpaiguri, 1408 B.S.), p. 13.

107. Rup Kumar Barman, *Jati Parichiti Gathan, Uttaran O Elite Netrittya,* p. 286.

108. Sibendra Narayan Mandol, *Rajbanshi Kshatriya Jatir Sanchipta Itihas* (Gauripur: India Press, 1972), p. 21.

109. Rup Kumar Barman, Jati Parichiti Gathan, Uttaran O Elite Netrittya (Bengali), in *Itihas Anusandhan* 18, (Kolkata: West Bengal History Council, 2004), p. 287.

110. Sibendra Narayan Mandol, *Rajbanshi Kshatriya*, pp. 27-32.

111. *Ibid.*, p. 26.

112. Upendra Nath Barman, *Thakur Panchanan Barmar Jibancharit*, p. 59.

113. Kshetra Nath Singha, *op.cit.*, pp. 22-26.

114. Cited in, Upendra Nath Barman, *Thakur Panchanan Barmar Jibancharit,* p.29.

115. *Ibid.*, p. 31.

116. Upendra Nath Barman, *Uttar Banglar Sekal O Amar Jiban Smriti,* (Jalpaiguri, 1392), p. 48.

117. Rup Kumar Barman: Malo Samajer Atma Chetana O Adwaita Malla Barman (Bengali), in Susanta Haldar (ed): *Bhasaman 8,* (Kolkata: Adwaita Malla Barman Educational and Cultural Society, 2006), pp. 35-36.

118. J. Kishore and P. C. Ray, *The Pioneering Social Reformers of India* (New Delhi: Wisdom Publications, 2001), p. 166.

119. Christophe Jaffrelot, *India's Silent Revolution,* p. 193.

120. Translated (by self) from Kshetra Nath Singha, *Roy Saheb Panchanan,* p. 12.

121. *Ibid.*, p. 21.

122. *Ibid.*, p. 34.

123. For details about the writings of Panchanan Barma *see* Ramendranath Adhikary (ed.), *Raysaheb Panchanan Rachanbali* (Cooch Behar, 1398 BS).
124. Rup Kumar Barman, *Malo Samajer Atma Chetana,* p. 36.
125. Kshetra Nath Singha, *Roy Saheb Panchanan,* p. 33.
126. *Bhagirathi,* Special Issue on the 3rd Conference of the West Bengal Fishermen Conference held at Baharampur 6-8 June 1986.
127. Annual Report of the Cooperative Societies 1930 in the Presidency Division of Bengal.
128. Upendra Nath Barman, *Thakur Panchanan Barmar Jiban Charit,* p. 60.
129. Sekhar Bandyopadhaya, *Caste, Protest and Identity in Colonial Bengal,* p. 34.
130. *Ibid.*
131. *Ibid.*, p. 35.
132. Kalyan Sinha Roy, Hari Buddha and the Namasudra Movement in Bengal, in Biswajit Chatterjee and Debi Chatterjee (eds.), *Dalit Lives and Dalit Visions in Eastern India* (Kolkata: Centre for Rural Resources, 2007), p. 41.
133. H.H. Risley, *The Tribes and Castes of Bengal*, vol.I. p.188.
134. A.K. Mitra, *The Tribes and Castes of West Bengal* (Alipore: West Bengal Government Press, 1953), p. 31.
135. Sekhar Bandyopadhaya, *Caste, Culture and Hegemony,* pp. 93-94.
136. Nripendra Kumar Dutta, *Origin and Growth of Caste*, p. 290.
137. *Ibid.*
138. *Ibid*, p. 294.
139. *Ibid.* p. 300.
140. A.K. Mitra, *The Tribes and Castes of West Bengal*, p. 32.
141. H.H. Risley, *The Tribes and Castes of Bengal*, vol. II, p. 170.
142. *Ibid.*
143. Nripendra Kumar Dutta, *Origin and Growth of Castes*, p. 302.

3

From Partition of Bengal to Partition of India: A New Look on the Pre-Partition Politics and Location of the Scheduled Castes in Bengal

Partition as a political tool to resolve the ethnic, communal, cultural and political conflicts has long been used in different parts of the world. Some partition theorists have argued in favour of partition while a host of others had bitterly criticized the partition as a means of conflict resolution. The advocates of partition[1] have raised some common points to justify their arguments such as – (i) partition may appear as a humane way to solve the ethnic problem. Partition is better than war since partition may bar war and save lives. (ii) Partition is directly based on Wilsonian Idea (Woodrow Wilson–1856-1924) of 'self determination.' Hence it may be a chosen route of self determination. (iii) Partition is a useful means of decolonization in the colonized countries.[2] (iv) Partition can control the conflicts even if not uproot the roots of the conflicts. Thus Donald Horowitz, a prominent partition theorist, has suggested that

> 'if it is impossible for groups to live together
> in a heterogeneous state, perhaps it is better for

> them to live apart in more than one homogeneous state, even if this necessitates population transfers. Separating the antagonists—partition—is an option increasingly recommended for consideration where groups are territorially concentrated'.[3]

But this suggestion and the arguments mentioned above are always not acceptable. After the collapse of USSR and observing the resurgence of ethnic violence in different parts of the world, a group of scholars have bitterly criticized these arguments.[4] To them, partition is not a remedy of ethnic or community conflicts. Radha Kumar, a notable scholar on partition issue, has argued that the partition generates the 'forced migration' and unbearable human sufferings which violate the human rights in mass scale.[5] Again in many cases it has been noticed that the post-partition successor states had formed the rule of the majority undemocratically that went against the interests of the minorities. So Nicholas Sambanis, another critic of partition, has argued that the partition often fails to establish ethnic homogeneity in the post-partition multiethnic countries where possibility of ethnic conflicts and civil war may sustain for long.[6]

So the partition, as a political tool to resolve the ethno-cultural and political conflicts between two groups or among groups; is a subject of great controversy since the cost of partition often resulted into forced migration of uncountable people from one state to another, unbearable pain, destruction of properties, death, rape, murder, trauma, or horrific violation of human rights as a whole. In the context of this partition debate, here we'll briefly deal with the background of partition of Bengal in 1947 as an essential part of the partition of India and the formation of independent India and Pakistan.

Generally the historians engaged on the studies of partition of India have argued that the demand of partition in British India became a major issue in the first half of the twentieth century due to the growth of communal differences having legacies of socioeconomic, political and cultural factors. Conflicts among the Indians on the grounds of caste and class along with the colonial rule and the international political developments had also stimulated the heterogeneous forces and barred the process of integration of the Indians as a homogenous national identity. The anti-colonial movement or freedom struggle led by the nationalists and nationalist organizations, demand of Muslim homeland or 'separate nation state' by the Muslim League as well as some other separatist regional organizations, and the urgency of leaving of the colonial rulers from the Indian subcontinent were reached their climax in the post Second World War period. All these forces finally got their respective success with the partition of Bengal and Punjab. The dream of the nationalists and the freedom fighters was materialized with the birth of independent India. The Muslim League was successful to achieve Pakistan and the British were successful to leave India with their due respect! But partition was not a sudden development in India. It has a long historical background. Here we are more concern about the partition of India's eastern side i.e. Bengal.

Here, apart from the 'Congress led nationalist politics' and 'Muslim League's communalist politics' had to interact with another major political force like the 'Caste politics' of the Scheduled Castes. Beginning of electoral politics in India particularly after the adoption of the *Government of India Act of 1919* and the *Government of India Act, 1935* had transformed the caste from a social entity to an active tool of politics of both provincial and all India level. It was reinforced by the political participation of the caste based social organizations of the so-called lower caste communities of different provinces of India. So the lower caste communities who were often categorized as 'Hinduised Castes', 'Semi Hinduised Castes', 'Depressed Castes' and 'Depressed Classes' in the colonial administrative records, with the beginning of their official classification as Scheduled Castes (1936) emerged as an essential part of political life of colonial Bengal. Sociopolitical leaders of the Scheduled Caste communities were successful to place themselves as a 'bargaining power' in between the nationalist and the communal political developments. So the National Congress, All India Muslim League, provincial level Krishak Praja Party (KPP) and other non-

Scheduled Caste political forces of colonial period had tried their best to mobilize the Scheduled Castes of Bengal in their favour. But on the eve of partition of India, the Scheduled Castes began to consider themselves as the essential part of nationalist (Congress) and class (Communist) based politics. So they lost their own political identity when they merged themselves to the Congress led political decision i.e. political support to the partition of Bengal. So in the following section of this chapter I'll briefly highlight the background of the partition of Bengal in 1947, along with, location of the Scheduled Castes and territorial arrangement of both East and West Bengal after the partition.

3.1. Bengal from 1905 to 1936

'Partition', as a political tool with communal implication, for the first time in twentieth century India, was used in case of Bengal in 1905. It is well-known that the colonial Bengal was divided in 1905 into two separate provinces—Eastern Bengal and Assam and the Western Bengal which was annulled in 1911. It was basically an administrative arrangement although the Bengalese particularly the upper caste Hindu educated gentlemen *(bhadralokas)* did not tolerate this partition. The anti-partition movement led to the growth of *swadeshi* movement that contributed to the rapid growth of Indian nationalism. At the same time formation of the All India Muslim League in 1906 had encouraged the elite Muslims to look after the better treatment of the Muslims of India including Bengal.

But during and after the First World War (1914-1918), with the emergence of Mahatma Gandhi (1869-1948) in all India level politics, Muslim interest of India was temporality absorbed by the Indian national movement. However, adoption of the *Government of India Act* in 1919 and the introduction of diarchy in different provinces of India (in the form of provincial autonomy) had again stimulated the forces of communal differences in Bengal. Although number of voters in each constituency was very limited but the beginning of electoral politics had promoted the communal sentiments of the upper caste Hindus, the Muslim middle class as well as the so-called Depressed Castes or lower castes.

According to the *Government of India Act of 1919* the constituencies of the Legislative Council of Bengal were divided into several categories like—non-Muhammedan constituency, Muhammedan constituency, university constituency, Anglo-Indian constituency, European constituency, land-holder constituency, commerce and industry constituency, and nominated members including official and non-official. Distribution of constituencies of the council in accordance with the population strength of religious communities and economic condition had no doubt encouraged the communal forces in Bengal.

There were no definite political parties in the election of first council (1921-1923). However, several prominent personalities and political leader from both the Hindu and Muslim communities like—Sir Surendra Nath Banerjee (1848-1925), Provash Chandra Mitter, and Sayid Nawab Ali Choudhury (1863-1929), were entrusted the charges of the ministries. Sir Bijay Chandra Mahtab of Burdwan and Sir Abdur Rahim were given prominent place in the Executive Council. It is interesting to note that the *Government of India Act, 1919* had provided with an opportunity to the Depressed Castes to send their representative to the Legislative Councils as nominated non-official member. Some of the lower caste social organization of Bengal had also contested the election in the non-Muhammedan constituencies. Here we may mention the name of some leaders of the Depressed Castes particularly of Rajbanshi, Namasudra and Poundra communities who were successfully elected to the Bengal Legislative Council like—Panchanan Barma and Jogesh Chandra Sarkar from Rangpur, Prasanna Dev Raikot of Jalpaiguri, Jogendra Krishna Roy of Faridpur South, Hem Chandra Nasker of 24 Parganas (Rural Central). Bishmadev Das, a Namasudra lawyer, was nominated to the Council as a Depressed Caste nominated member.[7]

Table 3.1: Distribution of Constituencies of the Bengal Legislative Council (1921-23)

Sl No	*Description of the Constituencies*	*No of Seats*	*Type of seats*
1.	Non-Muhammedan	46	Elected
2	Muhammedan	38	Elected
3	Calcutta University	1	Elected
4	Anglo-Indian	2	Elected
5	European	5	Elected
6	Land Holders	5	Elected
7	Commerce and Industry	16	Elected
8	Official	16	Nominated
9	Non-Official	6	Nominated
10	Members Executive Council	4	Nominated
11	Total	139	

Source: Dilip Banerjee, *Election Recorder* (Calcutta, 1990), p. 587.

In the second council total number of seat was increased to 140 and we notice some alteration in the distribution of seats. There was no change in the non-Muhammedan constituency while one Muhammedan constituency was increased. In the university constituency one seat was increased since Dacca University now began to be counted as a separate constituency. Similarly number of non-official nominated members was increased to 7 from 6. But the seats of the commerce and industry constituency and the nominated official were decreased to 15 in each from 16.

The election of the second council (1924-26) was a significant part of politics of the twentieth century Bengal. In this council a significant number of the members were elected with the tickets of the newly formed Swarajjya Party (52) under the leadership of Chittaranjan Das. Sir Abdur Rahim, Sayid Nawab Ali Choudhury and Sir Bijay Chandra Mahtab had retained their position in the second council. However, Sir Surendra Nath Banerjee, the father of Indian Nationalism, was defeated by Dr. Bidhan Chandra Roy in 24 Parganas Municipal North seat. Some new faces got prominence in the Council as ministers like A. K. Fazlul Huq and Manmatha Nath Choudhuri of Santosh. Many Depressed Caste members were also elected in the second council as non-Muhammedan (general) candidate. Panchanan Barma, Prasanna Dev Raikot and Hem Chandra Nasker retained their own position in the election. Some new members from different social and communal background including the Depressed Castes, having different political affiliation were also entered to the council who in the subsequent elections of Bengal played significant role. Here we may mention the name of H.S. Suhrawardy (Calcutta South), Dr. Bidhan Chandra Roy, Nagendra Nath Ray (Rangpur of Rajbanshi Kshatriya Samity).[8]

The third legislative (1926-1929) council had no exceptional feature in its composition. However, we find that some new faces were elected to the council who in the future politics of Bengal and India as well played significant role such as Subhash Chandra Bose (Calcutta North) and Naliniranjan Sarkar (Mymensingh East). It is interesting to note that one prominent Depressed Caste leader Panchanan Barma was defeated by Jotindra Nath Chakraborti in this election.[9]

Most significant political development during the tenure of the Third Council was the debate on the *Bengal Tenancy Reform Bill* in 1928. This debate actually originated in the tenure of the first council when the Bengal Legislative Council had appointed a committee under the chairmanship of Sir John Kerr in 1923. Kerr drafted an amendment to the *Bengal Tenancy Act*. The Kerr Committee recommended that the 'produce paying cultivators' who supplied their own seeds and cattle and themselves chose the crop should be treated as tenants.[10] This recommendation had created uproar among the *zamindars, jotedars* and tenure holders of Bengal. To them it was a kind of intervention of the government to the rights of the landholders and a way to give of holding to those cultivators who had no right to acquire that status.[11] The protest of the landholders was so strong that the Government had assured them in 1925 that it has no intention to implement the recommendations of the Kerr Committee.[12] However, mere assurance did not satisfy the land owning class of Bengal. Thus the government had withdrawn the bill. Again another 'special committee' of the officials was appointed in 1928 to draft the amendment of the bill. This bill recommended that those who paid a fixed proportion of the produce to the landholders (such as *adhiar, bhagchashi, bargadar*) were not tenants but those who paid a fixed quantity of produce as rent were to be regarded as tenant.[13]

The Bengal Tenancy Reform Bill of 1928 had created a lot of controversy among the members of the Legislative Council. Simultaneously it divided the members almost along the communal line. The members of the council were clearly divided into three blocks-- (a) Muhammedan, (b) Swarajists, and (c) Official and European. Muhammedan block was obviously consisted with Muslim members where one or two isolated Hindu members had support. The Swarajist bloc was consisted with the Swarajists elected from non-Muhammedan seats, some Hindu landlords and some members elected from various organizations. The official, European and some nominated non-official members formed the third block.[14] The voting pattern of the members in regards to the Tenancy Bill was also very interesting. The Hindu members, Swarajists and non-Swarajists, combined to safeguard the reasonable interests of the landlords while the Muslim members with solitary exceptions were in favour of the enhancement of interests of the *ryots* (cultivators).[15] The official and the Europeans generally voted against any amendment of the original bill. Among the Depressed Caste members Nagendra Narayan Roy was always with Muhammedan block. Thus he voted in favour of the *ryots* and proved himself as an anti-landlord.[16] But Hem Chandra Nasker, being a landlord, had supported the pro-landlord motions in the Council along with all other caste Hindu landlords and Calcutta based professional and businessmen.[17] *The Bengal Tenancy Reform Bill* thus divided the members of the council along the communal and class lines.

In such a background of the Bengal politics, the election (last election according the *Government of India Act 1919)* of the fourth council was held in 1929.The fourth council of Bengal lasted for almost six and half years (from 2nd July 1929 to 4th December 1936). The tenure of this council was full with significant political developments. While a large number of the members had resigned from the council in 1930 appointment of Simon Commission in 1927 and the Round Table Conferences (1930-1932) had contributed to the growth of political development in India ultimately led to the adoption of the *Government of India Act* in 1935.

Table 3.2: Distribution of Seats in Bengal According to the Communal Award, 1932.

Sl .No	*Constituency*	*Number of seats*
1	Muslims	117
2	Muslim Women	2
3	General*	80
4	Depressed Classes	*
5.	General women	2
6.	European	11
7	European Commerce	14
8.	Indian Commerce	5
9	Landholders	5
10	Universities	2
11	Labour	8
12	Anglo-Indians	3
13	Anglo-Indians women	1
14	Total	250

Note: * According to the Clause 9 of the Communal Award 1932 the number of general seats was 80, less the number of Special Depressed Castes seats. The Number of Special Depressed Castes seats in Bengal were maximum 10.Source: B.R.Ambedkar, *Pakistan or the Partition of India*, reprinted in Dr.Babasaheb Ambedkar, Writings and Speeches Vol. 8, (Bombay: Government of Maharashtra, 1990), p.461.

In the meantime British policy of division among the Indians on communal line and division among the Hindus along the caste line through the declaration of the separate electorate (popularly called the Communal Award 1932) became a serious issue for the politics of Bengal and India as well. In case of Bengal the Muslims were granted 117 seats while the number of general seat was only 70. 10 general seats were declared to be reserved for the Depressed Castes. So total Hindu seats was only 80 which obviously was a serious challenge for the upper Caste Hindu Bengalese in their political domination in Bengal.

Thus the upper caste Hindu politicians irrespective of their political affiliation and the Hindu middle class intelligentsia had strongly reacted against the Communal Award.[18] The Muslims of Bengal initially were halfhearted about the Award but ultimately they also welcomed it.[19] While the upper caste Hindus could not get success to increase their seats in the proposed Legislative Assembly of Bengal at the cost of the others, Mahatma Gandhi had refused to accept the concept of separate electorate for the Depressed Castes. According to Gandhi the question of untouchability and the lower social status of the Depressed Castes are social problems of the Hindus that can be resolved through the social reforms not through the political award. Thus he undertook fast unto death against the 'separate electorate'. Ambedkar on the other hand was stick on the separate electorate. However, this problem was eventually resolved through the conclusion of the 'Poona Pact' in 1932. By this pact the Depressed Castes who now began to be classified as the Scheduled Castes (SC) got more reserve seats in the provincial legislative councils. In case of Bengal the SCs got 30 reserve seats.[20] In order to establish its control, Congress now showed its attention to the SCs. It would not be irrelevant to note here that Mahatma Gandhi now began to pay more attention to the cause of the SCs through the publication of various newspaper and magazines such as *Harijan* (English), *Harijan Bandhu* (Gujarati) and *Harijan Sevak* (Hindi) during the period between 1933 and 1940.

In such a background of Indian political development of the 1930s, some Muslim intellectual began to raise the point of deprivation of the Muslims under the then contemporary political arrangement and suggested the formation of 'a separate homeland' for the Muslims. Here we find Allama Sir Muhammad Iqbal (1877-1938) who in the Presidential Address of the All India Muslim League held at Allahabad in 1930 (29 December) had suggested the formation of a 'Muslim State' within India. He said

> 'I would like to see the Punjab, North-West Frontier Province, Sind and Baluchistan amalgamated into a single State. Self-government within the British Empire, or without the British

> Empire, the formation of a consolidated North-West Indian Muslim State appears to me to be the final destiny of the Muslims, at least of North-West India.'

Iqbal's hypothetical idea got a defined name when Chaudhary Rahmat Ali Gujjar (1897-1951), a Cambridge undergraduate student, had coined the term Pakistan in 1933 which referred to the administrative units of Northwestern India such as Punjab (Afghanistan), Kashmir, Sind, and Baluchistan. He strongly voiced for Pakistan through the publication of his pamphlet entitled *"Now or Never: Are We to Live or Perish Forever?"* in 1933 (January 28). By the end of 1933, 'Pakistan' became a common vocabulary. However, in that Pakistan, Bengal had no place. Pakistan movement could not get proper attention of any political organization of Bengal before the advocacy of the 'Two-Nation Theory' by Muhammad Ali Jinnah (1871-1948) in 1940. So it appears that there was no question of partition of Bengal in the 1930s.

Table 3.3: Distribution of Seats in Bengal Legislative Assembly 1937

Sl No	*Types of Seats*	*No of Seats*	*Classification of Seats*
1.	General Seats	48	Urban 12, Rural 36
	General But Reserve for SCs	30	Rural 30
2.	Muhammedan Seats	117	Urban 6, Rural 111)
3.	Anglo-Indian Seats	3	---
4.	European Seats	11	---
5.	Indian Christian Seats	2	
6.	Representatives from Commerce, Industry, Mining and Planting	19	European 14, Hindu 4, Muslim, 1
7	Land Holders Seat	5	---
8.	Representatives of Labour	8	---
9.	University	2	Dacca University 1, Calcutta University 1
10.	Women Seats	5	(General 2, Muhammedan 2 Anglo-Indian 1)
11	Total	250	---

Source: Dilip Banerjee, *Election Recorder* (Calcutta, 1990), p. 532.

From the foregoing discussions it appears that the homogeneity among the Bengalese in the 1930s was a matter of great question. Here caste, class and religious division became more prominent particularly after the enactment of the *Government of India Act* in 1935. The Krishak Praja Party (KPP) under the leadership Abul Kashem Fazlul Huq (1873-1962) began to draw the attention of the middle class, radicals and peasantry of the Bengali Muslim society which now emerged as a significant political force in Bengal. At the same time the SCs had continued with their caste-based organizations for contesting elections although the Hindu Mahashabha began to mobilize them. So for the Congress and the Muslim League, both the KPP and the SC social organizations were appeared as series challenges. At the same time the Hindu Mahashabha (Bangiya Janasangha, Hindu Nationalist Party) and the Bengal Trade Union Federation were other prominent political forces of the pre-Second World War (1939-45) Bengal. In such a background, on the basis of the 1935's Act first election was held in 1937 for the Bengal Legislative Assembly.

3.2. Bengal from 1937-46

Result of the election of 1937 was very significant for the political development in Bengal which generated the forces of social conflicts on communal grounds. Many noteworthy leaders of Bengal politics were discarded by the voters. Out of 250 seats in the Assembly, no party was in the position to form the ministry without compromise. Individually the Congress was the largest political unit having 54 members in the assembly while the KPP and the Muslim League had 38 and 40 seats respectively.[21]

In such a situation, Fazlul Huq had approached the Congress for the formation of ministry with the KPP. The Provincial Congress was also willing to work with the KPP. But the Congress High Command did not allow it.[22] So the Congress could not utilize this opportunity to establish the Hindu-Muslim unity and to fight against the Muslim League and other reactionary forces. The KPP and the League now had decided to work together to form the government in Bengal.[23] Fazlul Huq together with League, and a number of independent (including Scheduled Caste) members had formed the Coalition Party to form the ministry of eleven members. Fazlul Huq was elected as Prime Minister (primer or chief minister) who had maintained a communal balance in the ministry by taking five members from both the Hindu and the Muslim communities. The KPP as a party got two ministers while the Muslim League (ML) got four. The Non-Congress Caste Hindus were allotted three ministries.[24] Congress got the position of the opposition.

Table 3.4: Result of the Election of 1937

Sl. No	*Party*	*Seats won*	*Details*
1	Congress	54	Congress Caste Hindu 43, SC in reserve seats 6, SC in general seat 1, Congress labour 4,
2.	Hindu Nationalist	3	
3	Hindu Mahashabha	2	(Both SC)
4.	Muslim League	40	
5	Krishak Praja Party	38	
6	Independent Muslim	43	Independent Muslim in Muslim general 41, Muslim Labour 2
7.	Independent Caste	14	Including tea garden labourer Hindu
8	Independent SCs	23	SC Reserve seats 22, Independent SC in general seats 1
9	European, Anglo-Indian and Christian	31	
10	Others	2	
11	Total	250	

Sources: Election Recorder, p. 532.

Table 3.5: Ministry of Fazlul Huq (1937-41)

Sl. No	*Name of the Minster*	*Affiliation*	*Department*
1	Mr.Fazlul Huq	KPP	Chief Minister (also in charge of education)
2	Mr.Nalini Ranjan Sarkar	Caste Hindu	Finance

3	Khwaja Sir Nazimuddin	ML	Home
4	Sir Bijoy Prasad Singha Roy	Caste Hindu	Revenue
5	Nawab Khwaja Habibulla Bahadur	M.L	Agriculture and Industry
6	Maharaja Srish Chandra Nandy (of Kashim Bazar)	Caste Hindu	Communication and Works
7	Mr. H.S.Suhrawardy	M.L.	Commerce and Labour
8	Nawab Musharruf Hussain Khan Bahadur	KPP	Judiciary and Legislature
9	Mr. Sayed Nausher Ali	KP	Local Self Government
10	Mr. Prasanna Dev Raikat	SC	Excise and Forest
11	Mr. Mukunda Bihari Mullick	SC	Cooperative, Credit and Rural Indebtedness

Source: Dilip Banerjee, *Election Recorder,* p. 566.

After the election of 1937 the Scheduled Castes (SC) had established themselves as a political force in Bengal. An analysis on the election result of 1937 also indicates a significant achievement of the Scheduled Castes. Besides the 30 reserved seats, they won two general seats (1 Congress and 1 Independent). We find that two ministers were chosen from the Scheduled Caste members. Sri Prasanna Dev Raikot (of Jalpaiguri cum Siliguri constituency) was entrusted the charge of the Department of Excise and Forests while Sri Mukunda Bihari Mullick (Khulna) was given the charge of the Cooperative, Credit and Rural Indebtedness ministry.

However, the Scheduled Castes of Bengal were failed to establish themselves as a politically homogenous social group. From the point of political affiliation, the SC MLAs (Members of the Legislative Assembly) had wide diversity. While the Congress was successful to own 6 reserved seats, the Hindu Mahashabha got 2 seats. Most of the SC candidates own the election as independent candidate under the banner of their caste organizations. For example we may mention the composition of the Rajbanshi MLAs like-- Shyamapada Barman and Premhari Barman (Dinajpur district), Nagendra Nath Ray, Pushpajit Barma and Kshetra Nath Singha (Rangpur), Tarini Charan Barman (Maldah) and Upendra Nath Barman (Jalpaiguri); who mostly contested the election as Kshatriya Samity candidate. The Independent Scheduled Caste MLAs, however, were successful to unify themselves in the Assembly under the banner of the newly formed 'Independent Scheduled Caste Party' (ISCP, 1938) with Hem Chandra Nasker as its President and Jogendra Nath Mandal as secretary. Upendra Nath Barman (1898-1988) was the leader of the party in the Assembly.[25]

Table 3.6: Composition of the SC MLAs Elected in the Bengal Legislative Assembly 1937

Sl. No	*Types*	*Own by SCs*	*Details*
1.	General Seats Reserved for the SCs	30	Congress 6, Independent SC 22, Hindu Mahashabha 2.
2.	General Seats	2	Congress 1, Independent 1.
3.	Total	32	------------

Source: Compiled by self from *Election Recorder;* Gautam Chattopadhyay, *Bengal Electoral Politics and Freedom Struggle 1862-1947* (Delhi: Indian Historical Studies, 1984).

The Government headed by Fazlul Huq had to face critical situation soon after its formation. Ideological differences, individual ambition, shifting loyalties, interplay of British imperial interests, and League's determination to control Bengal politics had created dissension within the Coalition Party. Again the issues like reforms of tenancy and land revenue system, tenancy rights, educational policy and rural indebtedness were contradictory for the partners of the Government as the structure of the Bengali society was very much plural in nature where class, caste and communal identity were intermingled. So Fazlul Huq's experience as premier (chief minister) of Bengal was not very sweet. He could not satisfy any political party. The Muslim League members were not satisfied with the distribution of the portfolios. KPP members were more critical to Fazlul Huq. The radical members of the KPP had raised questions against sharing power with League which is reactionary to the political agenda of their Party.[26] They continued their old demand of abolition of zamindari system and all repressive laws. They created pressure over the government to introduce free primary education and to release of all political prisoners and detainees. The situation became more complicated when 21 members of the left wing of the KPP left the Coalition in 1937 on the ground of breach of election promise by Fazlul Huq.[27] Huq thus became dependent to the League. On 15 October 1937, at Lucknow, he formally subscribed to the Muslim League creed and urged all the Muslim members of the Bengal Coalition to join the League and made a strong plea for Muslim unity under the banner of the League. Even Fazlul Huq chosen by Muhammad Ali Jinnah (1876-1948) for proposing the 'Lahore Resolution' popularly called the 'Pakistan Resolution', on 23 March 1940, at the Lahore Session of the All India Muslim League.

During the course of the Second World War (1939-45), the Bengal politics became more complicated when Fazlul Huq joined the Viceroy's National Defense Council without any consultation with Jinnah, the supreme leader of the League. On August 25, 1941, the Working Committee of the Muslim League asked Fazlul Huq to resign within ten days. Thus he resigned from the All India Muslim League Council. In his resignation letter dated 8th September 1941, he criticized Jinnah's arbitrary whishes according to him which were detrimental to the interests of Bengal.[28] Finally he resigned from the Government (on 2nd December, 1941).[29]

Although the then Governor of Bengal (Sir John Herbert 1939-1943) provided an opportunity to the Muslim League to form the ministry with Khwaja Nazimuddin as Premier but it was not possible for the League. Finally Fazlul Huq formed the 'Progressive Coalition Ministry' in Bengal on 12th December, 1941 with the support of the Forward Block-led Congress (28), Nationalists (14), KPP-Shamsuddin (19), ISCP(12), KPP-Huq (42), Anglo-Indians(3) and Labour(1).[30] New ministry of Huq, with total nine members, had represented a variety of views. In this ministry, the Scheduled Caste members had occupied an important position. Upendra Nath Barman was entrusted the charge of the Department of Forest and Excise which was earlier held by Mr. Prasanna Dev Raikot.[31] Khwaja Nazimuddin with 43 Muslim League members became the leader of the opposition.

Table 3.7: Progressive Coalition Ministry of Fazlul Huq 1941-43

Sl.No	*Name of the Minster*	*Department*
1.	Fazlul Huq	Chief Minister (also in charge of Home and Publicity Department)
2	Khwaja Habibullah	Agriculture and Industry
3	Khan Bahadur Abdul Karim	Education Commerce and Labour
4	Khan Bahadur Hashem Ali Khan	Cooperative, Credit and Rural Indebtness
5	Shamsuddin Ahmed	Communication and Works
6	Shyama Prashad Mookherjee	Finance
7	Santosh Kumar Bose	Public Health and Local Self Government
8	Pramatha Nath Banerjee	Revenue, Judicial and Legislative Department
9	Upendra Nath Barman.	Forest and Excise

Source: Election Recorder, p. 566.

Progressive Coalition Ministry led by Huq did not last long. Resignation of Shyama Prasad Mookerjee (20 November, 1942)[32] from the cabinet, failure of the Cripps Mission (1942), growth of Quit India movement in India including different parts of Bengal (1942), formation of the *Jatiya Sarkar* (national government) in Tamluk (Midnapur district), outbreak of famine in Bengal in 1943, shortage of food and irregularity in food supply, etc. had worsen the political situation of Bengal. The issue of scarcity of food was properly utilized by the League to bring down the ministry. In such a situation Fazlul Huq resigned from the post (28th March) and 31st March (1943) the Progressive Coalition Ministry came to an end.[33]

Fall of Progressive Coalition Ministry had provided the Muslim League to regain the power in Bengal. Khwaja Nazimuddin of Muslim League as Chief Minister now formed the ministry of 13 members with the support of Bengal Swarajya Party, ISCP, Europeans, Anglo-Indians, Indian Christians, Labour Party and the independents.[34] Progressive Party, KPP, Nationalists, Congress (Official and Bose Group) one Indian Christian and 8 SC members totaling 108 constitute the opposition in the

Assembly. In this ministry the Scheduled Castes held significant position. Three Scheduled Castes MLAs were given place as minister in the Government which was highest in terms of presence of the SCs in the Government of pre-partition Bengal.[35]

Table 3.8: Members of the Council of Ministers 1943-45

Sl.No	*Name*	*Social/communal status*	*Department*
1	Sir Nazimuddin	Muslim	Chief Minister (also in charge of Home including Civil Defense Coordination)
2	H.S.Suhrawardy	Muslim	Civil Supplies
3	Tulsi Charan	Caste Hindu	Finance Goswami
4	Tamizuddin Khan	Muslim	Education
5	Barada Prasad Pain	Caste Hindu	Communication and Works
6	Khan Bahadur Sayed Muazzamuddin Hussein	Muslim	Agriculture
7	Tarak Nath	Caste Hindu	Revenue Mukherjee
8.	Musharuff Hussein	Muslim	Judicial and Legislative
9	Khwaja Sahabuddin	Muslim	Commerce, Labour and Industries including Postwar reconstruction
10.	Premhari Barman	Scheduled Caste	Forest and Excise
11	Khan Bahadur Maulvi Jalaluddin	Muslim Ahmed	Public Health and Local Self Government
12	Pulin Behary Mullick	Scheduled Caste	Publicity
13	Jogendra Nath Mandal	Scheduled Caste	Cooperative, Credit and Rural Indebtedness

Source: Election Recorder, p. 567.

But Like the Progressive Coalition Government of Fazlul Huq, the Ministry of Nazimuddin was fell on 28th March (1945) on the occasion of discussion of the Agricultural Budget when the ministry defeated by a cut motion moved by the opposition.[36] Nausher Ali, the Speaker of the Assembly, clearly declared on 29th March that 'the House cannot function no longer unless a new ministry is formed.'[37] With the fall of the Nazimuddin Government, the first phase of the provincial autonomy as enshrined in the *Government of India Act 1935* came to an end. March 19 to 22, 1946 were fixed for the next general election for Bengal.

3.3. The Last Phase of Undivided Bengal 1946-1947

The history of last phase of undivided Bengal and pre-partition politics is very much interesting for many reasons. End of the Second World War, tragic end of the Azad Hind Fauz of Subhash Chandra Bose and its trial, arrival of Cabinet Mission in 1946 (January 5), pressure of the Muslim League for Pakistan, beginning of the *Tabhaga movement* (1946), etc.; had deep impact on the proposed general election in Bengal. Here we find different political trends and propagandas---(a) Congress highlighted the question of independence and was eager to get support from all sections of the society including the Scheduled Castes and the Muslims; (b) Jinnah as well as the Muslim League had declared that the 'general election' would be taken as a plebiscite of the Muslims of India for Pakistan, (c) The Communists and the Scheduled Castes were busy with the class and caste-based social mobilization respectively; and (d) the British Government was worried about the transfer of power to the Indian authority.[38]

In the general election of 1946, the Muslim League got an overwhelming victory in Bengal. Out of 117 Muhammedan seats, the League won 114 seats and got the support of two independent Muslim members. The Congress won 86 seats. The KPP won only 4 seats while the Communists entered into the Legislative Assembly by gaining victory in three seats. Result of the Scheduled Caste organizations like the All India Scheduled Caste Federation (AISCF) and Kshatriya Samity were very much deplorable. Although Jogendra Nath Mondal from AISCF and Nagendra Nath Ray from the Rajbanshi Kshatriya Samity got victory but most of Scheduled Caste candidates contested under the banner of caste organization were defeated. Congress alone got 26 out of 30 reserved seats. It indicates that the Scheduled Caste, on the eve of the partition of Bengal, began to be controlled by the nationalist organization like the Congress. This trend may be interpreted as 'a shift of attitudes of the Scheduled Castes of Bengal from caste-based politics to the nationalist politics.'

Immediately after the election, H.S. Suhrawardy, as a leader the League; was invited by Fredrick Burrows (1887–1973), the Governor of Bengal (19 February 1946 to 14 August 1947); to form the ministry. In the initial stage, Suhrawardy tried to make an understanding with the Congress but no concrete result was produced. Later on 23 April Muslim League's Ministry was formed in Bengal with very minor Hindu support. Initially (23rd April to 15th October) Suhrawardy appointed seven other ministers in his Government including one member from the Scheduled Caste community.[39]

Table 3.9: Members of the Council of Ministers 1946 (23rd April to October)

Sl. No	*Name*	*Department*
1.	H.S. Suhrawardy	Chief Minister (also in charge of Home)
2	Mohammed Ali	Finance, Public Health and Local Self Government.
3.	Sayeed Muazzamuddin Hussein	Education, Land and Land Revenue.
4	Ahmed Hussein	Agriculture, Forest and Fisheries
5.	Jogendra Nath Mondal	Judicial and the Legislative , Works and Building
6.	Abdul Gofran	Civil Supply
7.	Abul Fazal Muhhammad	Cooperative, Credit and Relief, Abdul Rahman Irrigation and Waterways
8	Shamsuddin Ahmed	Commerce, Labour and Industries

Source: Election Recorder, pp. 568-69.

Suhrawardy as the premier of the Bengal Government had to work in a very critical situation when communal tension, violence, Tebhaga movement (1946), and other political developments had engulfed whole Bengal. Condition of Bengal had worsened further with the publication of the proposal of the Cabinet Mission on May 16, 1946. The Cabinet Mission proposed to divide the Indian states into three major categories such as (a) the Hindu majority provinces (Madras, Bombay, Central Province, United Provinces, Bihar and Orissa), (b) the Muslim majority provinces like Punjab, Northwest Frontier Province, Baluchistan and Sindh; and (c) Bengal and Assam which would be allowed to frame their own constitution. An Interim Government headed by Viceroy and a constituent assembly to be formed to finalize the process of transfer of power from the British to the Indians.[40]

The Congress welcomed the proposal since there is no mention about the partition of India while the Muslim League rejected it on similar ground. The Congress Working Committee passed the resolution in favour of the Cabinet Mission Proposal on 25th June 1946. The Muslim League on the contrary adopted a resolution in Bombay (on 19th July) on 'Direct Action' for achieving Pakistan. The Working Committee of the Muslim League had chosen 16th August as the 'Direct Action Day'. Suhrawardy had declared 16th August as public holyday.[41] But 'Direct Action' turned violent in Calcutta. It resulted into the murder, rape, indiscriminate killing of the Hindus and destruction of their property for which this became infamous as 'Great Calcutta Killing' in the history of Indian subcontinent. However, in other provinces 'Direct Action Day' passed off peacefully.

As a reaction of the 'Great Calcutta Killing', the Hindus now began to take revenge against the Muslims in Calcutta. Jinnah condemned the communal violence of Calcutta. But in order to oppose the Congress and to enhance pressure on the British, he and his lieutenants had continued to incite violence.[42] The only way for the government to turn down the violence was to get the League in the Interim Government where Congress had already entered. On 13th October 1946, Jinnah decided to enter into the interim government. With this decision we notice that the structure of the ministry of Suhrawardy had changed. Jogendra Nath Mondal had joined the Interim Government as Muslim League representative. On 25 November,

1946 Sri Tarak Nath Mukherjee, Sri Nagendra Nath Roy, Fazlur Rahman and Dwarkanath Barui were given place in the ministry of Suhrawardy.[43]

However, League's entry to the government did not stop the communal tension. Even the Muslims with the support of the League had started forced conversion, murder, burning and destruction of the properties of the Hindus, raping, abduction and forced marriage of the Hindu womenfolk at Noakhali and Tiperrah in East Bengal in organized way.[44] This trend resulted into the forced migration of the Hindus from Noakhali and some other places of East Bengal. But the Muslim League Government of Bengal did not try to stop it. Suhrawardy stated that the League had nothing to do with this disturbance. Even the League put pressure on the police to withdraw all criminal cases connected with the said violence.[45]

News of the Noakhali violence had created the situation of revenge in Bihar against the Muslims. On 25 the October on the occasion of the Noakhali Day communal riot breakout in Hindu majority Bihar against the Muslims. The Congress Government of Bihar took very bold step to put down the riot.[46] However, League capitalized the Bihar violence and continued the pressure for Pakistan. In order to restore peace Mahatma Gandhi spent three moths at Noakhali (October 29 1946–February 1, 1947).[47] but hastened to Bihar on 1st February 1947 for establishing there. League in the meantime denied working with the Interim Government.

3.4. The Partition in 1947

In such a background of horrific clashes between the Hindus and the Muslims, the British Prime Minster Clemet Attlee (1945–47) had announced on 20th February 1947 that His Majesty's Government's definite intention is to take the necessary steps to effect the transfer of power into responsible Indian hands by a date not later than June 1948. It clearly hinted at the possibility of partition.[48] The Muslim League in the meantime had renewed the 'Direct Action' in Punjab and Northwest Frontier Province to sustain the pressure for Pakistan.[49] The Congress

Working Committee on the other hand welcomed the Attlee's announcement, i.e. transfer of power to the Indians even at the cost of division of India.

Thus three options were opened to the British administration, Muslim League and the Congress; to determine the future of Bengal---(a) to join India or Pakistan without being divided; (b) be divided and join India and Pakistan; and (c) remain independent without being divided. But the Congress, under the leadership of Jawaharlal Nehru, vehemently opposed the possibility of undivided independent Bengal and wanted that Bengal and Punjab must go to Hindustan or Pakistan totally or be divided and shared by Indian and Pakistan. On 8 March, the Congress Working Committee announced that, if India was to be divided, Punjab and Bengal also to be divided.[50] Accordingly 4th April the Executive Committee of the Bengal Branch of the Indian National Congress had resolved to divide Bengal on the ground that without partition there is no option to save the Hindus of this province. S.P. Mookerjee, K.C. Neogi, Dr. P.N. Banerjee, Dr. Bidhan Chandra Ray, Nalini Ranjan Sarkar, Makhan Lal Sen, Kumar Devendra Nath Khan and Atul Chandra Gupta were also present in that meeting as special invitee.[51] The Bengal Provincial Hindu Conference under the leadership of N.C. Chatterjee made a similar declaration. Bengal Hindu Mahashabha, even the Communist Party of India had also supported the partition of Bengal.[52]

However, the third option i.e. the 'undivided Bengal plan' was not disappeared from the political scenario of India. H.S.Suhrawardy, the then Chief Minister of Bengal, launched his idea of a sovereign state for undivided Bengal in a press conference held in Delhi on 27 April 1947.[53] A few days later, Sarat Chandra Bose put forward his proposal for a Sovereign Socialist Republic of Bengal.[54] Mr. Abul Hashim had also started campaigning in favour of this proposal. Suhrawardy met Frederick Burrows, Jinnah and Lord Mountbatten with his idea. Initially Mountbatten showed some interest to the plan of undivided independent Bengal.

This plan got a definite shape when the supporters of the 'undivided independent Bengal' plan had reached to an agreement on satisfactory terms[55] on 20th May, 1947. H.S. Suhrawardy, Kiran Shankar Roy and Sarat Chandra Bose tried their best to secure the approval of the League and the Congress High Command for the causes of the independent Bengal scheme. But the atmosphere of mutual distrust between the Hindus and the Muslims of Bengal was a major challenge to popularise the scheme of independent undivided Bengal. Majority of the Congressmen of Bengal had opposed this scheme. Most of the Leaguers of Bengal led by Khwaja Nazimuddin and Maulana Akram Khan took similar stand.[56] Congress and Hindu Mahasabha denounced it on the plea that it is nothing but a design of extension of Pakistan territory. On 28 May 1947, the Working Committee of the Bengal Provincial Muslim League under the leadership of Akram Khan denounced the scheme and announced full confidence in the leadership of Jinnah. Again, Kalipada Mukherjee, the General Secretary of the Bengal Congress discarded it by a statement issued on 1st June, 1947. Mountbatten had already discarded the idea (8th May) of independent Bengal plan and produced the plan of Partition in May (16th). The planners of the undivided Bengal lost their complete hope. The Congress and the League High Commands now accepted the 3rd June Plan of Mountbatten (or Mountbatten Plan) of 1947 for partition of India and for transfer of power to the Dominions of India and Pakistan.

When partition of Bengal was more or less accepted by the Congress, Muslim League, Hindu Mahasabha, the Communists and other political organizations; some prominent Scheduled Caste leaders of Bengal realized that the Scheduled Caste as a whole would be in a great danger in the divided Bengal. The Working Committee of the Bengal Scheduled Caste Federation under the leadership of Jogendra Nath Mondal had resolved on 14th May, 1947 that

> 'the division of the province into Hindu and Muslim Bengal ..(was) no solution of the communal problems. It would the growing political consciousness and ruthlessly crush the solidarity of the Scheduled Castes of

> Bengal....While the Scheduled Caste of Eastern Bengal would be at the mercy of the majority community, the Scheduled Caste of Western Bengal would be subject of perpetual slavery of the caste Hindus.'[57]

Jogendra Nath Mondal, together with some Scheduled Caste leader of the Rajbanshi community of northern Bengal, had thus come forward with a proposal for the formation of a separate homeland (called Rajasthan) for the Scheduled Caste of Bengal as an alterative.[58] But the Scheduled Caste of Bengal were neither homogenous nor politically a unified social group where Jogendra Nath and his supporters had very little control. It has already been mentioned that most of Scheduled Caste MLAs were elected under the banner of the Congress who strongly supported the partition of Bengal.

Now partition became a matter of implementation only. 15th August was proposed as the final date of transfer of power. Partition of the Muslim dominated provinces became the main task of Mountbatten to complete the process of transfer of power to the Indians. In accordance with the 3rd June Plan, administrative measures were promptly taken by the Government. Since there was no mutual agreement on the question of distribution of territory it was decided that the Members of the Bengal Legislative Assembly would finalise the matter. Accordingly the Bengal Legislative Assembly met on 20th June, 1947. Districts of Bengal were divided into two groups---Muslim majority districts and non-Muslim majority districts. Representatives of the non-Muslim majority districts had decided the partition of Bengal by 58 to 21 votes and agreed to constitute a separate assembly. Initially the members representing the Muslim majority districts had moved against the partition by 106 to 35 votes. But finally they also accepted the partition of Bengal by 107 to 34 votes and decided the amalgamation of Sylhet district with Pakistan if the referendum result in favour of such amalgamation.[59] The Punjab Legislative Assembly had also decided the partition on 23rd June.

The Scheduled Caste Congress MLAs of Bengal had no hesitation to accept the partition. But the non-Congress Scheduled Caste MLAs had reservation about the partition. They always remained intact with the Muslim League. One communist MLA, Rup Narayan Roy, did not vote.[60]

Finally the Indian Independence Act was ratified on 18th July in the British Parliament and Bengal and Punjab were divided by 15th August 1947 to form independent India and Pakistan. Partition of Bengal and Punjab appeared before the people of the respective provinces as a serious threat in the form of communal riots, violence, forced conversion, rape, molestation, murder, mutual distrust that ultimately generated the forces of forced migration from both sides of the newly formed borders.

3.5. Divided Bengal and the Territorial Distribution

The process of partition of Bengal became a serious matter since the British authority had no much time in its hand. The census of 1941 was accepted as the baseline but its authenticity was not beyond doubt. The Second World War (1939-45), political turmoil, poor financial condition of the Government, manipulation in information, etc. were major limitations of the census of 1941. It is a fact that the total Muslim population of Bengal had been increased in a gradual manner since the beginning of census i.e. 1872 to the last census of undivided Bengal (1941). In case of undivided Bengal, total Hindu population was estimated as 2, 50, 59,024 in the census of 1941 while the Muslim population was 3, 30, 05,434.

Table 3.10: Hindu and Muslim Population of Undivided Bengal

Year	*Hindus*	*Muslims*	*Hindu-Muslims*
1872	1,81,00,438	1,76,09,135	+4,91,303
1881	1,80,71,296	1,83,94,426	-3,23,130
1891	1,89,78,300	2,01,74,832	-11,96,532
1901	2,01,55,674	2,19,54,955	-17,99,281

1911	2,09,48,357	2,42,37,228	-32,88,871
1921	2,08,12,526	2,54,86,124	-46,73,598
1931	2,22,12,069	2,78,10,100	-55,98,031
1941	2,50,59,024	3,30,05,434	-79,46,410

Sources: Census of undivided Bengal 1872 to 1941.

The census data of both 1931 and 1941 as given in the following Table 3.11 shows that certain districts of undivided Bengal like--- Bakerganj, Dacca, Faridpur and Mymensingh of Dacca Division; Chittagong, Noakhali and Tripura of Chittagong Division; Jessore, Murshidabad and Nadia of Presidency Division; Bogra, Dinajpur, Maldah, Pabna, Rajshahi and Rangpur of Rajshahi Division; had clear Muslim majority. Rest of the districts of Bengal (including Cooch Behar State) had Hindu majority.

Table 3.11: Hindu and Muslim Majority Districts of Undivided Bengal at per Census

Hindu Majority Districts			*Muslim Majority Districts*		
Districts	*1931 per cent*	*1941 per cent*	*Districts*	*1931 per cent*	*1941 per cent*
1. Burdwan	79	81	1. Nadia	62	61
2. Birbhum	67	72	2. Murshidabad	56	56
3. Bankura	91	95	3. Jessore	62	65
4. Midnapur	89	92	4. Rajshahi	76	74
5. Hooghly	83	84	5. Dinajpur	51	50
6. Howrah	78	79.7	6. Rangpur	71	71
7. 24-Parganas	64	66.7	7. Bogra	83	84
8. Calcutta	69	72.7	8. Pabna	77	77
9. Khulna	50.2	50.5	9. Maldah	54	53
10. Jalpaiguri	67.5	75	10. Dacca	67	64
11. Darjeeling	74	84.9	11. Mymensingh	77	77
12. Cooch Behar	64	62	12. Faridpur	64	61
13. Tripura	68	74	13. Bakerganj	72	72
			14. Tipperah	76	77
			15. Noakhali	78	81
			16. Chittagong	74	74

Sources: Kanti B.Pakrasi, *The Uprooted: A Sociological Study of the Refugees of West*

Bengal, India, (Calcutta: Editions Indian, 1971), p. 20.

For demarcation of boundary and mapping the new border between East Bengal and West Bengal and for territorial distributions, a Boundary commission was constituted on 30 June 1947 under the chairmanship of Sir Cyril Radcliffe. Other members of this Commission were Justice Bijan Kumar Mukherjee, Justice C.C. Biswas, Justice Abu Saleh Mohammad Akram and Justice S.A. Rahman. This Commission was 'instructed to demarcate the boundaries of the two parts of Bengal on the basis of ascertaining the contiguous areas of Muslims and non-Muslims.'[61] The Radcliffe Award was published on 17 August 1947, two days after the Independence. It drew a dividing line between the two parts of Bengal with the following arrangements.[62]

1. East Bengal (East Pakistan) was assigned the whole of the Chittagong and Dacca Division comprising seven districts; the whole of the Rangpur, Bogra, Rajshahi and Pabna districts of the Rajshahi Division and the whole of the Khulna district of the Presidency Division.
2. West Bengal was assigned the whole of the Burdwan Division; the districts of Calcutta, the 24 Parganas and Murshidabad of the Presidency Division and the Darjeeling district of the Rajshahi Division.
3. The five districts of undivided Bengal viz. Nadia, Jessore, Dinajpur, Jalpaiguri and Maldah were divided between West Bengal and East Bengal (Pakistan).
4. Twelve Police Stations of Nadia districts, viz. Alamdanga, Bhoiramana, Chandanga, Damurhuda, that part of Daulatpur, east of the river Mathabhanga, Gangani, Jilannagar, Khoksa, Kumarkhali, Kushtia and Mirpur comprising with 1352 square miles were assigned to East Pakistan.
5. Bongaon and Gaighata police stations of Jessore district comprising 319.8 square miles were added to 24 Parganas district of West Bengal. Rest of Jessore was incorporated with East Pakistan.
6. In the case of Dinajpur district, ten police stations

(Banshihari, a part of Balurghat, (west of the main north-south railway line), Hemtabad, Itahar, Kaliaganj, Kosmandi, Kumarganj, Raiganj, Sangrampur and Tapan) were included in West Bengal. The remainder of the district went to East Bengal.

7. The whole of Jalpaiguri district was included in West Bengal except five police stations and some enclaves, south of Cooch Behar State. These five police stations were Boda, Debiganj, Pachagar, Patgram and Tentulia. They constituted 672 square miles area.
8. In Maldah district five police stations (Bholaghat, Gomastapur, Nachol, Nawabganj and Shibganj) with an area 596 square miles were assigned to East Pakistan. The remainder of the district came to West Bengal.
9. The whole district of Sylhet was transformed from the province of Assam to the new province of East Pakistan, excepting for the four police stations of Patharkandi, Rataleari, Karimganj and Badanpur. These police stations were inhabited mostly by the Bengali speaking Hindus.
10. Murshidabad district did not lose to East Pakistan any entire police station. However, several maujas (village clusters) of a number of bordering police stations were subject to dispute or in de facto possession of East Bengal.[63]

The Award gave West Bengal an area of 28000 square miles, containing a population of 21.19 million people of which nearly 5.3 million (or 29%) were Muslims. East Bengal got 49000 square miles for a population of 39.11 million, of which 29.1% (11.4 million) were Hindus. West Bengal got 36.36% of the land to accommodate some 35.14% of people, while East Bengal got 63.6% of land to accommodate 64.85% of population.[64] But the migration of the minorities in mass scale from East Bengal to West Bengal after the partition had misbalanced the expectations of the Boundary Commission.

Map 3.1. Bengal after Partition

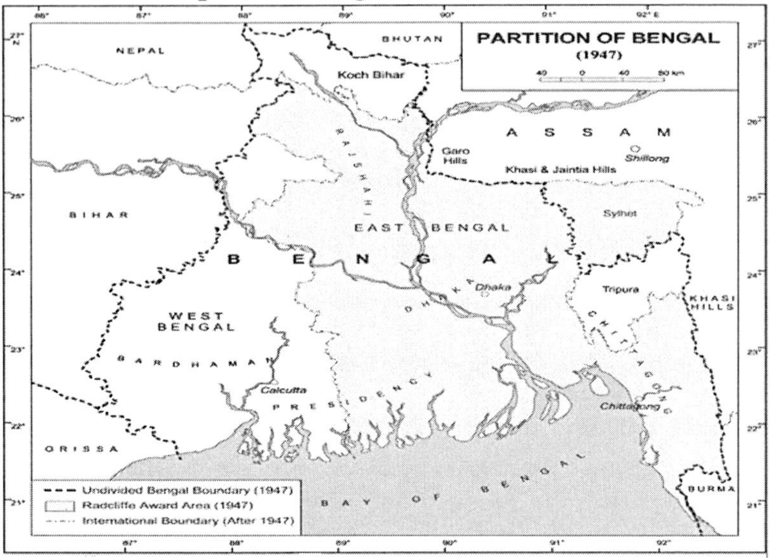

3.6. Conclusion

With the partition of India the nationalists were perhaps very much happy since India achieved independence from the foreign rule through this means. The communal organization like the Muslim League was happy with the birth of Pakistan, the long desired 'Muslim homeland'. The British authority perhaps was also very happy since it played the last card of 'divide and rule policy' in India and was successful to transfer the power with due respect! But there was an ugly side of this happy chapter of the history of India since the partition had compelled the minorities to migrate from one state to another by crossing the manmade political frontiers. The essential by-products of the partition like-- death, murder, rape, unbearable and unexplainable sufferings, destruction of property, trauma, insecurity, mental torture, etc. had darken the colourful achievements of the national, communal and colonial powers.

The process of partition of Bengal in 1947, as we discussed in the forgoing sections of this chapter, is theoretically a very significant aspect of the history of partition. Here the arguments of both the exponents and the opponents of partition are applicable. Firstly partition here was a way of decolonization i.e. end of the British colonial rule and the recognition of the self-determination of the nationalities. Secondly on the eve of the partition particularly in the post-Second World War period some communities having huge concentration in some geographical region began to think that it is almost impossible for them to live with other communities where the suggestion of Donald Horowitz was almost applicable i.e. to live apart. Thirdly the partition of India had generated the forces of forced migration from both the newly formed nation states that led to the unexplainable sufferings what Radha Kumar has argued as an 'inevitable consequence of the partition.' Fourthly the partition could not establish homogeneity in the newly born nations particularly in Pakistan where homogeneity among the Muslims was expected. It justifies the argument of Nicholas Sambanis. So it appears that the history of partition of Bengal of 1947 may contribute to the theoretical understanding of the partition debate.

NOTES AND REFERENCES

1. Among the advocates of the partition as a means of conflict resolution we may mention the name of Chaim Kaufmann, John Mearsheimer, Stephen Van Evera, Donald Horowitzer, etc.

   Chaim Kaufman has written in favour of partition particularly to solve the ethnic problems. In this connection following works of Kaufman are worth mentioning ---Possible and Impossible Solutions to Ethnic Civil Wars, *International Security 20:4* (Spring 1996), 136-75;----Why Iraq Partitioned Itself, Columbia *International Affairs Online,* (September 2007);---- "An Assessment of the Partition of Cyprus," *International Studies Perspectives* 8:2 (May), 206-223; "What Have We Learned About Ethnic Conflict? What Can We Do In Iraq?",*Harvard International Review 28:4 (Winter)*, 44-50; ------"Living Together after Ethnic Killing: in Theory, in History, and in Iraq Today," in Mia Bloom and Roy Licklider, (eds.), *Living Together after Ethnic Killing: Exploring the Chaim Kaufmann Argument* (Taylor and Francis, 2007); "When All Else Fails: Ethnic Partitions and Population Transfers in the Twentieth Century," *International Security* 23:2 (Fall 1998.), 120-156.

John J. Mearsheimer is basically an American international relations theorist. He is one of the leading proponents of a branch of realist theory called 'offensive realism'. Regarding partition we may mention his following works ---- "Shrink Bosnia to Save It," *New York Times*, March 31, 1993; ---- "The Impossible Partition," *New York Times*, January 11, 2001. John J. Mearsheimer and Robert A. Pape, "The Answer: A Three-Way Partition Plan for Bosnia And How the U.S. Can Enforce It," *The New Republic*, June 14, 1993, pp. 22-28; John J. Mearsheimer and Stephen Van Evera, "When peace means War", *The New Republic,* December 18, 1995; etc.

Stephen William Van Evera is also an International Relations theorist. His research includes the U.S. foreign and national security policy and causes and prevention of war. Here we may mention some of his writings like ----*Causes of War: Power and the Roots of Conflict* (Cornell, 1999). He is also the co-editor *Nuclear Diplomacy and Crisis Management* (1990), *Soviet Military Policy* (1989), and *The Star Wars Controversy* (1986). "Offense, Defense, and the Causes of War," *International Security,* vol. 22, No. 4 (Spring 1998), pp. 5-43.

Donald Horowitzer is a specialist in the study of ethnic conflict and the author of several books like *Ethnic Groups in Conflict* (California University Press, 1985), *A Democratic South Africa? Constitutional Engineering in a Divided Society* (California University Press, 1991), *The Deadly Ethnic Riot* (California University Press, 2001); etc. He has acted as a consultant on the problems of divided societies and on policies to reduce ethnic conflict in locations including Russia, Romania, Nigeria, Tatarstan and Northern Ireland.

2. Radha Kumar, The Troubled History of Partition, *Foreign Affairs* v. 76 (Jan. /Feb. 1997), p. 22; Nicholas Sambanis : Partition as a Solution to Ethnic War: An Empirical Critique of the Theoretical Literature, *World Politics* 52 (July 2000), p. 437.

3. Donald L. Horowitz, *Ethnic Groups in Conflict* (Berkeley: University of California Press, 1985), p. 588.

4. Among the antagonist of partition we may mention the names of Nicholas Sambanis, Radha Kumar, etc. For details see Nicholas Sambanis, Partition as a Solution to Ethnic War: An Empirical Critique of the Theoretical Literature, *World Politics 52* (July 2000), 437–83. Among the partition related writings of Radha Kumar we may mention the following works: The Troubled History of Partition, *Foreign Affairs, Dec.-Jan.* 1997, Reprinted in Intervention and American Foreign Policy, a *Foreign Affairs* book, 2001, Prasenjit

Duara (ed.), *Decolonization: Perspectives from Now and Then* (Routledge, 2004), Joshua S. Goldstein (ed.), *At the Helm: Foreign Policy Choices in a Turbulent World* (Longmans, 2003); and Richard K. Betts (ed.), *Conflicts after the Cold War* (Columbia University Press, 2002);------- Settling Partition Conflicts: Key Elements, Key Actors, in Michel Seymour (ed.), *The Future of the Nation State* (McGill-Queen's University Press, 2004);-------- Ethnic Partitions and Peace Processes: Lessons Learnt, the Options Ahead in Ghislaine Glasson Deschaumes and Rada Ivekovic (eds.), *Divided Countries, Separated Cities*, (Oxford University Press, 2003);---------The Partition Debate: Colonialism Revisited or New Policies? *The Brown Journal of International Affairs*, Winter/Spring 2000.

5. Radha Kumar, *The Troubled History of Partition,* in Prasenjit Duara (ed.), *Decolonization: Perspective from Now and Then* (New York: Rutledge, 2004), pp. 162-170.
6. Nicholas Sambanis, Partition as a Solution to Ethnic War: An Empirical Critique of the Theoretical Literature, *World Politics* 52 (July 2000), p. 440.
7. Dilip Banerjee, *Election Recorder* (Calcutta: Book Front Publication Forum, 1990), pp. 588-89.
8. *Ibid.*, pp. 591-95.
9. For details about the political career of Panchanan Barma see --Upendra Nath Barman, *Thakur Panchanan Barmar Jiban Charit,* 4th ed., (Jalpaiguri, 2001); ----- *Sekaler Uttar Bangla O Amar Jiban Smriti* (Jalpaiguri, 1985); Kshetra Nath Singha, *Ray Saheb Panchanan Barmar Jibani* (Rangpur, 1940); etc.
10. D.Bandyopadhyay, Tebhaga Movement in Bengal: A Retrospect, *EPW,* Vol.36 No 1 (October 13-19, 2001), p. 3902.
11. *Ibid.*
12. *Ibid.*
13. Partha Chatterjee, *Bengal 1920-1947, Volume I: The Land Question,* (Calcutta, KP Bagchi & Company, 1984), p. 3.
14. *Ibid.*, p. 88.
15. *Ibid.*, p. 84.
16. *Ibid*, p. 94.
17. *Ibid*, p. 95.
18. Joya Chatterji, *Bengal Divided: Hindu Communalism and Partition*, 2nd edn., (New Delhi: Cambridge University Press, 1996), pp. 26-27.

19. *Ibid*, p. 33.
20. *Ibid.* p. 35.
21. Dilip Banerjee, *Election Recorder*, p. 532; Gautam Chattopadhyay, *Bengal Electoral Politics and Freedom Struggle 1862-1947* (Delhi: Indian Historical Studies, 1984), p.145.
22. Anita Inder Singh, *The Origins of the Partition of India 1936-1947*, 2nd edn. (Delhi: Oxford University Press, 1991), p. 26.
23. *Ibid.*
24. Gautam Chattopadhyay, *Bengal Electoral Politics,* p. 147.
25. Rup Kumar Barman, *Caste and Class Awareness among the Fishermen, Voice of Dalits*, Vol.1, No. 1 (Jan-June 2008), p. 80.
26. Gautam Chattopadhyay, *Bengal Electoral Politics*, p. 151.
27. *Ibid.*, p. 150.
28. Anita Inder Singh, *The Origins of the Partition of India 1936-1947*, pp. 68-69.
29. Gautam Chattopadhyay, *Bengal Electoral Politics,* p. 17.
30. *Ibid*, 172.
31. Dilip Banerjee, *Election Recorder*, p.566.
32. *Ibid.*, p. 568
33. *Ibid*
34. *Ibid.*
35. *Ibid*, p. 567.
36. Gautam Chattopadhyay, *Bengal Electoral Politics*, p.196.
37. *Ibid.*, 204.
38. Dilip Banerjee, *Election Recorder,* pp. 541-547.
39. *Ibid.* pp. 568-569.
40. Gautam Chattopadhyay, *Bengal Electoral Politics*, pp. 205-206.
41. Anita Inder Singh, *The Origins of the Partition of India 1936-1947*, p. 183.
42. *Ibid*, p. 187.
43. Dilip Banerjee: *Election Recorder,* p. 569.
44. Anita Inder Singh, *The Origins of the Partition of India 1936-1947*, p. 195.
45. *Ibid.*, p. 196.
46. *Ibid.*, p. 198.

47. For details about the last days of Gandhi at Noakhali *see* N.K. Bose, *Satchalliser Diary,* edited by Abhik Kumar Dey (Kolkata: Punascha, 2009)
48. S.R.Meherotra, *Towards India's Freedom and Partition* (New Delhi: Vikash Publishing House Pvt. Ltd., 1979), p. 219.
49. Anita Inder Singh, *The Origins of the Partition of India 1936-1947*, pp. 214-215.
50. Joya Chatterji, *The Spoils of Partition: Bengal and India 1947-1967* (New Delhi: Cambridge University Press, 2008), p. 15.
51. Dilip Kumar Halder, "Dalits are the worse victims of Partition: A Human Rights Question", in Biswajeet Chatterjee and Debi Chatterjee, *Dalits Lives and Dalit Visions in Eastern India,* (Kolkata, Center for Rural Resources, 2007), p. 53.
52. *Ibid.*
53. http://www.banglapedia.org/httpdocs/HT/U_0020.HTM.
54. Joya Chatterji, *Bengal Divided,* pp. 259-60.
55. *Ibid*, p. 260.
56. *Ibid*, p. 26.
57. Sekhar Bandyopadhyay, *Changing Border, Shifting Loyalties: Religion, Caste and Partition of Bengal in 1947,* Asian Studies Institute Working Paper 2, (Victoria University of Wellington, 1998).
58. *Ibid.*
58. Kanti B. Pakrasi, *The Uprooted: A Sociological Study of the Refugees of West Bengal,* India, (Calcutta, Editions Indian, 1971), p. 9.
59. Sekhar Bandyopadhyay: *Changing Border.*
60. Kanti B. Pakrasi, *The Uprooted,* p. 17.
61. *Ibid.*, pp. 17-18.
62. *Ibid.*, p. 18.
63. *Ibid.*, p. 22.

4

Partition, Forced Migration and Policies of Rehabilitation: A General Outlook

Migration of people from the place of origin to alien land, from village to town, from one region to another and from one state to another state for socioeconomic, political, cultural and other grounds; is a common trend throughout the ages across the world. Forces of migrations may generate from multiple sources including internal conflicts within the society and state policies. At the same time large-scale migration of people to a particular region may create bitterness of the pre-settled communities (non-migrants or locals) of that region against the newcomers. Conflicts between the immigrants and the locals again stimulate the forces of remigration of the immigrants. But when the 'forced migrants' do not have any other option they are forced to stay in the land where they take shelter even without minimum provisions for survival. Birth of independent India and Pakistan in 1947 through the partition of British India had initiated such great episode of migration of people from one state to another by crossing the artificial political frontier. In this chapter, I have highlighted the types and categories of 'forced' and 'voluntary migrants' from East Bengal to West Bengal and to other places of India. Rehabilitation policies of the governments, both West Bengal and the Union Government; have also been highlighted in this chapter with somewhat objective outlook.

4.1. Types of Forced Migration and Migrants

'Forced migration' is a general term that refers to the 'movements of refugees and internally displaced people (those displaced by conflicts) as well as people displaced by natural or environmental disasters, chemical or nuclear disasters, famine, or development projects.' But forced migration at the same time is also a very complex one especially in terms of its wide ranging phenomena. 'Forced Migration' as a subject of study has drawn the attention of the academicians, social scientists, economists, human right activists, politicians, Non-Governmental Organizations (NGOs), International Non-Governmental Organizations (INGO) and International Governmental Organizations (IGO) all across the world.

The causative factors of forced migration have been categorized by the academicians broadly into three categories like---'conflict-induced displacement', 'development-induced displacement' and 'disaster-induced displacement'. 'Conflict-induced displacement' is very much common in the entire world. In may be caused by the armed conflicts including civil war, generalized violence; and persecution on the ground of nationality, race, religion, political opinion or social group. But 'development-induced forced migration' generally originates due to the construction of infrastructure projects such as dams, roads, ports, airports; urban clearance initiatives; mining and deforestation; and introduction of conservation parks/reserves and biosphere projects; etc. 'Disaster-induced displacement' on the other hand are the outcomes of the disasters of both natural and men-made. A detail classification of types of forced migration has shown in the following Table No. 4.1.

Table 4.1: Types of displacement/Forced Migration

Conflict-Induced Displacement.	*2. Development-Induced Displacement*	*3. Disaster-Induced Displacement*
1. Armed conflicts including civil war. 2. Generalized violence. 3. Persecution on the ground of nationality, race, religion, political opinion or social group.	1. Infrastructure projects such as dams, roads, ports, airports. 2. Urban clearance initiatives. 3. Mining and deforestation. 4. Introduction of conservation parks/ reserves and biosphere projects.	1. Natural disasters (floods, volcanoes, landslides, earthquakes). 2. Environmental change (deforestation, desertification, land degradation, global warming). 3. Human-made disasters (industrial accidents, radioactivity).

Sources: Compiled by self from http://www.forcedmigration.org/whatisfm.htm. Date of access 07.12.2009.

Like the causative factors, there are wide variations among the displaced persons or forced migrants. Most significant type of forced migrants is 'refugee.' According to the United Nations Convention on Refugees (of 1951) a refugee is a 'person residing outside his or her country of nationality, who is unable or unwilling to return because of a 'well-founded fear of persecution on account of race, religion, nationality, membership in a political social group, or political opinion.'[1] The United Nations High Commission for Refugees (UNHCR) in its Protocol of 1967 (31st January) relating to the status of refugees has removed the temporal and geographical limitation of the term refugee contained in the 1951's convention. This Protocol came into force in October 1967. The OAU (Organization of the African Unity) further extended the scope of the definition of refugee by stating that 'the term refugee shall apply to every person who owing to external aggression, occupation, foreign domination or events seriously disturbing public order in either part or whole of the country of origin or nationality is compelled to leave his place of habitual residence in order to seek refuge in other place outside his country of origin or nationality.[2] Scope of definition of the term refugee has been further extended by the Council of Europe's Definition on Refugees of 1976 and the Cartagena Declaration (1984).[3]

Table 4.2: Types of Forced Migrants

Sl. No	*Types of Migrants*	*Description*
1.	Refugee	A person residing outside his or her country of nationality, who is unable or unwilling to return because of a 'well-founded fear of persecution on account of race, religion, nationality, membership in a political social group, or political opinion'.
2.	Asylum seekers	Who have moved across an international border in search of protection but whose claim for refugee status has not yet been determined (under the 1951 Refugee Convention).
3	Internally Displaced Persons /Internal refugee	'Persons who have been forced to flee their homes suddenly or unexpectedly in large numbers, as a result of armed conflict, internal strife, systematic violations of human rights or natural or man-made disasters, and who are within the territory of their own country.
4	Development displaces	People who are compelled to move as a result of policies and projects implemented to supposedly enhance 'development'
5	Environmental and disaster displaces	People displaced as a result of natural disasters (floods, volcanoes, landslides, earthquakes), environmental change (deforestation, desertification, land degradation, global warming) and human-made disasters (industrial accidents, radioactivity).
6.	Smuggled people	Those who have been forcibly displaced as well as those who have left their homeland in search of better economic and social opportunities.
7.	Trafficked people	Who are moved by deception or coercion for the purposes of exploitation.

Source: Compiled by self from http://www.forcedmigration.org/whatisfm.htm. Date of access 07.11.2009.

Second type of forced migrants are the 'asylum seekers' means who have moved across an international border in search of protection but whose claim for refugee status has not yet been determined.[4] Third category of forced migrants is also very significant who are called 'internally displaced persons' or 'internal refugees'. According to the United Nations Guiding Principles on Internal Displacement 'internally displaced persons are persons or groups of persons who have been forced or obliged to flee or to leave their homes or places of habitual residence, in particular as a result of or in order to avoid the effects of armed conflict, situations of generalized violence, violations of human rights or natural or human-made disasters, and who have not crossed an internationally recognized state border.[5] Recently a new type of 'forced migrants' has entered into the typologies of forced migration called 'development displaces' who are compelled to move as a result of policies and projects implemented to supposedly enhance 'development'. At the same time 'environmental and disaster displaces' now are being identified as 'ecological refugees' means 'people displaced as a result of natural disasters (floods, volcanoes, landslides, earthquakes), environmental change (deforestation, desertification, land degradation, global warming) and human-made disasters (industrial accidents, radioactivity). We got two additional types of forced migrants called 'smuggled people' and 'trafficked people' whose figures are very small than first five categories.

4.2. Forced Migrants of Present Study

In case of our present study we'll deal with the first one category of causative factors of forced migration i.e. 'conflict-induced displacement'; and first two categories of forced migrants like --- 'refugees' and 'asylum seekers'. Here refugees and 'asylum seekers' are those people who have been driven off from their country of residence for no apparent faults of theirs and for reasons, which were created mainly due to the partition of Bengal in 1947 at the cost of independence of India. Although we find two way traffics of people i.e. from West Bengal and Northeast India to East Pakistan and from East Pakistan to India; but we are more concerned about the migration from East Bengal to West Bengal and other parts of India. Again among the East Bengali refugees or asylum seekers or voluntary migrants our main emphasis would be on the Scheduled Castes who along with the upper caste Hindu refugees were compelled to leave their country of forefathers. Like the upper caste Hindus, they also took shelter in West Bengal, Northeast India and other parts of India. In this chapter I would highlight some basic points of forced migration from East Bengal and rehabilitation policy of the government in India. State policies towards the Scheduled Caste refugees and the nature of treatment they got from the state and other agencies would be discussed in the chapter five.

4.3. Exodus from East to West Bengal

Forces of 'forced migration' of the minority communities from East Bengal to West Bengal were actually generated with the rapid growth of communal violence since the 'Great Calcutta Killing' of 1946. Forced conversion, murder and burning and destruction of properties of the Hindus; raping, abduction and forced marriage of the Hindu womenfolk at Noakhali and Tiperrah had threatened the lives of minorities in East Bengal.[6] The Muslim League Government of Bengal, led by H. S. Suhrawardy, stated that the League had nothing to do with this disturbance. Even his Government did not take action against the persons who were connected with this violence.[7] So for the creation of a situation of threat and insecurity, migration of the Hindus and other minority communities from Noakhali, Tiperrah and other Muslim dominated districts of East Bengal to West Bengal and other contiguous districts of Assam and Tripura became a general trend.

It is really a very hard task to determine the exact figure of the people who migrated from East Pakistan to West Bengal and other states of India during and after the partition of Bengal as forced migrants. However, we possess some official figures estimated by various government organizations by which we can make an idea about the number of the migrants at least who took shelter in the refugee camps or received assistance from the government for rehabilitation. But the exact figures of the 'forced migrants' or who resettled themselves by their own initiative may not be equal with the official figures. So here we are mainly dependent on the population growth rates as estimated in the census.

According to the government sources, by the end of June 1948, around 1.1 million Hindus left East Bengal.[8] West Bengal received another 55000 people from East Pakistan by the end of October of the same year in its camps.[9] However, migration from East Pakistan gradually reduced in 1949. But due to the organized killing of the Hindus and looting of their properties in different places of East Pakistan particularly after the Bagerhat incident (February 1950) the population flow from East Bengal to West Bengal was further increased. So from March 1950 admission to the refugee camps began to increase. We can make an idea about the growth of refugees in the camps from the table 4.4. In March 1950 West Bengal alone admitted 75595 persons while Orissa and Bihar had received around 25000 East Bengali refugees in their camps.[10]

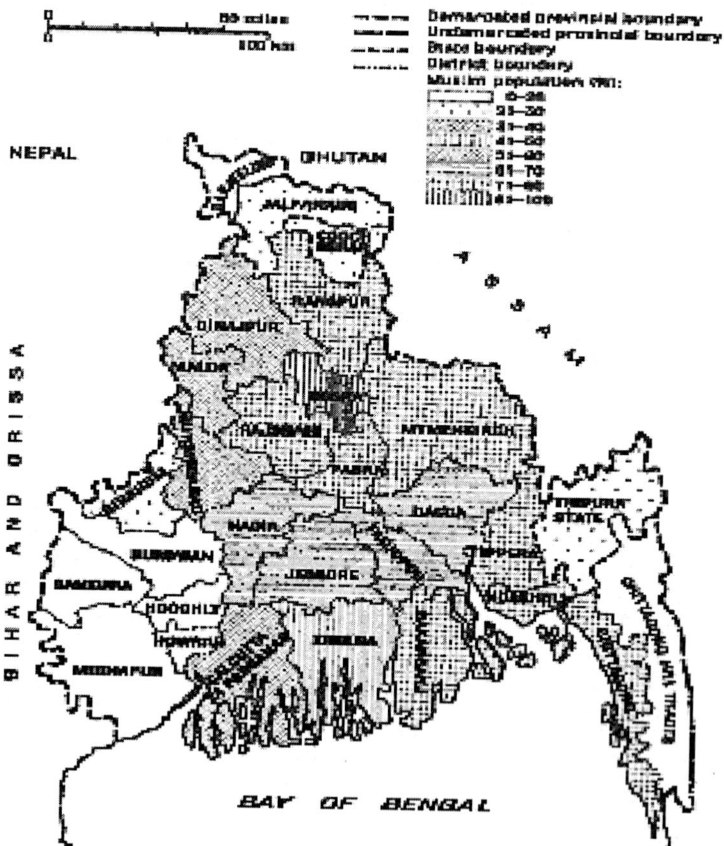

Map: 4.1.Distribution of the Muslims in Bengal 1931

Table 4.3: Hindu and Muslim Majority districts of Bengal

Hindu Majority Districts			Muslim Majority Districts		
Districts	*1931 per cent*	*1941 per cent*	*Districts*	*1931 per cent*	*1941 per cent*
1. Burdwan	79	81	1. Nadia	62	61
2. Birbhum	67	72	2. Murshidabad	56	56
3. Bankura	91	95	3. Jessore	62	65
4. Midnapur	89	92	4. Rajshahi	76	74
5. Hooghly	83	84	5. Dinajpur	51	50
6. Howrah	78	79.7	6. Rangpur	71	71
7. 24-Parganas	64	66.7	7. Bogra	83	84
8. Calcutta	69	72.7	8. Pabna	77	77
9. Khulna	50.2	50.5	9. Malda	54	53
10. Jalpaiguri	67.5	75	10. Dacca	67	64
11. Darjeeling	74	84.9	11. Mymensingh	77	77
12. Cooch Behar	64	62	12. Faridpur	64	61
13. Tripura	68	74	13. Bakerganj	72	72
			14. Tipperah	76	77
			15. Noakhali	78	81
			16. Chittagong	74	74

Source: Kanti B. Pakrasi, *The Uprooted: A Sociological Study of Refugees of West Bengal, India* (Calcutta: Editions Indian, 1971), p. 20.

However, from April 1950 number of the refugees seeking shelter in the government camps began to decline. It is due to the conclusion of the Liaquat–Nehru Pact on 8th April 1950 for lessening the fears of the religious minorities in both India and Pakistan and to promote the communal peace. From April to September 1950 average 25000 people per month got shelter in the government sponsored refugee camps of West Bengal.[11] From October 1950, this figure was reduced to 9000 or less.

Table 4.4: Rate of admission of the refugees to the government camps of West Bengal in different months of 1950 and 1951

Sl.No.	*Year*	*Month*	*No of Refugees admitted to the government camps*
1	1950	January	1150
2	1950	February	1002
3	1950	March	75596
4	1950	April	14960
5	1950	May	27440
6	1950	October	8754
7	1950	November	9543
8	1950	December	6549
9	1951	January	4399
10	1951	February	4215
11	1951	March	5117

Hiranmoy Bandyopadhyay, *Udvastu* (Calcutta, 1970), pp. 92-93, 137-138.

Beside the government camps, the refugees from East Pakistan began to resettle themselves in different districts of West Bengal according to their own conveniences. They migrated in large scale to those districts of West Bengal, Tripura and Assam (including present Meghalaya) which are contiguous to the district of East Bengal. During the period between 20th December 1950 and 15th January 1951, the State Statistical Bureau of the Government of West Bengal had conducted a survey to estimate the figures of the refugees who took shelter in West Bengal (outside the camps). Report of this survey shows that during the period between 15th October 1946 and 15th January 1951 a total 21432228 persons had migrated to West Bengal from East Bengal of which 56% came during the period between 31st December 1949 and 15th January 1951.[12]

Table 4.5: Migration from East Bengal to West Bengal since 15th October1946 to 15th January 1951 (Outside Camps)

Sl.No.	*District*	*Number of families one or more migrants*	*Number of persons including migrants*	*Total migrants since 15th October 1946 to 15th January 1951*	*Migrants since 31st December 1949 upto 15th January 1951*
1	Burdwan	24616	106514	100805	39777
2	Birbhum	2655	12351	11524	5545
3	Bankura	2294	10223	9814	6017
4	Midnapur	6058	31797	28722	5581
5	Howrah	16827	92778	86444	49094
6	Hooghly	12115	68666	63334	28636
7	24 Parganas	100564	598833	541720	265966
8	Calcutta	76078	476759	415970	178799
9	Nadia	84913	411733	403804	267872
10	Murshidabad	14424	67763	65578	32170
11	West Dinajpur	27305	138448	134756	109875
12	Malda	14876	70201	68197	56806
13	Jalpaiguri	20596	107178	100675	65234
14	Darjeeling	3425	18910	17643	8757
15	Cooch Behar	22526	95890	94242	80350
16	Total	429272	2308044	2143228	1200479
17	Percent			100.00	56.00

Source: Government ofWest Bengal, *Report on the Sample Survey for Estimating the Socio-economic Characteristics of displaced persons migrating from Eastern Pakistan to the state of West Bengal,* 1951(Calcutta: State Statistical Bureau, 1951), Table A, p.13.

Map 4.2: Map of West Bengal showing police station wise distribution of the migrant families (Each dot represents 100 families)

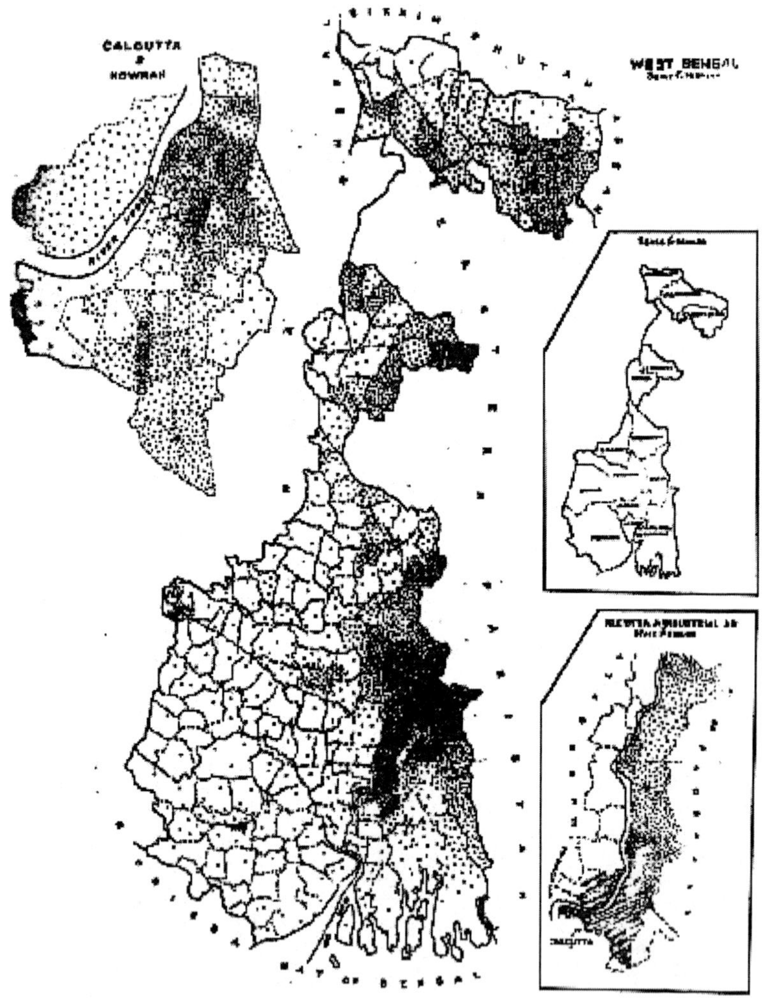

Source : Government of West Bengal, *Report on the Sample Survey for Estimating the Socio-economic Characteristics of displaced persons migrating from Eastern Pakistan to the State of West Bengal,* 1951 (Calcutta, State Statistical Bureau, 1951).

Apart from the survey of the State Statistical Bureau of the Government of West Bengal, the national level census of 1951 has estimated an almost similar figure of the East Bengali refugees those who migrated from 1946 to 1951. According to this census, West Bengal alone had received 2104241 forced migrants from East Bengal.[13] From January 1951 to April 1952 West Bengal received another 85475 persons from East Pakistan. Rumor on the introduction of passport system for traveling from Pakistan to India from 15th October 1952 onward, had suddenly increased the influx from East Pakistan. So during the period between May and October 1952, i.e. six months; a total 193668 persons entered to West Bengal.[14] However, after the introduction of the passport system the rate of migration from East Pakistan had considerably decreased. So from November 1952 to December 1953 only 13004 parsons came to West Bengal with proper documents. Actual number was much higher as many entered to India from East Pakistan without proper documents. As a whole upto 31st December 1954 total 2662601 East Bengali refugees got shelter in West Bengal.[15]

Table 4.6. Figure of the migrants from East Bengal upto 31st December 1954

Sl. No.	*Year*	*Number*
1	Up to December 1950	2304514
2	From January 1951 to April 1952	85457
3	1952 From May 1952 to October	193668
4	From November 1952 to December 1953	13004
5	1954	65918
6	Total	2662601

Hiranmoy Bandyopadhyay, *Udvastu* (Calcutta, 1970), p. 343.

According the report of the Government of West Bengal total number of refugee families (outside the government camps) till May 1955 was 563748 with 273869 people. Together with the camp dwellers it was around 608100 families with a total 2890400 members.[16] According to a report of the Government of India, till December 1958 the total number of displaced person in West Bengal was 3132008 and the total East Bengali displaced families was calculated as 455000 in 1960.[17]

Table 4.7: Distribution of the Refugees in different districts of West Bengal (1946-55)

District of West Bengal	*Number in thousand*			*Families*	
	single member	*others*	*total members*	*total*	*Migrants**
I. Outside Govt. camp					
1. Burdwan	3.8	25.7	29.5	124.3	100.4
2. Birbhum	1.0	3.0	4.0	16.3	12.8
3. Bankura	0.6	2.0	2.6	10.2	7.9
4. Midnapur	1.4	7.1	8.5	40.2	30.9
5. Howrah	1.3	15.0	16.3	82.1	64.6
6. Hooghly	1.4	15.9	17.3	93.8	74.2
7. 24-Parganas	9.5	128.6	138.1	704.3	569.0
8. Calcutta	10.2	94.2	104.4	570.9	446.1
9. Nadia	7.3	98.5	105.8	466.6	386.5
10. Murshidabad	1.6	14.2	15.8	72.7	58.9
11. West Dinajpur	2.4	29.1	31.5	146.1	123.6
12. Malda	1.1	14.8	15.9	72.5	60.4
13. Jalpaiguri	3.7	29.8	33.5	150.2	124.6
14. Darjeeling	0.7	5.2	5.9	30.1	23.7
15. Cooch Behar	3.1	31.5	34.6	143.6	124.7
Total	49.1	514.6	563.7	2723.9	2208.3
II. In Govt. camp	2.4	42.0	44.4	166.5	159.7
Grand Total (I + II)	51.5	556.6	608.1	2890.4	2368.0

Source: State Statistical Bureau, Government of West Bengal, *Rehabilitation of refugees: A Statistical Survey,* 1955

The census of 1961 had estimated a total of 3068750 migrants from East Pakistan to West Bengal.[18] According to the Annual Report of the Department of Rehabilitation of the Government of India between 1946 and 1971, India received a total 51.44 lakhs persons from East Pakistan of which West

Bengal alone had received 38.41 lakhs.[19] The Relief and Rehabilitation Committee also estimated a figure of 52.83 lakhs between 1946 and 1970.[20] A massive exodus took place at the time of war of independence of Bangladesh in 1971. With the beginning of military operation in the streets of Dacca on 25th March 1971, the political situation took a dangerous turn in East Pakistan. Aground 30000 people were killed within two days (25th and 26th March 1971) including the students, teachers and intellectuals.[21] It resulted into the massive influx from East Pakistan including the Muslims and the minorities. So from 26th March 1971 to 31st March on an average 17000 people per day left East Pakistan. In April it reached to 40000 per day. From May 1971 it further increased.[22] However, many of them returned to their homeland after the emergence of impendent Bangladesh. The facts of migration has also been officially recognized by the Government of Bangladesh when it says 'if there were no migration of the Hindus from East Pakistan and Bangladesh during 1961-1991 there would have been 16.5 million of Hindus in Bangladesh instead of 11.2 million in 1991. According to our (Bangladesh) calculation a total of 5.3 million i.e. average 200000 persons have gone missing during 1964-1991.'[23]

4.4. Migration and Resettlement: Responses of the Governments

Huge migration of the East Bengali Hindus to West Bengal and other states had undoubtedly generated unwanted situation in the host regions. The Government of West Bengal was not prepared to handle the situation with proper care. Moreover, it was going through a transitional phase for which West Bengal was dependent to the Union Government to deal with the refugee rehabilitation. But the Government of India under Jawaharlal Nehru's premiership (1947-1964) was not agreed to realize the severity of the situation. In a letter dated 1st December, 1949 to Prime Minister Nehru, Dr. Bidhan Chandra Roy the then Chief Minister of West Bengal (14 January 1948 – 1 July 1962), complained that "the upper and middle class Hindu families came here hungry and starved, having lost all including their hope of finding subsistence in this new place. For months the Government of India would not recognize the existence of the refugee problem in East Pakistan and therefore, would not accept the liabilities on their account..." But Pandit Nehru replied (2nd December 1949) in such a way that there is no responsibility of the Union Government for the East Bengali refugees. He wrote, "in East Pakistan a very large numbers (Hindus) remained and it is your (state govt.) policy ours (Central Government) not to do anything...."[24] This irresponsible phenomenon had been continued in the subsequent years too. Nehru had an impression that there is no permanent danger for the survival of the Hindu minorities in East Pakistan. From the very beginning assurances of Nehru Government to provide rehabilitation and to grant citizenship were not implemented for the East Bengali refugees. So the Government of West Bengal could not arrange their proper rehabilitation. Even it adopted the policy of repatriation and prevention of influx.[25]

However, the Government was not completely silent on the question of rehabilitations of the refugees. The West Bengal and the Union Government had come forward with certain schemes and temporary measures for handling the situation. In the initial stage, it was only opening of camps with the provision of subsistence (dole). Later the Governments had taken some steps for the rehabilitation of the camp-refugees (campers) as well as relief for some non-camp refugees what continued unto 1958. Let us have a look on the Government policy of rehabilitation regarding the refugees from East Pakistan.

4.4.1. Opening of Camps and Colonies

In the initial stage, huge flow of the refugees from East Pakistan was considered by the newly formed West Bengal Government as a 'law and order problem'.[26] However, the West Bengal Government under Dr. Prafulla Chandra Ghosh (1891-1983) had stretched out its hand to the upper Caste Hindus of upper and middle class background. Dr. Ghosh 'tried to help the refugees by filling all the official vacancies with 'optees' from East Pakistan'.[27] It means Dr. Ghosh had provided ample opportunity to the educated section of the Hindus of East

Pakistan to migrate to West Bengal without suffering. But it was less effective for the Scheduled Castes since they were largely illiterate. A very few of them got the proper education and were employed in the government sector. Dr. Ghosh's pro-East Bengali policy, however, generated much criticism for which his ministry felled. Successor of Prafulla Chandra Ghosh, Dr. Bidhan Chandra Roy (1882-1962) now decided to handle the refugee problem very carefully. Dr. Roy had preferred to discourage the refugees to migrate to West Bengal by giving them minimum subsistence or relief. He also wanted dispersal of the East Bengali refugees in different states of India other than West Bengal.[28]

In order to cope with the situation, Dr. Roy had entrusted the charge of refugee rehabilitation to a newly formed department called Refugee Rehabilitation instead of former Relief Department. Mr. Hiranmoy Bandyopadhyay, the then District Magistrate of 24 Parganas, took the charge of this Department in 1949 (15th June). Mr. Bandyopadhyay left a remarkable description of refugee rehabilitation in his work called *Udvastu* published in 1971. According to Bandyopadhyay, till 1949 around 70000 people got shelter in the refugee camps in West Bengal out of which 7500 persons were not suitable of rehabilitation i.e. they became permanent liabilities of the Government. But rests of the camp refugees were suitable for rehabilitation.[29] There were three categories among these people --- (i) refugees having ability of self rehabilitation without government support, (ii) refuges having no financial capability but had self confidence, (iii) very poor and had no confidence of survival without government assistance.[30] Apart from the third category most of the camp refugees were given rehabilitation by the end of January 1950 in different places of 24 Parganas, Nadia and Burdwan.[31]

But fresh influx of the refugees from East Pakistan had generated more complicated problem in the work of rehabilitation. During the period between March 1950 to December 1950, 252000 refugees got shelter in the camps. Out of these figure, around 30000 persons were not suitable for rehabilitation. So rehabilitation of this vast population was a Herculean task for the West Bengal Government. In this connection the West Bengal Government had some major problems like— (i) scarcity of resource, (ii) acquisition of land, (iii) maintenance of law and order in the camps and colonies, (iii) reduction of the rate of influx from East Pakistan.

However, on March 2, 1950 Mr. Mohan Lal Saksena, minister in charge of the Department of Rehabilitation of the Union Government; had convened a meeting in Calcutta with the officials of West Bengal, Assam, Tripura, Bihar and Orissa to resolve the refugee crisis. Saksena proposed that the refugees from East Pakistan entering to India after 1949 would be given relief but the Government would not take any responsibility for rehabilitation.[32] Saksena argued that the newcomers may get back to East Pakistan since they left their all belongings in the land of their forefathers. Secondly the Government is unable to take any firm policy to handle the situation since no body knows the future trend in forced migration.[33] Although this stand of the Government of India was strongly criticized by many well-known personalities of West Bengal but finally it was decided that West Bengal would receive 100000 East Bengali refugees, Tripura, Bihar and Orissa would take the responsibility of 25000, 50000, and 25000 refugees respectively.[34] As an outcome of this meeting, the Government of India had also opened a branch of the Refugee and Rehabilitation office of the Union Government in Calcutta for easy communication between the Union and the State Government and agreed to bear the expense for handling the refugee crisis.[35]

But the expectation of the Union Government could not materialize i.e. the East Bengali Hindu refugees did not return to their own land. Rather flow of the refugees was increased inspite of conclusion of the 'Nehru-Liaquat Pact' (on 18th April 1950). It on the other hand resulted into the return of many Muslims of West Bengal who got shelter in East Pakistan. Thus Nehru-Liaquat Pact could not stop the flow of migration from East Pakistan. It got little success from Indian perspective only to reduce the rate of migration.

In such a situation, both the State and Union Governments began to think about the opening of camps for the refugees.

There were three categories of camps--- (i) relief and transit camps, (ii) colony camps, and (iii) permanent liability camps. The East Bengali refugees who entered India by train mainly arrived at Sealdah Railway Station. So Sealdah Station itself became a transit camp in the early months of 1950. It was really a hard task for the officials of the Refugee and Rehabilitation Department to send the refugees in the relief camps or colony camps of West Bengal, Bihar and Orissa in proper time. Situation became so delicate that the Government had to take rent of some godowns of the jute mills for temporary relief of the East Bengali refugees where around ten thousand refugees got temporary shelter.[36]

During the period between 1950 and 1958 the relief and transit camps were open mainly outside Calcutta (particularly at Bagda and Tangra village of Bongaon subdivision, Chandipur of Basirhat, Ranaghat (Coopers Camp), Krishnagar and Dhubulia of Nadia district). Table 4.8 shows that 24 Parganas, Burdwan, Hooghly and Nadia districts of West Bengal had received largest number of refugees in their camps during the period between 1950 and 1958. Camps were also opened in Bankura, Birbhum, Midnapur, Murshidabad, Cooch Behar and West Dinajpur districts. In Calcutta only 7 camps were opened where 5090 refugees took shelter.

Table 4.8: Refugees in West Bengal upto 1958

District	*No. of Camps and Homes*	*Population in camps and homes*	*No. of govt. colonies*	*Population in Govt. colonies*	*Refugees outside camps and colonies*	*Total refugee population*
Burdwan	30	43127	8	6895	108481	158503
Birbhum	17	17400	6	1775	4375	23550
Bankura	7	11165	2	50	4796	16011
Midnapur	11	16838	38	4390	22654	43882
Hooghly	11	18013	38	21580	65017	104610
Howrah	7	7779	16	7575	75781	91135
24 Parganas	45	43284	209	105345	714161	862790
Calcutta	7	5059	----	-----	571555	576614

Nadia	7	53160	32	61640	539730	664530
Murshidabad	8	12709	21	9945	53443	76097
Malda	----	---	12	2939	69004	72924
West Dinajpur	1	989	111	3865	158095	162949
Jalpaiguri	----	----	9	7850	142306	150156
Darjeeling	----	-----	2	3375	26668	30043
Cooch Behar	1	1159	12	6550	222118	227827
Purulia	----	----	----	----	1332	1332
Total	152	240682	389	243765	2778506	3262952

Source: Government ofWest Bengal, *Relief and Rehabilitation of Displaced Persons in West Bengal* (1958); Joya Chatterji, *The Spoils of Partition* (New Delhi: Cambridge University Press, 2008), p. 134.

Apart from relief camps, West Bengal had also opened colonies in almost all districts according to the nature of refugee population. From the table 4.8 we notice that unto 1958 West Bengal Government had opened largest number of refugee colonies (209) in 24 Parganas district where 105345 refugees took shelter. Some of the notable colonies of this district were Jaytara Colony (of Habra), Chauhatta Colony (of Rajpur), Kanchrapara Colony, Goyeshpur Colony, Baigachhi Colony (Habra), Ashoke Nagar Colony, Kalyangar Colony, Bongaon Colony, Chandipur Colony (Basirhat), Bagda Colony (Bongaon), Tangra Colony, Madhyamgram Colony, Acharya Prafulla Nagar Colony (Sonarpur), Media Colony, Alipore Utvastu Colony, Ramchandra Pur Colony, Kakdwip Colony, Diamond Harbour Colony, Narayanpur Colony, etc. The refugees themselves had established some colonies by their own efforts such as 8 no Ghat Colony of Kakdwip, Narayanpur Colony, etc.

Table 4.9: Colonies of 24 Parganas, Nadia and Murshidabad upto 1958

District	*No. of Colonies*	*No. of Refugees*	*Notable colonies*
24 Parganas	209	1,05,345	Jaytara Colony (Habra), Chouhatta Colony (Rajpur), Kanchrapara Colony, Gayeshpur Colony, Baigachhi Colony (Habra), Ashoke

			Nagar Colony, Kalyangar Colony, Bongaon Colony, Chandipur Colony (Basirhat), Bagda Colony (Bongaon), Tangra Colony, Madhyamgram Colony, Acharya Prafulla Nagar Colony (Sonarpur), Media Colony, Alipore Utvastu Colony, Ramchandra Pur Colony, Kakdwip Colony, Diamond Harbour Colony, Narayanpur Colony, 8-no Ghat Colony (Kakdwip), Bijaygarh Colony (Naihati), Sahid Jatin Das Colony(Beleghata), Palta Colony etc.
Nadia	32	61640	Rupashree Pallly, Fulia Colony, Kuyash Colony, Dhubulia Colony, Chanmari Colony, Kalyani Colony, Swarup Nagar Colony, Taherpur Upanagari, Majherchak Colony.
Murshidabad	21	9945	Kumitala, Nasipur, Debipur, Diyar colonies.

Source: Compiled from Hiranmoy Bandyopadhyay, *Udvastu* (Calcutta, 1970), Government of West Bengal, *Relief and Rehabilitation of Displaced Persons in West Bengal* (1958).

Nadia district was second in terms of receiving the refugees during the period between 1946 and 1958. Here around 61640 refugees were given shelter in 32 government sponsored colonies (see table 4.9) while total number of the refugees of the district including the non-camps and non-colonies was much higher. Since Nadia is a border district of West Bengal having close social, economic and cultural relations with the people of neighboring districts of East Pakistan many East Bengalese had just shifted to Nadia.

Inspite of being a border district, Murshidabad had received less number of refugees than Nadia and 24 Parganas. Here we find that the number of Government sponsored camps was 8 where 12709 persons were registered as refugees. In this district number of colonies was 21 where 9945 persons were resettled.

Table 4.10: Colonies of Burdwan, Birbhum and Bankura

District	*No. of Colonies*	*No. of Refugees*	*Notable colonies*
Burdwan	4	6895	Asansol Utvastu Colony, Salanpur Utvastu Colony, Durgapur Utvastu Colony
Birbhum	6	1777	Guskara Colony, Ratibati Colony, Peardoba Colony, Nababnagar Colony.
Bankura	2	50	Salboni Colony, Shiromony Colony

Source: Compiled from Hiranmoy Bandyopadhyay, *Udvastu* (Calcutta, 1970), Government of West Bengal, *Relief and Rehabilitation of Displaced Persons in West Bengal* (1958).

Burdwan district is although situated far-away from the Bangladesh-West Bengal border but received a good number of refugees. Initially 30 camps were opened in this district where 43127 refugees took shelter. Later few colonies were opened where 6895 refugees were given accommodation.

Not only Burdwan, infertile tract of Birbhum was also chosen by the West Bengal Government for the opening of colonies. However, only six colonies were ultimately opened in this district and only 1775 refugees could accommodate. Among the refugee colonies of this district, we can mention the names of Guskara Colony, Ratibati Colony, Peardoba Colony, Nababnagar Colony, etc.

Another infertile district of West Bengal like Bankura had received some East Bengali refugees. In its 7 camps around 1165 refugees were accommodated. Only 50 persons got place in the colonies like Salboni Colony, Shiromony Colony of this district.

However, Howrah, Hooghly and Midnapur districts had received far more refugees than Bankura and Birbhum. In Midnapur, total camp population during the period between 1947 and 1958 was around 16834 (in 11 camps). There were

38 colonies where 4390 persons were resettled. In Howrah district, number of the refugees in the colonies was around 7575. In this district the colonies were opened mainly in the industrial areas of Bali, Bauria and Fuleswar. Hooghly, the district with fertile land and industries; had accommodated 18013 refugees in its 11 camps and 21580 persons in its colonies. Besides camps and colonies, 65017 refugees took shelter in this district to take advantage of employment facilities in its industries.

Table 4.11: Colonies of Midnapur, Hooghly and Howrah

District	*No. of Colonies*	*No. of Refugees*	*Notable colonies*
Midnapur	38	4390	Sutahata Colony, Aurobinda Pally
Hooghly	38	21580	Guptipara Colony, Bandel Colony, Konnagar Colony
Howrah	16	7575	Bali, Bauria, Fuleshwar etc.

Source: Compiled from Hiranmoy Bandyopadhyay, *Udvastu* (Calcutta, 1970), Government of West Bengal, *Relief and Rehabilitation of Displaced Persons in West Bengal* (1958), Joya Chatterji, *The Spoils of Partition* (New Delhi: CUP, 2008).

Districts of northern part of West Bengal like---- Maldah, West Dinajpur (present South Dinajpur and North Dinajpur), Cooch Behar, Jalpaiguri and Darjeeling had also received a significant number of East Bengali forced migrants. But in these districts Government had opened very less number of camps and colonies. There was no camp in Maldah, Jalpaiguri and Darjeeling. In Cooch Behar around 1159 people got shelter in a camp while in West Dinajpur around 989 refugees were given shelter in a small camp.

In Maldah, only 12 colonies were opened where accommodation of 2939 became possible while the district received around 72924 persons as refugees. In West Dinajpur it was much higher. Here total 162949 persons took shelter. Only 4854 persons got rehabilitation in the camps and colonies. Rest of the refugees did not get attention of the Government.

Table 4.12: Colonies of the districts of North Bengal upto 1958

District	*No. of Colonies*	*No. of Refugees*	*Main areas of the colonies*
Malda	12	2939	Bahadurpur, Maheshpur, Chatia, Habibpur, etc.
West Dinajpur	11	3865	Fatehpur, Kaliyaganj, Radhikapur.
Cooch Behar	12	6550	Mathabhanga, Tufanganj, Cooch Behar
Jalpaiguri	9	7850	Rajganj, Fakir Para, Mandal Ghat, Alipurduar, Panda Para, Fatapukur.
Darjeeling	2	3375	Mohitlal Colony, Phansidewa

Source: Government of West Bengal, *Relief and Rehabilitation of Displaced Persons in West Bengal* (1958), Joya Chatterji, *The Spoils of Partition* (New Delhi: CUP, 2008).

In Cooch Behar, condition of the refugees was much deplorable. Here number of the East Bengali migrants was around 227827 while only 7709 refugees got place in the government sponsored camps and colonies. Jalpaiguri district had also similar experience regarding the rehabilitation of the refugees. This district had received around 150156 refugees till 1958 but only 5850 people got shelter in the government colonies. Although Darjeeling had received less number of refugees but 90% of them were non-camp and non-colony refugees. So the forced migration from East Pakistan to North Bengal had produced different results than the districts of southern part of West Bengal (It would be discussed in detail in the chapter six).

West Bengal had also opened some camps for the refugees who did not have any chance of rehabilitation. They were declared as 'permanent liabilities.' Population in those camps was around 34000 upto 1952 what increased to 50000 by 1958.[37]

4.4.2. Squatters' Colonies

Government policy of opening of camps and establishment of colonies for the 'forced migrants' from East Bengal was no way a complete package for proper rehabilitation. The refugees were not happy with the assistance provided by the Government.

So there were many East Bengali forced migrants who had no interest in the camps and colonies. Many refugees (who did not lose the will power) inspite of losing all belongings; had come forward to resettle themselves in West Bengal by their own efforts. They were not looking for any assistance except the 'dole'.

Map 4.3: Map of West Bengal showing refugee rehabilitation 1951

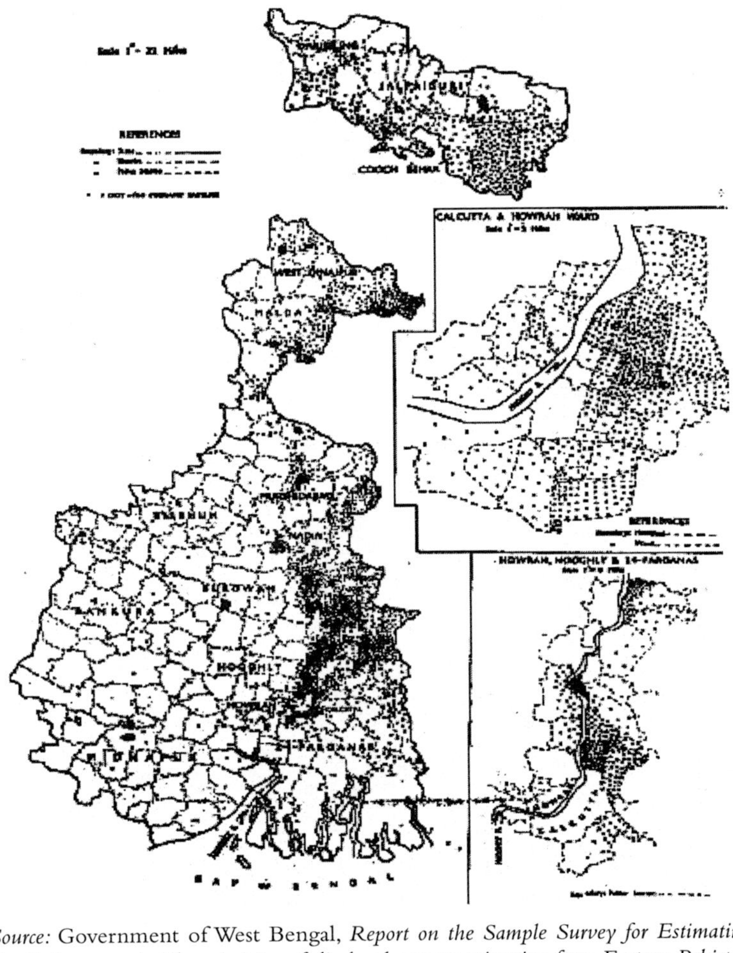

Source: Government of West Bengal, *Report on the Sample Survey for Estimating the Socio-economic Characteristics of displaced persons migrating from Eastern Pakistan to the state of West Bengal,* 1951(Calcutta: State Statistical Bureau, 1951).

In the initial stage the refugees having middle class background in East Pakistan had tried to resettle them nearby Calcutta. They occupied deserted government lands, army barracks and houses and transformed them as colony.[38] These colonies ultimately came to be known as squatters' colony. First colony of this kind was founded at the southern suburbs of Calcutta called Jadavpur Bastuhara Palli[39] what eventually renamed as Bijaygarh.[40]

Table: Pre-1951 Squatter's Colonies of Calcutta and 24 Parganas

Sl. No.	*Place*	*Number of Colonies*
1	Jadavpur	58
2	Behala	4
3	Habra	2
4	Noapara	4
5	Naihati	3
6	Khardah	18
7	Titagarh	40
8	Jagaddal	4
9	Belgharia	3
10	Baranagar	8

Source: Anil Sinha, *Paschim Banglar Jabardakal Udvastu Upanibesh* (Calcutta: Book Club, 1995).

Bijaygarh marked the beginning of a new trend in the settlement of the refugees in West Bengal. In 1949 squatters colonies sprang up at Sodepur (Deshbandhu Nagar), Naihati (Vijaynagar) and Kanchrapara (Shahidnagar). Gradually many squatters' colonies were founded by the East Bengali refugees in different pockets of Calcutta and suburban areas of 24 Parganas in 1950. Here we may mention the names of Bagha Jatin Colony, Azadgarh Colony, Ramgarh Colony,[41] Sahid Jatin Das Colony (Belgharia), Biveknagar Colony (Jadavpur), Nehru Colony, Netaji Colony, Naktala Colony, Gurudas Road Colony, Rabindra Sarobar Road Colony, Southern Avenue Colony, Santoshpur Utvastu

Colony, Ballygunge Utvastu Colony, Regent Park Utvastu Colony, Dhakuria Colony, Tollygunge Colony, etc. Most of the colonies were regularized by the government.

In the squatters' colonies most of the refugees were of upper caste Hindu families. They had enough opportunity of adaptation with the metropolitan city of Calcutta by utilizing their skills. They just wanted the shelter where would be no interference by the state or any other agencies. In these colonies, number of the Scheduled Caste refugees was very less.

Apart from Calcutta, the East Bengali refugees had also established squatters' colonies in other districts of West Bengal. 24 Parganas, Nadia, Murshidabad and Burdwan had allowed the refugees to open largest number of squatters' colonies. The refugees had also established many squatters' colonies in Jalpaiguri, West Dinajpur, Cooch Behar and Malda districts of North Bengal.

Table 4.13: Squatter's Colonies set up between 1st January, 1951 and 25th March, 1971

Sl. No.	*Place*	*Number of Colonies*
1	Birbhum	22
2	Murshidabad	50
3	Nadia	65
4	Bankura	29
5	Howrah	31
6	Malda	38
7	Midnapur	10
8	Calcutta	13
9	Burdwan	66
10	Darjeeling	17
11	Cooch Behar	26
12	Jalpaiguri	76
13	24 Parganas	109
14	West Dinajpur	52

Source: Prafulla K. Chakraborti, *The Marginal Men: The Refugees and the Left Political Syndrome in West Bengal* (Kalyani: Lumiere Books, 1990).

Map 4.4: Occupational distribution of the migrant families

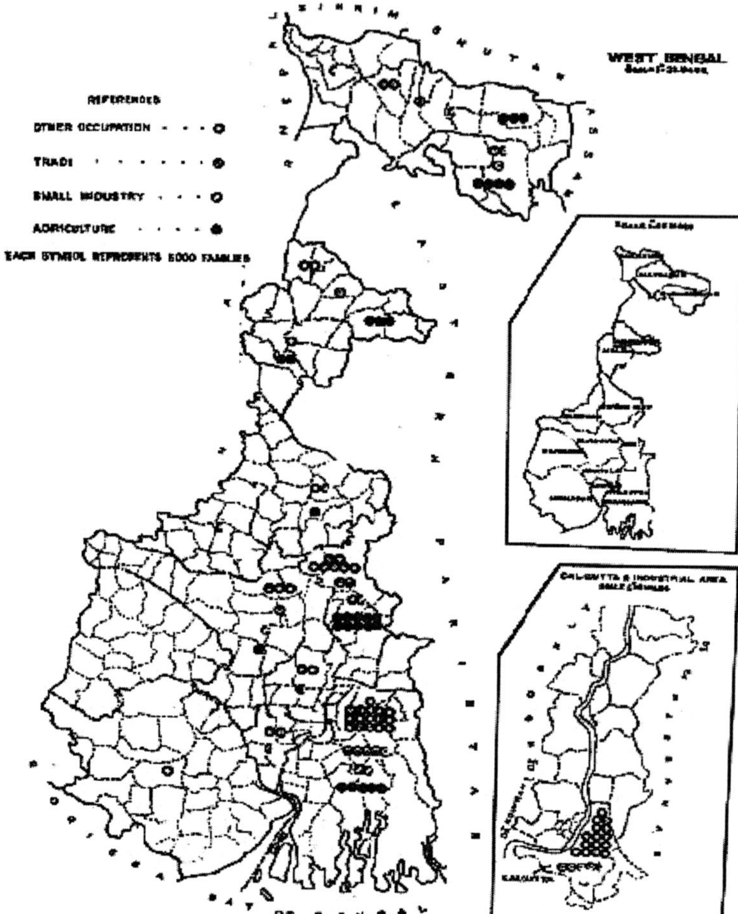

Source: Government of West Bengal, *Report on the Sample Survey for Estimating the Socio-economic Characteristics of displaced persons migrating from Eastern Pakistan to the state of West Bengal,* 1951(Calcutta: State Statistical Bureau, 1951).

4.4.3. Life at the Camps

Life of the refugees at the camps was of utter miserly. The government had although supplied 'doles' for survival of the refugees but practically their life was no way better than the ordinary domestic animals. Refugees had to spend the days at the camps without proper sanitation along with the shortage of food, drinking water and cloths. The 'nishen huts' in case of the Coopers Camp of Ranaghat was nothing but hell where the refugees spent years after year with a hope of good days in future!

There was no place to stay, any food, water and medical facilities at the temporary shelter like Sealdah Station. There was inhuman existence, hardship and death. There were no facilities for jobs within the camps. Even they were not allowed to move outside the camp in search of jobs.[42] So overcrowded and vulnerable life at the camps eventually demoralized many refugees or had broken the abilities of thinking about the future and rehabilitation.

4.4.3. Assistance to the Refugees: Various Schemes

Influx of the forced migrants in large scale to West Bengal was a serious matter for both the West Bengal and the Union Government. There were some general problems for the state. Firstly the Union and the West Bengal Governments were not ready to face the situation since they were passing through a transitional phase from colonial rule to independence. Secondly the governments were somewhat embarrassed with the situation. So the policy of rehabilitation for the refugees in some cases was impractical. Upto 1955 lack of rationality was a common feature in the rehabilitation policy of the Government. It is only some time in 1955 and thereafter that the Government of India really settled down to take the problem of refugees from East Pakistan on a rational basis.

The government had given more emphasis for rehabilitation for the camp refugees or campers. The non-camp refugees tried to fend by their own efforts. Up to 1958((March), out of 31.32 lakh refugees around 7.92 lakhs got shelter in government camps for whom government had taken some schemes for rehabilitation. In the rural areas these schemes were --- (i) Type Scheme, (ii) Union Board Scheme, (iii) Barujibi (betel leaf cultivators) Scheme, and (iv) Horticultural Scheme. There were three schemes for non-agriculturists in rural areas, like (i) type Scheme, (ii) Union Board Scheme, and (ii) Variant of Union Board Scheme.[43]

Among these schemes, 'Type Scheme' for the rural area was a significant one or permanent in nature. Under this scheme, the refugees were distributed land, acquired by the Government, or loan was granted for purchasing land by the refugees. Loan was also granted for house-building, agriculture and small trade. The refugees, those who purchased land under their own initiative, were given grants maximum upto Rs.1900 per family, Rs.555 for house building, Rs.600 as agricultural loan, Rs.150 for irrigation and land reclamation loan per acre, and cash dole for one month. Average amount of land, in case of government sponsored settlement, was around two acres per family and for private settlement it was 0.5 acre.[44] Till 1952 (September) 5442 families were rehabilitated under the government scheme whereas under private initiative around 68014 families were rehabilitated. But in case of government scheme 19.5% families deserted the scheme because they found the land given to them are almost impregnable or unsuitable for survival. In case of private scheme rate of desertion was only 4.3%.[45]

'Union Board Scheme' on the other hand was unique in nature. Here the Government sought to resettle the refugees in different *moujas* (village) with the assistance and cooperation of the Union Board Presidents and the local school teachers. Here the refugees were entitled to get a small piece of land. But no loan facility was available. More over they were not allowed to purchase agricultural land of adequate quantum.[46] This scheme could not produce good result. Around 55% families deserted the scheme.

Barujibi and horticultural schemes were adopted for the agriculturists. The Barujibi or the traditional betel leaf cultivators (who now have been classified as OBC) were given 0.66 acres of agricultural land in average per family and 0.13 acre of land for homestead. Although the refugees did not desert these schemes in large scale but these could not produce good result.[47]

West Bengal Government had given rehabilitation to 101916 families upto September 1952 where average 11.5% left the government schemes. Particularly the Union Board and variant of Union Board Schemes were deserted in large percentage.[48] Thus the government policy of rehabilitation upto 1952 in many cases had produced dispersal of the camps and places of rehabilitation. This phenomenon continued for more years. It is only from 1955 the Government of India began to think seriously about the rehabilitation of the East Bengali refugees particularly in outside Bengal.

However, after 1958 the Government suddenly became silent about the new flow of the refugees from East Pakistan. From March 1958 to December 1963 the migrants from East Pakistan were not recognized as refuges. It was only after the Hazrat Bal incident in 1964 (what generated widespread violence in India and Pakistan) West Bengal again resumed the camp policy. Along with the new migrants (from 1964 to 1971) the migrants of the period between 1958 and 1963 were also now recognized as refugees and considered for rehabilitation. So here we find four stages in the relief and rehabilitations of the East Bengali refugees i.e. 1947 to 1958, 1958 to 1964, 1964 to 1971 and post 1971.Let us have a look on the Government policy of rehabilitation for rehabilitation of the East Bengali refugees in outside West Bengal.

4.5. Migration of the Refugees to Northeast India

Apart from West Bengal, the minorities of East Pakistan had chosen Northeast India as the safer place for their survival. Assam and Tripura having their border with East Pakistan had to receive the refugees in large scale. Migration of the East Bengalese to Assam actually started long before the partition. Introduction of colonial rule, beginning of new production system and the growth of modern age in colonial Assam had generated a pull factor. So migration of the East Bengalese in different capacities particularly as agriculturists, agricultural workers, carpenters, artisans, and civil administrators; was a common trend in the late nineteenth and the early twentieth century. But the migration of the East Bengalese after the partition of Bengal was something different. Here we notice two type of migration, 'voluntary migrants' and the 'forced migrants'.

Voluntary migration to Northeast India particularly in Assam was started with the separation of Sylhet district from Assam. When this district joined East Pakistan (after a referendum) the civil servants who used to work at Sylhet had opted for Assam. The railway personnel of different designations had migrated to Pandu-Maligaon railway colony from Chittagong. These voluntary migrants were very much insignificant in terms of total migration from East Pakistan. Figure of forced migrants was much higher. Since the time of communal riots of 1946 migration of the Hindus of both upper and lower castes has been a common trend in Assam. Moreover, the tribal communities particularly the Garos and Khasis of Mymensingh district, the Chakmas of Chittagong Hill Tracts and Manipuris of Sylhet and the Koches of Northern districts of East Pakistan began to migrate to the contiguous districts of Assam.[49] Huge migration to Assam can be estimated from the population growth rate. We find that during the period between 1951 and 1971 the population growth rate of Assam was abnormally high.

Table 4.14. Population Variation in India and Assam (in %)

Sl. No.	*Decade*	*Assam*	*India*
1	1941-51	19.93	13.31
2	1951-61	34.98	21.51
3	1961-71	34.95	24.80
4	1971-81	23.36	24.69
5	1981-91	24.24	23.82

Source: Census of India of various years.

Tripura, being bordered by Chittagong, Noakhali, Tipperah (Comilla), and Sylhet districts of East Pakistan; had to open its border for the forced migrants since the very beginning. First batch of the refugees entered to Tripura in 1941 after the Raipura riot.[50] After the Noakhali riots of 1946; Tripura became the immediate destination of the East Bengali minorities. The rulers of Tripura had formed a relief committee to handle the situation. Although some refugees got back to their ancestral homeland but a large number of them settled themselves in Tripura.

Table 4.15: Migrants from East Pakistan to Northeast India during 1931-1971

Years	*AP*	*Assam*	*Manipur*	*Meghalaya*	*Mizoram*	*Nagaland*	*Tripura*	*Total*
1931	512	700473	308	6641	739	170	97612	706452
	(0.07)	(85.00)	(0.04)	(0.94)	(0.10)	(0.02)	(13.82)	(100.00)
1951	1492	799735	1394	24133	6512	1416	210161	1044843
	(0.14)	(76.54)	(0.013	(2.31)	(0.62)	(0.14)	(20.11)	(100.00)
1961	1299	740750	3056	25596	8523	1682	394883	1175789
	(0.11)	(63.00)	(0.26)	(2.18)	(0.72)	(0.14)	(33.58)	(100.00)
1971	7388	896823	2330	473922	6606	1979	527355	1916403
	(0.39)	(4680)	(0.12)	(24.73)	(0.34)	(0.10)	(27.52)	(100.00)

Figures in () are percentages: Source: Census of India of different years.

But the situation became more worrying in 1950 with the beginning of huge influx from East Pakistan what continued in the subsequent years. Upto June 1950, the number of the refugees in Tripura, was estimated as 21000 although actual number was much higher. From March to June 1950, Tripura Government had provided rehabilitation to 3866 refugee families in 39 colonies at the cost of Rs.1952783.[51] But from 1951 flow of the refugees was so high that their normal rehabilitation became almost impossible in Tripura. Up to 1958 total number of refugees in Tripura was estimated as 374000(83000 families). From 1st May 1958, the Government had stopped the registration of the refugees what was resumed only in 1963-64. According to the Government sources between 1957 and March 1971 Tripura had received a total 609998 refugees.[52]

4.6. Rehabilitation of the Refugees in Central and Northern India and in Islands

While the policy of rehabilitation for the East Bengali refugees had many limitations in West Bengal, the Government of India had come forward to disperse the refugees in different pockets of India particularly in Eastern, Northern and Southern India. So from the transit camps of West Bengal many refugees were sent to Orissa, Bihar, Andaman and Nicobar Islands, Madhya Pradesh and Uttar Pradesh. However, many refugees from these states began to re-migrate in other states (details would be given in the next chapter).

4.7. Observations

Forces of forced migration from erstwhile East Pakistan were generated for several reasons. Generalized violence and a sense of insecurity were major factors of migration of the minorities. Communal violence was created mainly due to the persecution of the minorities for their economic and social affiliations. Although a small section of the urban and educated people of the minority community had migrated to India as voluntary migrants especially with the option of transfer but most of the migrants were 'forced migrants.' They were scattered in different states of India and tried to settle in the new land by their own efforts.

The policy of relief and rehabilitation as taken by the Governments was ad hoc in nature since they did not have any experience of handling such a crisis although the international human society began to think about the better treatment of the refugees and the protection of human rights in all across the world. It is also a noticeable fact that the post-partition refugee problem in India and the Universal Declaration of Human Rights (UDHR 1948) and the formation of the United Nations' High Commission for Refugees (UNHCR 1951) were contemporary development. But in case of India, the international standard for the protection of human rights and ensuring sufficient assistance to the refugees were merely a nightmare. So the refugees in West Bengal had to face a critical stage in their life.

Again the policy of relief and rehabilitation was full with inequality. While the upper caste non-agriculturists were allowed to stay in the squatters colonies the agriculturalists had to move towards distant lands. Luck of the agriculturist refugees was again unequal. The agriculturist families who took shelter in 24 Parganas, Nadia and Burdwan got more suitable land whereas the land allotted to the refugees in Bankura, Birbhum, Midnapur and Jalpaiguri were less fertile (more precisely infertile).

Table 4.16: Tripura: Proportion of Tribal Population

Sl. No.	*Year*	*Tribal Population (in percent)*
1	1901	52.89
2	1911	48.48
3	1921	56.37
4	1931	50.26
5	1941	50.09
6	1951	36.85
7	1961	31.53
8	1971	28.95
9	1981	28.44
10	1991	30.94
11	2001	31.05

Source: Census of India, various years.

Condition of the refugees in Assam, and other states of Northeast India was no way better than the refugees who took shelter in West Bengal. However, in case of Tripura the refugees and the voluntary migrants had outnumbered the local people. In Tripura tribal population was 50.09% in 1941 what decreased to 36% immediately after the partition of Bengal. In the subsequent years it was further declined. So a sense of deprivation had developed among the hosts of Northeast India. It was stimulated by the determined attitude of the refugees for survival by any cost and their participation in all sectors of economy, politics and society. As a consequence, a section of the youths of Northeast India had raised the slogan in 1960s for expulsion of the refugees by branding them as foreigner *(bideshi)*. The *bideshi kheda* (expulsion of the foreigners) movement turned violent in Assam in the 1970s and 1980s.

In Arunachal Pradesh, the Chakma and the Hajong refugees, inspite of being tribal people, are receiving hostile attentions of the local tribals. In Mizoram also the Chakmas are receiving atrocities from the locals. In Meghalaya, the relationship between the refugees (except the tribal components) and the local tribals turned into a tribal-non-tribal relationship. As a whole in entire Northeast India, after their migration the refugees, are not out of insecurity.

NOTES AND REFERENCES

1. S.K. Roy (ed.), *Refugee and Human Rights* (Jaipur, Rawat, 2001), p. 9; E.G. Ferris (ed.), *Refugees and World Politics* (New York, Preager, 1985), p. 6.
2. V.T. Patil and R.Trivedi, *Refugee and Human Rights* (New Delhi, 2000), p. 31.
3. Alok Kumar Ghosh (ed.), *Dandakaranya: A Survey of Rehabilitation of Saibal Kumar Gupta* (Kolkata, Bibhasha, 1999), p. 2.
4. http://www.hreoc.gov.au/human_rights/immigration/asylum_seekers.html. Date of access 6th November, 2009.
5. For more details about the United Nations Guiding Principles on Internal Displacement see O.P. Misra and A.J. Majumdar (eds.) *The Elsewhere People: Cross-border Migration, Refugee Protection and State Response* (New Delhi: Lancer's Books, 2003).
6. Anita Inder Singh, *The Origins of the Partition of India 1936-1947* (Delhi: Oxford University Press, 1987), p. 195.
7. *Ibid.*, p. 196.
8. Prafulla K.Chakraborti, *The Marginal Men: The Refugees and the Left Political Syndrome in West Bengal* (Kalyani: Lumiere Books, 1990), p. 1.
9. *Ibid.,* p. 2.
10. Hiranmoy Bandyopadhyay, *Udvastu* (Calcutta: Sahitya Samsad, 1970), p. 93.
11. *Ibid.,* p. 111.
12. State Statistical Bureau, Government of West Bengal, *Report on the Sample Survey for Estimating the Socio-economic Characteristics of displaced persons migrating from Eastern Pakistan to the State of West Bengal, 1951* (Calcutta, 1951), p. 13.
13. Kanti B. Pakrasi, *The Uprooted: A Sociological Study of Refugees of*

West Bengal (Calcutta: Editions Indian, 1971), p. 25.

14. Hiranmoy Bandyopadhyay, *Udvastu*, p. 343.
15. *Ibid.*
16. State Statistical Bureau, *Rehabilitation of Refugees: A Statistical Survey* (Calcutta, 1955), p. 2.
17. Kanti B. Pakrasi, *The Uprooted,* p. 26.
18. Migration Table, as given in the Census of India 1961, West Bengal and Sikkim.
19. Rup Kumar Barman, *Fisheries and Fishermen: A Socioeconomic History of Fisheries and Fishermen of colonial Bengal and postcolonial West Bengal* (Delhi: Abhijeet Publications, 2008), p. 56.
20. Abhijit Dasgupta, The Politics of Agitation and Confession, Displaced Bengalis in West Bengal, in S.K.Ray (ed.), *Refugee and Human Rights* (Jaipur, 2001), pp. 102-103.
21. Sandip Bandyopadhyay, Millions seeking refuge: The Refugee question in West Bengal, 1971, in Pradip Kumar Bose (ed.), *Refugees in West Bengal: Institutional Processes and Contested Identities* (Kolkata: Mahanirban Calcutta Research Group, 2000), p. 33.
22. *Ibid.,* p. 34.
23. Shahdeen Malik, Overview of Refugees, Stateless Persons and Internally Displaced Persons in Bangladesh, in *Regional Consultation on Refugee and Migratory Movements in South Asia* (New Delhi, 12-14 November, 1996), p. 29.
24. Prafulla K. Chakraborti, *The Marginal Men*, p. 21.
25. Samar Mukherjee, Rehabilitation of the Bengali Refugees, in S.K. Roy (ed.): *Refugees and Human Rights*,(Jaipur, 2001), p. 135.
26. Joya Chatterji, *The Spoils of Partition: Bengal and India 1947-1967* (Cambridge: Cambridge University Press, 2007), p. 130.
27. *Ibid.*
28. *Ibid.,* p. 132.
29. Hiranmoy Bandyopadhyay, *Udvastu*, p. 46.
30. *Ibid.,* p. 48.
31. *Ibid,* pp. 48-55.
32. *Ibid.*, p. 60.
33. *Ibid.*
34. *Ibid.,* p. 63.
35. *Ibid.*, p. 64.

36. *Ibid.*, p. 66.
37. Samir Das, Refugee Crisis: Responses of the government of West Bengal, in Pradip Kumar Bose(ed.), *Refugees in West Bengal: Institutional Processes and Contested Identities* (Kolkata: Mahanirban Calcutta Research Group, 2000), p. 18.
38. Prafulla K. Chakrabarti, *The Marginal Men,* p. 35.
39. *Ibid.*, p. 39.
40. *Ibid.*, p. 35.
41. *Ibid.*, p. 65.
42. Subhendu Dasgupta, Making of a Refugee History : A Review in Biswajit Chatterjee and Debi Chatterjee (eds), *Dalit Lives and Dalit Visions in Eastern India* (Kolkata, Centre for Rural Resources, 2007), p. 3.
43. Prafulla K. Chakrabarti, *The Marginal Men*, p. 212.
44. *Ibid.*, p. 241.
45. *Ibid.*, p. 242.
46. *Ibid.*, p. 241.
47. *Ibid.*, pp. 241-242.
48. *Ibid.*, p. 243.
49. Rochna Das, Dalit Refugees and the Politics of Northeast India, in Biswajit Chatterjee and Debi Chatterjee (eds.), *Dalit Lives and Dalit Visions in Eastern India* (Kolkata: Centre for Rural Resources, 2007), p.130.
50. Bijan Mohanta, *Tripura in the Lights of Socio-Political Movements Since 1945* (Kolkata: Progressive Publishers, 2004), p. 73.
51. *Ibid.*, p. 75.
52. *Ibid.*

5

Struggle for Survival: Resettlement and Experience of the Scheduled Castes

The partition of Bengal in 1947 and the migration of uncounted number of people from the then East Pakistan had produced mixed results in the lives of the Scheduled Castes of Bengal. The East Bengali Scheduled Castes, after their migration to West Bengal or other states of India; had to face more critical stage in their life than the pre-partition days. At the same time huge migration from East Bengal had created an unhealthy competition among the Scheduled Castes of West Bengal. It has already been discussed in the chapter two that the Scheduled Castes of Bengal in the pre-partition days were mostly engaged in the primary sector of economy where beginning of fresh competition means further degradation of their socioeconomic condition. In such a situation, resettlement of the Scheduled Caste refugees was not an easy one. Again the Scheduled Caste refugees, having lower class and lower caste background; were treated apathetically as 'unwanted persons' or as 'aliens'. In this chapter I have examined 'resettlement experience' of the Scheduled Caste refugees in West Bengal and other states of India with a new perspective of historical writings on the partition of India and refugee resettlement.

5.1. Forces of Migration of the Scheduled Castes from East Pakistan

Immediately after the partition of Bengal, the 'forced' and 'voluntary migrants' from East Pakistan, were mostly higher caste Hindus of upper and middle class background. Since they were closely associated with the freedom movement and pre-partition politics they felt that they would be under the control of a new political force where they would not be able to enjoy political liberties in Pakistani regime. Frequent outbreaks of communal riots and a sense of insecurity had motivated them to depart East Bengal.[1] They had a close economic and social relations with West Bengal for which their journey towards West Bengal was quite natural. The Scheduled Castes of Bengal, on the other hand, were mostly very poor and lived by cultivation of land, catching fish in rivers of East Bengal and working as wage earner. No way was their migration to West Bengal a practical thought.[2] A major portion of the agriculturist Scheduled Castes were busy with the question of their economic survival as they engaged in agriculture work mainly as day labourer and share croppers except very few landholder i.e. *jotedars, talukadars, chakladars, chukanidars,* etc. Now the question is why did the Scheduled Castes leave East Pakistan? Obviously there were certain causative factors what compelled them to migrate to West Bengal and other parts of India.

It has already been highlighted that the Scheduled Castes of Bengal in the late colonial period had placed them as a 'bargaining power' between the nationalist and communal politics. But on the eve of partition, the Scheduled Castes leaders were confused about the acceptance of partition. Most of the seats reserved for the Scheduled Castes owned by the Congress(26 out of 30) for which the Scheduled Caste politicians had to accept the partition for granted. But those section of the Scheduled Caste leaders particularly the non-Congress Scheduled Caste MLAs and MLCs were not in favour of partition of Bengal. They always maintained close political ties with the Muslim League. So the Scheduled Castes particularly the Namasudras had preferred to stay in East Pakistan. Moreover,

Jogendra Nath Mondal (1904-1968), an influential Namasudra leader; had joined the Pakistan Government as Law and Labour Minister (1947-October 1950). He was also a member and temporary chairman of the Constituent Assembly of Pakistan. Jogendra Nath and some other Scheduled Caste leaders of East Pakistan, in a conference held on 19th October 1947; had expressed their faithful allegiance to the Pakistan Government.[3] They also declared that 'each and every member of the Scheduled Caste communities in Pakistan have an inherent right as a loyal citizen to the protection of life, property, religion and culture of his or her from the Government and demands with one voice that the Pakistan Government be pleased to make an immediate declaration reassuring their safety in all respect and to take effective measures to ally the panic prevailing in the country.'[4]

But due to the attacks on the Namasudras in the early 1950s and the atrocities on the Hindus in whole East Pakistan, Jogendra Nath criticized the Government of Pakistan and resigned from the ministry on 8th October, 1950.[5] In his resignation letter, Jogendra Nath had complaint that the 'Pakistan Government has adopted an anti-Hindu policy including the Scheduled Castes and promoting the policy of forced conversion to Islam. The official machinery is also being used as a tool for looting the properties of the Hindus and killing them mercilessly.'[6]

Jogendra Nath's resignation and his own migration to West Bengal had generated additional energy to the anti-Hindu or anti-minority sentiment in East Pakistan. Moreover, most of the educated members of the Scheduled Caste communities of Bengal (who once awakened the Scheduled Castes along the caste-based political consciousness) left East Pakistan for which the ordinary Scheduled Castes lost their all hopes. So in East Bengal, where once a few Scheduled Caste communities had placed them as an essential part of political power (particularly the Namasudras, the Rajbanshis and Poundras) now became irrelevant. So influx of the Scheduled Castes along with the higher caste Hindus to West Bengal and other places of India were continued.

These are some general notions conceptualized in the historical writings of India's partition in the East. Let us have a critical look on the causative factors of forced migration of the Scheduled Castes from East Pakistan. First major factor was communal violence and communal threat. It has been already highlighted by most of the scholars that repeated outbreak of communal violence since 1946 and atrocities committed against the minorities and the fear psychosis of the minorities had compelled them to move for safer places. The Scheduled Castes were no exception. They began to be considered as 'General Hindus' by the majority community of East Pakistan. Hence being Hindu, they had to face the challenges from contemporary majority community. Jogendra Nath Mondal, the then Law and Labour Minister of Pakistan, had illustrated the nature of insecurity of the Hindus in following style:

> "What is today the condition in East Bengal? About fifty lakhs of Hindus have left since the partition of the country. Apart from the East Bengal riot of last February, the reasons for such a large scale exodus of Hindus are many. The boycott by the Muslims of Hindu Lawyers, medical practitioners, shop-keepers, traders and merchants has compelled Hindus to migrate to West Bengal in search of their means of livelihood. Wholesales requisition of Hindu houses even without following due process of law in many and non-payment of any rent whatsoever to the owners have compelled them to seek for Indian shelter. Payment of rent to Hindu landlords was stopped long before. Interference in matters of education and methods adopted by the Education Authority for Islamisation frightened the teaching staff of Secondary Schools and Colleges out of their old familiar moorings. They have left East Bengal. As a result, most of the educational institutions have been closed. I have received information that sometime ago the Educational Authority issued circular in

> Secondary Schools enjoying compulsory participation of teachers and students of all communities in relation from the Holy Koran before the school work commenced. Another circular requires headmasters of schools to name the different blocks of the premises after 12 distinguished Muslims, such as Jinnah, Iqbal, Liaquat Ali, Nazimuddin etc. Only very recently in an educational conference held at Dacca, the President disclosed that out of 1,500 High English Schools in East Bengal, only 500 were working. Owing to the migration of Medical Practitioners there is hardly any means of proper treatment of patients. Almost all the priests who used to worship the household deities at Hindu houses have left. Important places of worship have been abandoned. The result is that the Hindus of East Bengal have got now hardly any means to follow religious pursuits and performance of social ceremonies like marriage where the services of a priest are essential. Artisans who made images of gods and goddesses have also left. Hindu Presidents of Union Boards have been replaced by Muslims by coercive measures with the active help and connivance of the police and Circle Officers. Hindu headmasters and Secretaries of Schools have been replaced by Muslims. The life of the few Hindu government servants has been made extremely miserable as many of them have either been superseded by junior Muslims or dismissed without sufficient or any cause."[7]

So it appears that the atrocities against the minorities had created a sense of insecurity among them. Naturally field survey carried out among the Scheduled Caste migrants and the present generation of their families, who took shelter in different districts of West Bengal (like Nadia, Murshidabad and Cooch Behar); shows that the fear of communal persecution had been a major issue for their migration (See Table 5.1).

Table 5.1: Reason of Migration from East Pakistan as Stated by the Persons Interviewed

Sl No	*District*	*Fear of communal persecution*	*Economic*	*Political*	*Being induced by others*	*Others*	*Total*
1	Cooch Behar	12	26	5	7	0	50
2	Nadia	26	0	0	4	0	30
3	Murshidabad	5	0	0	25	0	30
4	Midnapur	22	0	1	2	0	25
5	Total	65	26	6	38	0	135

Source: Compiled by self from the data acquired through filed survey carried out between November 2008 and October 2010)

However, there were many other factors what led to the forced and voluntary migration of the Scheduled Castes from East Pakistan particularly after 1950. According to Jogendra Nath Mondal 'after the partition particularly after the death of Qaid-e-Azam, the Scheduled Castes have not received a fair deal in any matter' what obviously demoralized the educated Scheduled Castes who remained in East Pakistan.[8] So they proceeded towards West Bengal and Northeast India as voluntary migrants.

Economic factor was another major force of forced migration of the Scheduled Castes of East Pakistan. They received a severe challenge when the lower class Muslims began to adopt their traditional occupations. Moreover, with the beginning of rule of the Pakistan Government in East Bengal, the land holding Hindu families found that the landless Muslim peasant labour force became allured towards their land. Again many Scheduled Caste families lost their assured set of economic relationship with their (upper Caste Hindu) employers. The Scheduled Caste agricultural labourer (who had no sharp class conflict with the Muslim poor class in the colonial days) now began to receive threat from the new Muslim landed class about getting job in cultivable land.[9] So their migration to West Bengal was quite natural.

5.2. Scheduled Castes Migrants from East Pakistan to India

While the official figures on the forced migrants from East Pakistan to India have been criticized by the academicians in their different micro level studies, it is really a hard task for us to make an idea about the Scheduled Castes migrants from East Pakistan as 'forced migrants' or as 'voluntary migrants'. Among the early official survey, for estimating the figure of the East Bengali Scheduled Caste refugees we may talk about the survey report of the State Statistical Bureau of the Government of West Bengal. Its 'Report on the Sample Survey for Estimating the Socio-economic Characteristics of displaced persons migrating from Eastern Pakistan to the state of West Bengal' indicates that out of 2143228 East Bengali displaced persons 405260 were Scheduled Castes i.e., 18.91% (who migrated from 15th October 1946 to 15th January 1951).[10] This report shows that the upper caste Hindus had migrated from all districts (except Sylhet, Chittagong, Malda and Jalpaiguri) while the Scheduled Castes Hindu families migrated in large scale from Faridpur, Dacca, Khulna, Barisal, Nadia, Jessore, Rajshahi, Rangpur and Pabna districts to West Bengal.[11] The Scheduled Tribes were mainly migrated from Dinajpur, Rajshahi, Bogra and Rangpur.

Table 5.2: Distribution of Displaced Persons of Bangladesh to Different Districts of West Bengal by Communities, 1950

Sl. No	*Districts*	*Hindus other SC*	*SC*	*ST*	*Others & Not-recorded*	*Total*
1.	Burdwan	85,876 (85.19)	14467 (14.35)	-----	462 (0.46)	100805
2.	Birbhum	8035 (69.72)	3167 (27.48)	115 (1.00)	207 (1.80)	11524
3.	Bankura	8421 (85.81)	411 (4.19)	982 (10.00)	207 (1.80)	11524
4.	Midnapur	27316 (95.15)	1272 (4.43)	-----	134 (0.47)	28722
5.	Howrah	81,261 (94.00)	4999 (5.78)	-----	184 (0.21)	86444

6.	Hooghly	57,483	5851	-----	-----	63334
		(90.76)	(9.24)			
7.	24 Parganas	439612	101,306	334	738	541720
		(81.15)	(18.70)	(0.06)	(0.18)	
8.	Calcutta	405303	7636	394	2637	415970
		(97.44)	(1.84)	(0.10)	(0.64)	
9.	Nadia	267166	133954	1030	1654	403804
		(66.16)	(33.17)	(0.26)	(0.41)	
10	Murshidabad	38936	23901	2741	----	65578
		(59.37)	(21.76)	(4.18)		
11.	West Dinajpur	75296	29328	30132	----	134756
		(55.88)	(21.76)	(22.36)		
12	Malda	26278	26641	14597	681	68197
		(38.53)	(39.06)	(21.40)	(1.00)	
13	Jalpaiguri	69495	30550	48	582	100675
		(69.03)	(30.35)	(0.05)	(0.58)	
14	Darjeeling	10933	6710	----	----	17643
		(62.00)	(38.00)			
15	Cooch Behar	78322	15337	426	157	94242
		(83.11)	(16.27)	(0.45)	(0.17)	
16	Total	1679773	405260	50799	7436	2143228
		(78.37)	(18.91)	(2.37)	(0.35)	

Source: State Statistical Bureau, Government of West Bengal: *Report on the Sample Survey for Estimating the Socio-economic Characteristics of displaced persons migrating from Eastern Pakistan to the state of West Bengal,* 1951, p. 19.

Table 5.3: Migrant Families of Different Communities by District of Origin in Pakistan (15th October 1946 to 15th January 1951)

Sl. No	*District*	*Upper Caste Hindus*	*Scheduled Castes*	*Scheduled Tribes*	*Others*	*Total*
1	Jessore	20161	9636	95	47	29939
2	Khulna	17530	6214	73	----	23817
3	Faridpur	35037	14495	148	70	49750
4	Barisal	39804	5827	99	172	45902
5	Dacca	66402	10209	----	121	76732
6	Mymensingh	24656	2281	23	118	27078

7	Nadia	30494	10987	142	142	41765
8	Rangpur	13265	6124	282	24	19695
9	Pabna	11910	5100	71	89	17070
10	Bogra	4519	1735	1388	23	7615
11	Dinajpur	4305	3210	3237	----	10752
12	Rajshahi	13377	7447	5174	105	26103
13	Noakhali	16546	1570	----	24	18140
14	Tipperah	18647	2472	----	25	21144
15	Chittagong	7525	190	----	263	7978
16	Sylhet	1665	47	----	----	1692
17	Hill Chittagong	21	----	----	----	21
18	Malda	166	119	----	----	285
19	Jalpaiguri	1036	1381	----	----	2417
20	West Pakistan	704	73	----	260	1037
21	Not Recorded	317	23	----	----	340
22	Total	327967	89140	10682	1483	429272

Source: State Bureau of Statistics, Government of West Bengal, *Report on the Sample Survey for Estimating the Socio-economic Characteristics of displaced persons migrating from Eastern Pakistan to the state of West Bengal,* 1951, p. 20.

It is very significant in this connection to note that the Namasudras had considerable concentration in the southern districts of Eastern Bengal like Jessore, Khulna, Dacca, Faridpur, Bakerganj, etc. So it may be safely concluded that among the Scheduled Caste migrants till 1950 from these districts the Namasudras were majority. They got shelter mainly in rural areas of 24 Parganas and Nadia districts which were convenient for them because of geographical location. On the other hand, the Rajbanshis had significant concentration in the districts of northern part of Eastern Bengal i.e. in the Rajshahi division; particularly in Rangpur, Dinajpur, Rajshahi and Mymensingh districts. They had close social and cultural ties with their caste fellows of Jalpaiguri and Cooch Behar and the districts of lower Assam. Moreover, the social reform movements of the Rajbanshis in the early twentieth century had considerably strengthened their fellow feeling. Naturally the Rajbanshis mainly migrated to the districts of northern part of West Bengal including former Cooch Behar State. Among other numerically prominent Scheduled Castes of Bengal the Poundras and the Bagdis were mainly concentrated in the districts of Western Bengal while the Jelia Kaibartyas and the Jhalo Malos were concentrated in Eastern Bengal who migrated to West Bengal and other states of India according to their convenience.

Map 5.1: Community Wise Distribution of the Migrants 1951

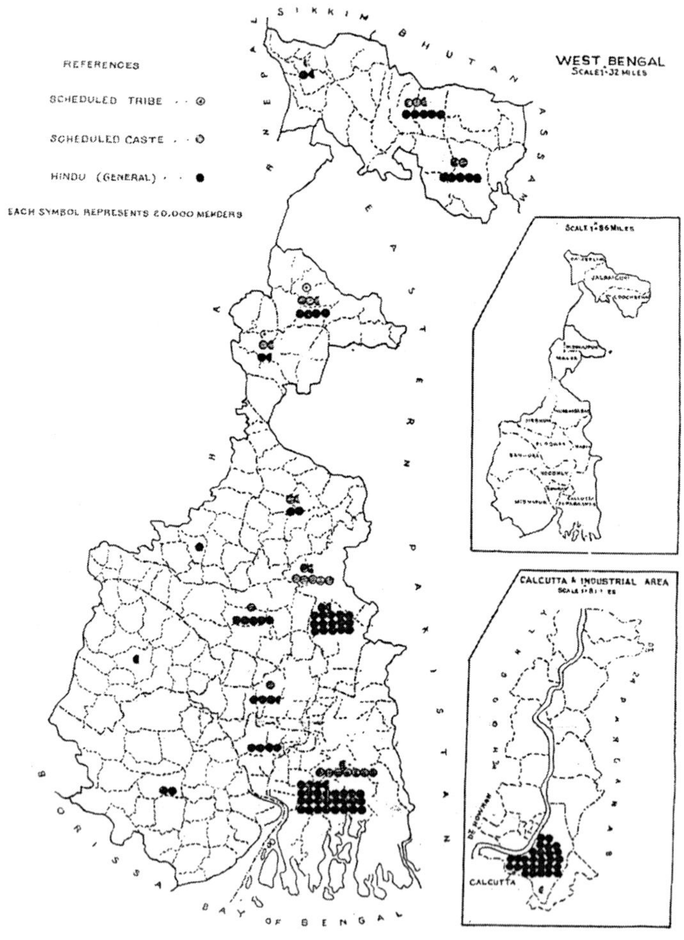

Source: State Bureau of Statistics, Government of West Bengal, *Report on the Sample Survey for Estimating the Socio-economic Characteristics of displaced persons migrating from Eastern Pakistan to the state of West Bengal*, 1951.

Table 5.4: Distribution of the Rajbanshis in Different Districts and Division of Eastern Bengal 1931

State/ Division/ District	*Male*	*Female*
Bengal	939396	864975
British Territory	773651	711622
Burdwan Division	24561	24625
Rajshahi Division	665572	598833
Rajshahi	13198	13331
Dinajpur	187487	172881
Jalpaiguri	177919	153249
Darjeeling	14640	12329
Rangpur	229670	215304
Bogra	4926	4487
Pabna	6577	6398
Malda	21155	20854
Dacca Division	36747	34104
Dacca	13826	13093
Mymensingh	15449	14286
Faridpur	8689	6330
Bakerganj	755	395
Chittagong Division	1000	827
Tipperah	708	494
Noakhali	87	32
Chittagong	205	241
Chittagong Hill Tract	---	---
Bengal States	165745	153153
Cooch Behar	165695	153151
Tripura	50	2

Source: Census of India, 1931.

According to the survey (carried out in 1955) of the State Statistical Bureau of Government of West Bengal, out of total 563748 migrant families in West Bengal (till May 1955) 130800 were Scheduled Castes (23%).[12] These families were mainly distributed in 24 Parganas (33.8 thousand families with 147.6

thousand people) and Nadia district (32 thousand families with 132 thousand person). West Dinajpur (Present North Dinajpur and South Dinajpur), Jalpaiguri, Cooch Behar and Malda districts had also received a significant number of Scheduled Caste refugees. Although Calcutta received a significant number of refugees from East Pakistan, the Scheduled Caste refugees had almost no concentration. Here out of 570[9] thousand migrants only 13.6 thousand were Scheduled Castes. It was obviously for the reason that the Scheduled Castes of Bengal were not suitable for survival in the urban areas.

Table 5.5: District wise Distribution of Migrants by Community in West Bengal 1955 (Outside Government Camps)

Sl. No	*Districts*	*Total*	*Hindu (General)*	*Scheduled Castes*	*Scheduled Tribes*	*Others*
1	Burdwan	124.3	100.3	23.4	0.1	0.5
2	Birbhum	16.3	14.3	1.9	0.1	----
3	Bankura	10.2	8.8	1.3	---	0.1
4	Midnapur	40.2	38.5	17	----	----
5	Howrah	82.1	78.0	3.9	----	0.2
6	Hooghly	93.8	70.0	23.5	---	0.2
7	24 Parganas	704.3	553.1	147.6	0.7	2.9
8	Calcutta	570.9	556.6	13.6	----	1.7
9	Nadia	466.6	332.8	132.0	0.1	1.7
10	Murshidabad	72.7	43.3	28.1	0.8	1.5
11	West Dinajpur	146.1	77.8	47.5	20.6	0.2
12	Malda	72.5	32.1	29.9	10.4	0.1
13	Jalpaiguri	150.2	103.2	46.5	0.1	0.4
14	Darjeeling	30.1	26.3	3.5	0.3	---
15	Cooch Behar	143.6	98.3	44.6	0.2	0.5
16	All Districts	2723.9	2131.4	549.0	33.4	10.1

Source: State Statistical Bureau, 1956 Table 2.

Apart from the official surveys, decennial census is another alternative method for making an idea about the approximate figure of the Scheduled Caste forced migrants from East Pakistan.

In this connection the census of 1961 is very much noteworthy. Growth rate of Scheduled Caste population in 1961 as given in the table 5.6 indicates huge influx of certain Scheduled Caste communities who had main concentration in East Bengal (Pakistan). Here we may talk about the population growth rate of the Bhuimalis (+101.93%), Doais (+632.03%), Jelia Kaibartyas (+39.38%), Jhalo Malo or Malos (+47.08%), Namasudras (+124.47%), Paliyas (+ 510.28%), Pod or Poundras (+ 47.62%), Rajbanshis (+ 61.80%), Sunris excluding Sahas (+ 136.30%), etc. High population growth rate of these communities was possible because of their large scale migration from East Bengal. Although the decadal growth rate of the Bahelias (+ 240.43), Gonrhis (+ 507.32&), Kadars (+ 838.13%), Kandras (+ 1,809.16%), Kaurs (+ 106.20%), Koches (+ 278.30%), etc. was abnormally high but their total population figure was very small.

Table 5.6: Growth of Population of Scheduled Castes, West Bengal, 1951-61

Schedule Caste	*1951 Population*	*1961 Population*	*Percentage Variation (+for increase, -for decrease)*
Bagdi or Duley	905,491	1,096,885	+ 21.14
Bahelia	371	1,263	+ 240.43
Baiti	4,394	8,269	+ 88.19
Bediya	11,016	4,380	- 60.35
Beldar	1,116	1,795	+ 60.84
Bhuimali	19.403	39.181	+101.93
Bhuiya	64,183	53,329	- 16.91
Bind	18,923	22,924	+21.14
Doai	1,937	14,191	+ 632.03
Gonrhi	2,282	13,859	+ 507.32
Hari	96,275	125,880	+ 30.75
Jalia Kaibartya	84,218	117,384	+39.38
Jhalo Malo or Malo	46,748	68,757	+ 47.08
Kadar	598	5,610	+ 838.13
Kandra	1,332	25,430	+ 1,809.16
Kaora	132,145	117,929	- 10.76
Karenga or Koranga	8,704	11,332	+ 30.19

Kaur	1,161	2,394	+ 106.20
Khaira	43,990	67,913	+54.38
Khatik	3,666	2,716	- 25.91
Koch	931	3,522	+ 278.30
Konai	32,422	43,101	+ 32.94
Konwar	3,462	3,895	+12.51
Kotal	7,810	7,700	- 1.41
Lohar	63.692	83,545	+ 31.17
Mahar	4,206	6,760	+ 60.72
Mal	91,166	117,704	+ 29.11
Mallah	21,842	12,366	- 43.38
Methor	35,884	30,850	- 14.03
Namasudra	324,790	729,057	+ 124.47
Nuniya	24,244	17,561	- 27.57
Paliya	12,125	73,997	+ 510.28
Patni	33,064	6,288	- 80,98
Pod or Poundra	593,093	875,525	+ 47.62
Rajbanshi	742,733	1,200,717	+ 61.80
Sunri excluding Saha	45,226	106,870	+ 136.30
Tiyar	41,978	39,633	- 5.59
Total of the Selected Castes	3,526,651	5,161,512	+ 46.36

Source: Census of India 1961, (Vol. XVI), West Bengal and Sikkim, Part V-A(i), (P.1– ii).

Table 5.7: Comparative Tables of Population Growth Rate of Certain Scheduled Caste Communities in West Bengal

State and Community	*1961-71*	*1971-81*	*1981-91*
West Bengal	+26.89%	+23.17%	+24.73%
SC	+70.80%	+36.12%	+33.93%
Rajbanshi	+12.66%	+66.83%	+25.70%
Namasudra	+34.49%	+72.58%	+52.55%
Bagdi	+17.17%	+41.85%	+16.38
Jelia Kaibartya	+74.37%	+55.53%	+39.05%
Jhalo Malo	+30.77%	+71.88%	+42.54%

Gonrhi	-12.31%	+22.04%	+63.32%
Tiyor	+101.31%	+2.88%	+94.27%
Patni	+103.265%	+75.7655	+31.58%

Source: Census of West Bengal, 1961, 1971, 1981 and 1991

The decade between 1961 and 1971 had also witnessed the high population growth rate of the East Bengali Scheduled Caste communities like the Jelia Kaibartyas (74.37%), Malos (30.77%), Namasudras (34.49%), Tiyors (101.31%) and Patnis (103.26%). The period between 1971 and 1981 was more serious for the Scheduled Castes in terms of their population growth rate. The high growth rate of the Rajbanshis (66.83%), Namasudras (72.58%), Malos (71.88%), Jelia Kaibartyas (55.53%), and Patnis were strengthened by the huge migration to West Bengal from Bangladesh as well as remigration from some states of Northeast India. The decade of 1981-1991 had also witnessed the same phenomenon. So it appears that the migration of the Scheduled Caste communities from East Pakistan was a general trend during the period between 1951 and 1971.

5.3. Resettlement of the Scheduled Caste Refugees in West Bengal

In the last chapter we have analyzed the rehabilitation policy of the government. The Scheduled Castes as refugees in West Bengal had some basic problems in regards to their rehabilitation. It has been indicated earlier that the Scheduled Castes of colonial Bengal were mostly engaged in the primary sector of economy mainly as wage earner. Rate of education was quite low although some of the Scheduled Caste communities had laid emphasis on the spread of education. So the resettlement of the agriculturists and the fishermen refugee Scheduled Castes in the urban area was not feasible. Thus the government had taken some steps for the agriculturists to settle them in the backward areas in some cases in impregnable land. In case of the old migrants i.e. migrants from 1946 to 1958, percentage of the agriculturists was comparatively higher among the 'Scheduled Caste camp refugees'. These families were given rehabilitation mainly in the agricultural belt of 24 Parganas, Burdwan and

Nadia districts.[13] The fishermen on the other hand were given rehabilitation in the river bed.

Non-camp Scheduled Caste refugees on the other hand received less attention from the Government. For them 'social relation' was more fruitful. Those who had close social relations with their caste fellows in West Bengal got better treatment than other refugees. It has been indicated earlier that the Rajbanshis had developed a kind social integrity through the Kshatriya movement what became a significant tool for survival of the Rajbanshi migrants from northern part of East Pakistan. The Namasudras on the other hand had established a social homogeneity through their socio-religious organization called the Matua Mahasangha. Its head quarter was shifted to Thakurnagar of 24 Parganas. This organization has been playing a constructive role for unifying the dispersed Namasudras in West Bengal. Inspite of that it has been noticed in my filed survey that the refugee Namasudras in Nadia district had expressed their feelings of receiving hostile attitude from the local hosts.

5.4. Resettlement of the Scheduled Caste Refugees in India Other than West Bengal

Apart from West Bengal, the Scheduled Caste refugees were also migrated to Northeast India. The districts of different states (Assam, Meghalaya and Tripura) contiguous to East Pakistan had received the Scheduled Castes in large scale. The Scheduled Castes took shelter in such places which were comparatively backward in terms of civil amenities. Even the government had consciously encouraged the policy of settlement of the Scheduled Caste refugees in the river beds, forest area covered with jungles, hills, and rivers. So both the West Bengal and the Union Governments had adopted the policy of settlement of the East Bengali Scheduled Caste camp refugees in such places of Bihar, Orissa, Madhya Pradesh, Uttar Pradesh and Andaman and Nicobar Island which were full with geographical constraints.

5.3.1. Andaman and Nicobar Islands

Plan for resettlement of the agriculturist Scheduled Caste refugees in the virgin land of Andaman and Nicobar Islands (what once were infamous for imprisonment of the convicts and freedom fighters of Indian mainland) was initiated immediately after the partition. Actual resettlement through the policy of colonization was started with the assistance of the Union Government since 1949. First batch of the East Bengali refugees comprising 198 families arrived at Andaman in 1949 (March). Between 1949 and 1952 total 420 families (28 non-agriculturist 392 agriculturists) were deported to Andaman. However, all the non-agriculturists and 42 agriculturist families had repatriated till August 1952.[14] So 350 families comprising 1583 members have been rehabilitated mainly in 21 villages in Port Blair Tehsil.[15]

Table 5.8.: The Number of Agriculturist Families from East Bengal Settled in Andaman Upto 1969

Sl. No	*Year*	*Name of states*	*No of Families*	*Area of Settlement*
1	1949	East Bengal	202	South Andaman
2	1950	East Bengal	119	South Andaman
3	1951	East Bengal	78	South Andaman
4	1952	East Bengal	51	South Andaman
5	1953	East Bengal	97	Ferrargunj
6	1954	East Bengal	438	Rangat
7	1955	East Bengal	390	Ferrargunj and Rangat
8	1956	East Bengal	357	Diglipur
9	1957	East Bengal	221	Diglipur
10	1958	East Bengal	194	Mayabunder
11	1959	East Bengal	217	Mayabunder
12	1960	East Bengal	250	Mayabunder
13	1961	East Bengal	228	Port Blair(Havelock)
14	1967	East Bengal	323	Mayabunder(Billi ground)
15	1969	East Bengal	375	Little Andaman
Total			3540	

Source: Census of India, 1961, Andaman and Nicobar Islands, p. 22 and from the Records of Revenue Dept. (settlement Wing)

In the second phase between 1953 and 1959, 851 families with 3453 members had rehabilitated in 27 village of Middle Andaman (Rangat). Between 1956 and 1959 another 700 families with 3166 members had settled in North Andaman (Diglipur).[16] Resettlement of the agriculturist had further continued in other places of Andaman and Nicobar Islands in the subsequent years.

5.3.2. Uttar Pradesh and Uttaranchal

Resettlement of the East Bengali Scheduled Caste refugees in the 1960s in Uttaranchal and Uttar Pradesh also deserve a careful historical enquiry. In Uttar Pradesh, the East Bengali Scheduled Castes refugees got agricultural land for settlement in several districts like Bijnor, Bereilly, Pilbhit, Meerut, Badaun, Kanpur, Lakhimpur Kheri, Rampur, Bahraich, etc. Two districts of Uttaranchal (formerly under Uttar Pradesh) like Nainital, and Udham Singh Nagar had also received a significant number of East Bengali refugees along with the West Pakistani Punjabi refugees. The East Bengali refugees were deported mostly from Cooper's Camp of Nadia and Charbedia Camp of Orissa.[17] Sucheta Kriplani as Chief Minister of Uttar Pradesh (2 October 1963 – 14 March 1967) had brought around 1600 East Bengali refuge families from Mana Transit Camp of Dandakaranya.[18] In the process of resettlement in Uttar Pradesh, the East Bengali refugees both the upper castes and the Scheduled Castes, had to face discriminatory treatment from the Government.

5.3.3. Dandakaranya

Resettlement of the East Bengali Scheduled Caste refugees in the virgin but sterile land of Dandakaranya in the 1960s is a significant part of history of forced migration, resettlement and repatriation of the Scheduled Castes. Around 77670 square kilometers land of Koraput and Kalahandi districts of Orissa and Bastar districts of Madhya Pradesh (now under Chhatishgarh) were chosen for resettlement of the refugees by the Union Government in 1957. Accordingly Dandakaranya Development Authority (DDA) was created in 1958 for materializing the project.

Table 5.9 a: Settlement Zones and Amount of Land Released for Rehabilitation of the Refugees in Dandakaranya (Orissa)

Sl No	*Zones*	*Amount of Land*
1	Umarkot	20,392 acres
2	Raigarh	27,376 acres
3	Malkangiri	43,884 acres
4	Total in Koraput District	91,652 acres

Source: Saibal Kumar Gupta, *Dandakaranya: A Survey of Rehabilitation,* edited by Alok Kumar Ghosh (Calcutta: Bibhasha, 1999), p. 4.

Table 5.9. b: Settlement Zones and Amount of Land Released for Rehabilitation of the Refugees in Dandakaranya (Madhya Pradesh)

Sl No	*Zones*	*Amount of Land*
1	Paralkot	55,279 acres
2	Pharasgoan	4,930 acres
3	Jamri	3,455 acres
4	Total in Bastar District	63,664 acres

Source: Saibal Kumar Gupta, *Dandakaranya: A Survey of Rehabilitation,* edited by Alok Kumar Ghosh (Calcutta: Bibhasha, 1999), p. 4.

In the initial stage, resettlement of the refugees in Dandakaranya was a hard task. The refugees were mainly transported from West Bengal via transit camps to Dandakaranya. Mana camp of Raipur was the main centre of transportation of the refugees to Dandakaranya from Bengal. First phase of the rehabilitation programme at Dandakaranya was started in 1961-62. Four zones viz. Umarkot, Malkangiri, Paralkot and Kondagaon; were chosen for settlement of the East Bengali agriculturist Scheduled Caste refugees. By the end of 1962, the Government of Orissa had released 91652 acres of land in Koraput district for resettlement of the refugees while the Government of Madhya Pradesh released around 63664 acres of land in Bastar district.[19]

Table 5.10: Distribution of the Refugee Families in Different Zones of Dandakaranya upto 30th June 1961

Sl No	*Place*	*Families*
1	In work Centers	603
2	In Paralkot Zone	703
3	In Umarkot Zone	1279
4	In Boregoan Jugani Villages	251
5	Working as truck operators, etc	119

Source: Saibal Kumar Gupta, *Dandakaranya: A Survey of Rehabilitation,* edited by Alok Kumar Ghosh (Calcutta: Bibhasha, 1999), p. 4.

Table 5.11: Settlement of the Refugees at Dandakaranya during the Period between July 1961 and June 1962

Sl. No.	*Month*	*Families*
1	July 1961	186
2	August 1961	145
3	September 1961	177
4	October 1961	52
5	November 1961	40
6	December 1961	182
7	January 1962	174
8	February 1962	307
9	March 1962	190
10	April 1962	374
11	May 1962	299
12	June 1962	187

Source: Saibal Kumar Gupta, *Dandakaranya: A Survey of Rehabilitation,* edited by Alok Kumar Ghosh (Calcutta: Bibhasha, 1999), p. 5.

Land released by the Government, was immediately taken up by the DDA. By the end of June, a total 2955 families were sent to the Project area particularly in Paralkot and Umarkot zones.[20] During the period between July 1961 and June 1962, the DDA received another 2313 families.[21] Each refugee family was roughly granted 6.5 acres of agricultural land along with

0.5 acre of homestead and kitchen garden.[22] They were also granted loans for initial settlement consisting Rs.1700/- for house building, Rs. 1115/- for purchase of bullocks and implements and Rs. 150/- for digging a well.[23] By the end of the harvest season of 1963-64, 6286 families got agricultural land.[24] Out of 7500 families of the DDA area, 7261 families were recorded as agriculturist mostly belonged to the Scheduled Caste communities. They were distributed in over 184 villages. By the end of 1972, DDA received other 9000 agriculturist families for resettlement.[25]

Table 5.12: Rate of Rice Production at Different Zones of Dandakaranya 1964-65

Zones	*Less than 10*	*Less than 30*	*30*	*31-40*	*41-50*	*50*	*Almost Nil*	*Total*
Farashgaon/Bastar	---	-----	131	16	5	21	32	205
Umarkot	111	452	30	219	108	121	121	

Source: Saibal Kumar Gupta, *Dandakaranya: A Survey of Rehabilitation,* edited by Alok Kumar Ghosh (Calcutta: Bibhasha, 1999), pp. 17-38.

Although the DDA tried its best to provide proper rehabilitation, the East Bengali refugees were not satisfied. The refugees those who went to Dandakaranya with a new hope were soon demoralized because of certain problems. Saibal Kumar Dasgupta, Chairman of the Dandakaranya Development Authority (December 1963-Septemebr 1964), had identified certain problems faced by the refugees in their rehabilitation. Since most of the families were agriculturists, the amount of agricultural land had allured them. But the 'quantity of land' was not the only factor for successful agricultural development. The 'quality of land' was very poor in terms of natural fertility and content. Agricultural practices of the refugees were not suitable for agricultural operation in Dandakaranya. In Dandakaranya, the local people, particularly the indigenous tribal communities, were basically 'subsistence producer' whereas the East Bengali refugees had the dreams of commercial production by which they could compensate their loss of East Pakistan. But the rate of production was quite unsatisfactory for many families by which their survival became a matter of question. The report of Saibal Kumar Gupta shows extreme state of backwardness in agricultural production particularly of food grains. Table 5.12 based on Gupta's report shows that in Farashgaon and Umarkot the rate of rice production was so poor that many families realized the futility of the rehabilitation in these zones of Dandakaranya.[26]

Table 5. 13A: Death Chart of Padia Transit Camps, Malkangiri from15.4.64 to 20.5.64

Date	*Died at Camp No 1*	*Date*	*Died at Camp No 2*	*Date*	*Died at Camp No 3*	*Date*	*Died at Camp No 4*
15.4.64	1	28.2.64	1	11.5.64	1	2.5.64	1
16.4.64	3	2.5.54	2	12.5.64	2	12.5.64	1
18.4.64	1	3.5.64	1	16.5.64	1	14.5.64	1
20.4.64	1	4.5.64	1			15.5.64	1
21.4.64	1	5.5.64	3			16.5.64	2
23.4.64	1	6.5.64	3			19.5.64	1
24.4.64	1	7.5.64	1				
25.4.64	2	8.5.64	3				
27.4.64	1	9.5.64	1				
28. 4.64	2	11.5.64	1				
2.5.64	2	12.5.64	1				
3.5.64	1	14.5.64	2				
5.5.64	2	15.5.64	6				
6.5.64	2	16.5.64	2				
9.5.64	2	17.5.64	1				
11.5.64	1	18.5.64	1				
15.5.64	1	19.5.64	1				
16.5.64	1	20.5.64	1				
17.5.64	6						
Total	32		32		04		8

Source: Saibal Kumar Gupta, *Dandakaranya: A Survey of Rehabilitation,* edited by Alok Kumar Ghosh (Calcutta, Bibhasha, 1999) p. 94.

Table 5.13 B: No of Families and their Members in Different Camps of Padia

Sl no	*Camp*	*Total No families*	*Total No head*
1	No 1	280	1131
2	No2	418	1641
3	No 3	118	471
4	No 4	185	771

Source: Saibal Kumar Gupta, *Dandakaranya: A Survey of Rehabilitation,* edited by Alok Kumar Ghosh (Calcutta: Bibhasha, 1999), p. 94.

Nature of tenancy right had also disappointed the refugees.[27] Lack of drinking water, scarcity of medical facilities and recurring epidemics had further discouraged the refugees to stay in Dandakaranya. Inadequate medical facilities and the nature of transport of the refugees from the transit camps to the settlement sites were also responsible for creation of a fear among the refugees. Dr. Sankar Ghosh Dastidar, a medical officer of the Dandakaranya Project, had left an account of bare condition of medical facilities in the Padia Camps. Table 5.13A based on his report shows that within a moth 76 parsons lost their lives at Padia Camps.

Experience of the East Bengali migrants at Dandakaranya and the causes of desertion of the settlement zones have been best reflected in the writings of Mr. Raiharan Barai, General Secretary of the Udvastu Unnayanshil Samity .In his own words 'in rehabilitation centers/sites whether in Dandakaranya or in other states we had to live like cows and buffalos in slaughter houses having little security of lives. In Dandakaranya-----

(1) 3 to 5 acres of land divided into 4 to 5 plots were allotted to each migrant families at a distance of 4 to 5 km. The villages were completely barren, covered with stony, sandy mud without any water supply facilities.

(2) The offices, markets, hospitals, ration distributing centers, etc. were located in far away places. The distance may be 15 to 20 km from different villages and rehabilitation centers.

(3) Irregular payments of inadequate cash doles/rations/ medicines etc. from places far away from migrant villages reflect the harassment to migrants. The system of paying low wages to the refugees irregularly adds to the harassment.

(4) Ill treatment of local authorities and the hostility of the Adivashis, lack of security and modesty of women and of justice compelled the migrants to dessert their respective Rehabilitations sites/centers.'[28]

Desertion of the villages of Dandakaranya was thus quite natural what was first officially noticed in 1965. Between October and December 1965, around 1400 refugees left Dandakaranya of whom 163 were from the camps, 957 families from Malkangiri and rest of them were from Umarkot.[29] Desertion of Dandakaranya was further continued. In 1966 around 2170 families left Dandakaranya[30] what reached to 8000 by 1973. It was further increased when the Left Front(LF) Government came into power in West Bengal in 1977 since the Communist Party of India(Marxist) (CPI(M)) and the left political parties of West Bengal had assured the refugees of Dandakaranya to bring back them to West Bengal.[31]

5.3.4. Marichjhapi Episode

After the establishment of the LF Government in West Bengal, around 15000 refugee families (most of whom were Scheduled Castes) left Dandakaranya in order to resettle themselves in West Bengal even at the cost of their all belongings. They raised the slogan 'Go to Calcutta, Go to Sundarban!'[32] The refugees from Dandakaranya began to move towards West Bengal in March 1978 and by the mid-April they reached to Hasnabad Railway Station and camped there for few days to find out the proper place of their resettlement. They crossed the Ichhamati river and finally identified Marichjhapi Island as their destination.[33] On 18th April 1978, first batch of the refugees of around ten thousand in number had proceeded towards Kumirmari, Bagna and Marichjhapi without any obstacle.[34] By the end of April, number of refugees at Kumirmari and Bagna reached to 5000. It was 11106 and 16929 at Hasnabad and Char Hasnabad respectively.[35] Around 40000 refugees now began to resettle themselves in Marichjhapi Island.[36]

They started a new life at Marichjhapi. By their own efforts they established living houses, salt pans, a health center, market, road, schools and tube wells, etc.[37] In order to make their life viable they also established different type of cottage industries like-- bidi factory, bakery, carpentry, weaving industry, etc. They also tried to earn by fishing, pisciculture and collecting forest products. So Marichjhapi, hitherto been an isolated jungle tract; turned into an automatons village. In order to respect their fighting spirit, the settlers named it as Netaji Nagar (in the name of Great Subhash Chandra Bose).

But life of the refugees was not a smooth one. The CPI (M)-led LF Government of West Bengal (1977-2011) was not willing to tolerate such settlement. It was determined to expel them from Marichjhapi on several grounds. To the West Bengal Government, the settlers of Marichjhapi were unauthorized occupiers since they violated the forest act as Marichjhapi is situated in the Sunderland Reserve Forest.[38] It was merely an open issue. There were many other factors for which the LF Government was afraid of the Dandakaranya-returned refugees.

First problem raised by the West Bengal Government was the growth of refugee population. Since West Bengal had already received a significant number of the East Bengali refugees since 1946 and population density has already reached to its climax where further migration from Dandakaranya means additional burden for the state. And if the refugees from Dandakaranya are allowed in West Bengal there would be a population explosion and the Government would have to arrange for their livelihood including social, educational and cultural development. Above all they had to be given the status of legal citizens. Considering all these, the Government of West Bengal planned to drive them away from Hasnabad and Burdwan Railway stations.[39]

The second issue raised by the West Bengal Government was the possible impact of human settlement at Marichjhapi. It was the question of deforestation in Sundarban and the mal impact on the eco-system of that region. It is generally believed that the Sundarban has a special recognition in the world for its natural resources and its role in maintaining the ecological balance. Both the State and the Union Governments had taken several steps for the protection of the eco-system and biosphere of the region. So Mr. Kalyan Chakrabarty, the then Field director of Tiger Project of Sundarban; had complained that if the refugees are allowed to stay in Marichjhapi, the Tiger Project would be affected badly. Since Marichjhapi is situated in the tiger project area, settlement of human population means the extinction of the tigers from that Islands. At the same time tigers would not be able to stay in the nearby islands because the poacher can easily interfere into the animal world of that region.[40]

Thirdly, the West Bengal Government had suspected that the settlement at Marichjhapi would enhance illegal activities particularly smuggling of goods between India and Bangladesh would be appreciated. Settlement at Marichjhapi itself is an example of illegal activity since the refugees had violated the land and forest related laws.[41] Fourthly the Government of India had spent a huge amount for proper rehabilitation of the refugees in Dandakaranya. Under this circumstance, if the refugees are allowed to stay in Marichjhapi, Dandakaranya project would face severe setback. This would lead to Centre-State clash.

Considering all these possibilities, the West Bengal Government decided to expel the refugees from Marichjhapi. Thus on 11th April, Jyoti Bose (8 July 1914 – 17 January 2010), the then Chief Minister of West Bengal (1977-2000), made an appeal to the settlers of Marichjhapi to go back to Dandakaranya.[42] Mr. Bose had also argued that 'there is no possibility of any new settlement in Sundarban. There is no surplus agricultural land. The salinity of land is so high that agricultural production would be a difficult one.' So he urged the refugees to go back to Dandakaranya where good days are waiting for them.[43]

But the refugees of Marichjhapi were not agreed with Mr. Bose's fabricated dream of good days. According to them it is a 'distant utopia.' They raised some counter arguments and stressed on the possibility of their successful settlement at Marichjhapi. Mr. Raiharan Barai, Mr. Rangalal Golder, Mr. Satish Mandal and few other refugee leaders of Marichjhapi had categorically raised the issue of assurance of Mr. Jyoti Bose what he made before assuming power in West Bengal. They argued that Mr. Bose, had promised the refugees of Dandakaranya in 1975 in a meeting held at Bhilai (situated at former Madhya Pradesh and present Chattishgarh), that West Bengal has sufficient space for resettlement of the settlers of Dandakaranya now why the Left Front after assuming power denying the promise on the ground of population growth? Secondly, question of Kalyan Chakrabarty, the Field Director of Sundarban Tiger Project, was answered that in Marichjhapi habitation of the tiger is not possible since there is no food for the tigers.[44] About smuggling, they blamed the Government and said that some ruling party leaders were engaged in this activities having involvement of some dishonest government officers. So settlement of the refugees at Marichjhapi had violated the process of smooth smuggling for which the refugees became the targets of the ruling party leaders.[45]

Apart from the arguments of the Government, the refugees had identified some other factors for negative attitude of the Government towards them at Marichjhapi. Firstly the LF Government after assuming powers in 1977, the UCRC (the United Central Refugee Council), a left refugee organization; wanted the merger of the organization of the Dandakaranya refugees called Udvastu Unnayanshil Samity. The UCRC also asked them to join the CPI (M) what the Udvastu Unnayanshil Samity refused.[46] Again Mr. Subhas Chakraborty (1942-2009), a LF minister; directly appealed them to join their party. But the refugees discarded it.[47] This refusal had enraged the LF Government.[48] Since the 'lefts' had projected themselves as the 'saviors' or 'Messiah' of the ordinary people of West Bengal in such a situation attempts of self rehabilitation of a community/ group of refugees means the violation of their image!. Mr. Raiharan Barai had also argued that the refugees at Marichjhapi attract atrocity of the Government since they are Scheduled Castes specially Namasudras who posses a strong fighting spirit.[49] The refugees also felt that 'the question of prestige of governance of the newly formed LF Government had generated much anxiety among the Left leaders and the government officials. The Government was worried that the refugees entered to Marichjhapi by superseding the decision of the State Government what would expose the weakness of the government to the public. In long run it would be a question of maintenance of law and order.'[50] Question of prestige thus awakened the brutal force of the state power. So when failed to stop the efforts of resettlement of the Dandakaranya-returned refugees at Marichjhapi, the West Bengal Government decided to expel the refugees by force from Netaji Nagar. However, the refugees had nothing to lose except their measurable life.

First police attack against the refugees of Marichjhapi took place on 20th August 1978 when 30 launches carrying a large number of police to take back the refugees to Dandakaranya. However, this attack could not break the will power of the refugees. No refugee family was agreed to go back to Dandakaranya. But the police again blocked the island on 7th, 8th and 9th September 1978 with launches what resulted into the death of two young refugee boys. Police also attacked the boats of the refugees and destroyed their 157 boats loaded with food grains and other essential items.[51] Inspite of that the refugees denied to dessert Marichjhapi. West Bengal Government on the other hand became more ruthless and decided to kill the refugees by curtailing them from rest of the world. So on 24 January 1979, West Bengal police again rushed to Marichjhapi with more power and means to oust the refugees forcibly. Mr. Raiharan Barai described the police atrocity at Marichjhapi with following words:-

> "—From the morning of 24th January '79 police started the oppression with the help of 30 launches and two steamers of B.S.F. by bursting teargas shell towards Marichjhapi, arrested people from their living houses in different plots by breaking down and setting fire to the houses. They also looted all the articles i.e. food grains, clothing, bell-metal, plates, glass, brass pitches, gold ornaments, iron made articles, hard cash

> etc. The police also did not hesitate to outrage the modesty of our women including three young girls. The launches ran over refugee boats carrying food grains and necessary commodities. They beat the drowning passengers severely and prevent them from getting to the shore. After 7 days, on 31.1.79, refugee women, afraid of starvation strict death, attempted to cross the Bagna river to collect food and water from Kumirmari, the nearest village. The police with their launches attacked the boats in the river by throwing teargas shells violently, drowning the boats by dashing with the launches and attacked the drowning women by running over them repeatedly. The refugees standing on the other side (plantation) became impatient for fear of their painful death....and beating of the people gathered there to protest the brutal actions of the police on hungry helpless refugees. The police became angry and opened fire indiscriminately resulting death of 15 refugees and two local people including one woman. The police arrested a large number of refugees, wounded persons, beating severely by gun barrels and pressed with boot-soles. The police by day and night strictly barricaded the island, started inhuman torture on the refugees everywhere, resulting arrest of nearly a thousand refuges including 500 persons."[52]

Beside the indiscriminate killing and confiscating the belongings of the hungry refugees the police also destroyed the fisheries and tube wells. The Government of West Bengal was successful to stop the supply of food and water to Marichjhapi.'[53] Section 144 of the Indian Penal Code was imposed at Marichjhapi. No body was allowed to visit that place including the journalists. However, Mr. Sufal Halder, made an appeal to the Calcutta High Court to withdraw the blocked. Finally the High Court directed the Government on 8th February to take necessary action for normalization of the situation including ensuring supply of food and drinking water.

Table 5.14: Age Groups of Persons who Died of Starvation at Netaji Nagar (Marichjhapi) Since 24.01.1979.

Upto one year	*2 years to 5 years*	*6 years-14 years*	*14 years to 70 years and above*	*Female*	*Male*	*Total*
52	38	8	37	37	99	136

Source: Memorandum submitted by Mr. Raiharan Barai, General Secretary of the Udvastu Unnayanshil Samity, 22nd March 1979 to the Enquiry Committee headed by Shri Prasannabhai Mehta.

The blockade at Marichjhapi is an ugly episode of experience of the East Bengali Scheduled Caste refugees. During the blocked, being isolated from rest of the world and due to the lack of food and water, they were compelled to consume wild grass locally called *jadu palang* and leaf called *jalipata*. They also tried to survive by having the soft portion of coconut tree (*mathi*). No charitable trust was allowed to distribute food and drinks and other assistance to the refugees.[54]

According to the sources of the Udvastu Unnayanshil Samity during the blocked from 24th January to 16th February (1979) 136 refugees were died due to starvation, 239 lost their measurable life for consuming unnatural (unfit) food for human being, 14 persons died due to police firing and 128 persons were missing while 500 refugees were arrested by the police.'[55] Mr. Raiharan Barai had given a list of the victims along with the memorandum date, 22nd March 1979 submitted to the 'Enquiry Committee Regarding Police Firing at Marichjhapi'. It shows that 52 children lost the lives who were less than one year and 38 children were between 2 and 5. Because of consuming unfit foods, the refugees attracted diarrhea, dysentery, cholera and typhoid. The refugees surely would have not lost their lives if they were allowed to receive medicine and normal food. It means a serious human rights violation had taken place in Marichjhapi.

Table 5.15 A.: Age Groups of Persons Died at Marichjhapi during the Blocked due to Ordinary Disease

Upto one year	*2 year to 5 years*	*6 years- 14 years*	*14 years to 70 years and above*	*Total*
157	18	6	58	239

Source: Memorandum submitted by Mr. Raiharan Barai, General Secretary of the Udvastu Unnayanshil Samity, 22nd March 1979 to the Enquiry Committee headed by Shri Prasannabhai Mehta.

Table 5.15B: Type of Diseases that Cost the Life of the Refugees

Typhoid	*Diarrhea*	*Dysentery*	*Cholera*	*Total*
25	132	28	54	239

Source: Memorandum submitted by Mr. Raiharan Barai, General Secretary of the Udvastu Unnayanshil Samity, 22nd March 1979 to the Enquiry Committee headed by Shri Prasannabhai Mehta.

Inspite of facing atrocities and unbearable suffering the refugees of Marichjhapi were not willing to go back to Dandakaranya. So on 18th April 1979 in a meeting held at his office, the Chief Minister, along with other ministers of his Government, had decided to take more action for expulsion of the refugees from their Netaji Nagar. The District Magistrate of 24 Parganas, Mr. Indrajit Choudhury, Police Super of 24 Parganas, Mr. Amiya Samanta; had visited Marichjhapi on 28th April to understand the seriousness of situation.[56] Finally on 13th May further police operation was started at Marichjhapi against the refugees. Their houses were destroyed and burnt. They were lathi charged and teargased. And within next four days all the refugees were compelled to evacuate Marichjhapi.

According to the media reports police had tried its best to show the number of the victims and atrocities as less as possible.[57] The West Bengal Government always publicly stated that there was no incident of atrocities committed by the police. Rather the police made proper arrangement of transportation of the refugees from Marichjhapi to Hasnabad and then to

Dandakaranya. Mr. Amiya Samanta, the then Police Super of 24 Parganas District, had firmly stated that

> 'no person of Marichjhapi was died due to police firing. By the middle of May 1979 they (asylum seeker or refugees) left Marichjhapi Island. Police administration had arranged transport for them. Police administration had created pressure on the refugees. But the police did not forcibly put them in launch... the question of setting fire by the police is an utter lie. The fugitive volunteers of the refugees actually set fire on some deserted houses in the darkness of night. One constable of the police was wounded by the fire....but no refugee was effected'.[58]

Whatever the fact might be it is a historical fact that the refugees who took shelter at Marichjhapi were mostly forced to return to their old place called Dandakaranya.[59] So it seem that the Marichjhapi incident was a horrible chapter of post-partition refugee resettlement in West Bengal; particularly of the Scheduled Caste refugees.

5.4. The Fishermen Refugees

Like the agriculturists, the fishermen Scheduled Caste communities of East Bengal could not escape from the curse of partition. Partition had generated their large scale migration to West Bengal and northeast India. The East Bengali fishermen now have huge concentration in certain districts of Northeast India (Barpeta, Dhubri and Jagir Road of Assam, West Garo Hills of Meghalaya and the districts of Tripura). It is to be noted that a large number of fishermen migrated to West Bengal particularly at Midnapur, Sundarban, Howrah and Hooghly for economic reasons not for communal persecution in East Bengal. Beginning of fish catching and drying in large scale in these districts had attracted them.[60] But in the post-partition days their experience was something different.

In the pre-partition days the fishermen were mainly 'captured fishers.' So they did not have any other option but to earn livelihood by their traditional occupation in new land. So they were looking for shelter in the river banks or even in the river beds. But the resettlement was not an easy task since in the post-partition days the fishermen, both migrants and the locals (host), had to face two major problems. First problem was the growth of fishermen population i.e. engagement of more people in same source of income. Secondly, all existing fisheries were not in the condition of fish production. Environmental pollution had decreased fish production.

However, the fishermen tired their best to survive by their own efforts. Although (in the initial stage) some fishermen families got assistance from the government as camp- refugees[61] but most of them tried to resettle in West Bengal by their own efforts. The fishermen communities had collectively taken some steps for the formation of cooperative societies as a practical tool for struggle for survival in post-partition West Bengal. It is to be noted that the fishermen had a strong background of cooperative type of production system since the time immemorial.[62] So formation of fishermen cooperative societies (FCS) with modern concept became easier for them. We can get some idea about the efforts of the refugee fishermen from the very name of fishermen cooperative societies such as--- Falta Refugee FCS Ltd (24 Parganas), Chandannagore Bastuhara FCS Ltd., Rabindra Nagar Refugee FCS Ltd. (Hooghly), Raghunathpur Refugee FCS Ltd. (Hooghly), Kashiganj Bastuhara FCS Ltd., (Jiaganj), Jalpaiguri Refugee FCS Ltd. (Jalpaiguri), Kayakata Barman Colony FCS Ltd. (Jalpaiguri), Nirmala Colony FCS Ltd. (Cooch Behar), Media Government Colony Refugee FCS Ltd., (24 Parganas), Adi Saptagram Gar Colony FCS Ltd., (Hooghly), etc.

Struggle of the fishermen got a new dimension when 100 representatives of fishermen communities from eight districts of West Bengal met in a convention held at Dumdum, Calcutta; and decided to form a state level organization called the West Bengal Fishermen Conference (WBFC or Paschim Banga Matsyajibi Samity) on 7th July, 1968.[63]

Table 5.16: Some Fishermen Cooperatives established by the Refugee Fishermen.

Name of the cooperative	*Year of Foundation*	*District*
Lalgola Padma Fishermen Cooperative Society	1949	Murshidabad
Kashiganj Bastuhara FCS Ltd	1949	Murshidabad
Surajpur FCS Ltd	1955	Murshidabad
The Bhakuri Fishermen Cooperative Society	1955	Murshidabad
The Kanchrapara Refugee FCS Ltd.	1950	Nadia
Khidirpur Beltola FCS Ltd	1955	Nadia
Manadnpur YFCS Ltd	1956	Nadia
The Beladenga Barrackpore Fishermen Cooperative Society Ltd.	1958	24 Parganas
Dooma Fishermen Cooperative Society Ltd.	1959	24 Parganas
The Mudialy Fishermen Cooperative Society Limited	1961	24 Parganas
24 Parganas Southern Central Fishermen Cooperative Society Ltd.	1962	24 Parganas
The Akaipur Darbasini Fishermen Cooperative Society Ltd.	1961	24 Parganas
The Phanshidewa Fishermen Cooperative Society Ltd.	1960	Darjeeling
Rampur Anchal FCS Ltd	1965	Cooch Behar
Nisiganj FCS Ltd	1969	Cooch Behar

The educated section of the fishermen communities of West Bengal came forward to organize the traditional fishermen for their overall progress. Accordingly state and district level preparatory committees were formed to draft the constitution and rules and regulation of the WBFC. The WBFC got its final shape in 1969 in its first conference held in Calcutta (7-8th June). An executive committee of 21 members was formed with three-tier organizational level—Central Committee, Districts Level Committees and Primary Committees. First president of the WBFC was Purna Chandra Shastri, a fishermen activist. Apurba Lal Majumdar, the then Deputy Speaker, West Bengal Legislative Assembly; was one of the Vice Presidents of the WBFC.[64] The WBFC adopted its constitution in its first conference, which had following objectives:

(1) upliftment of lives, livelihood and economic status of the fishermen; (2) development of the water bodies and introduction of modern and scientific pisciculture in the state to mitigate the fish crisis by increasing fish production; (3) upliftment of social and cultural status of the fishermen by spreading education and literacy campaign; (4) attainment and enjoyment of social justice and political right of the fishermen by uniting them; (5) to arouse the self-consciousness, social cohesiveness and fellow feelings among the fishermen communities; (6) establishment of financial organization to assist the needy fishermen; (7) to make adequate employment of the unemployed and jobless fishermen; (8) to assist the brilliant but poor students of the fishermen communities to pursue their higher studies; (9) to highlight the contribution of the intellectuals, poets, laureates, educationists and artists of the fishermen communities in the Bengali literature and culture; (10) to encourage the writers, laureates, artists and the poets of the fishermen communities to produce excellent pieces in their respect fields; and (11) to organize the cooperative movement by organizing primary (local), secondary (district) and central (state) level cooperatives for production and proper distribution of fishes.[65]

Throughout the 1970s and 1980s the WBFC had been agitating for the all round development of the fishermen communities including the refugee fishermen through the proper management of the water resources of the state. The WBFC raised the demand for the abolition of tank fishery provision of the *Estate Acquisition Act 1953* what allowed the landholders to retain their possession over the big fisheries. Although this Act imposed ceiling provision for retaining agricultural and non-agricultural land in order to abolish the zamindari system (particularly for vesting land) but sub-section 1(e) of Section 6 of the Act had the excluded tank fishery from ceiling provision. *Beels* and *baors* even being the natural water bodies have been defined as 'tank fishery' and had been excluded from the vesting of non-agricultural land. So the owners of the *beels, baors* and other tanks where pisciculture is practiced; were allowed to retain their possession. So the demand of abolition of tank fishery provision by the fishermen was directed against the interest of the feudal class.

Second demand of the WBFC was more radical. It raised the slogan *'jal jar jala tar'* i.e. fisheries for fishermen. It can be compared with the popular slogan like 'land for the tillers' *(langal jar jami tar*). The WBFC also mobilized the fishermen of West Bengal in the 1970s and 1980s for abolition of toll tax (including *khutigary* tax) in Sundarban area, ban on the use of harmful pesticides, distribution of the technology of scientific pisciculture to the fishermen, for proper rehabilitation of the refugee fishermen in West Bengal, etc.

5.5. Present Condition of the Scheduled Castes

We have already highlighted the fact that after the partition of Bengal in 1947 the Scheduled Castes were marginalized in East Pakistan. In case of India the scenario was something different. Here the independent government has maintained the 'policy of protective discrimination' i.e. policy of 'reservation. Reservation policy has been implemented in educational institutes, government job, and in politics. So the 'Scheduled Caste status' is now a tool of upward socioeconomic development of the so-called lower caste communities of India. Here the East Bengali Scheduled Caste refugees are fortunate enough since they have been recognized as Scheduled Castes in West Bengal. So we may assume that the Scheduled Caste refugees might have experienced a remarkable progress in different field of the society. But practical scenario is quite unsatisfactory what will be discussed in the following section of this chapter.

5.5.1. Educational Scenario

Educationally, the Scheduled Castes communities of Bengal were extremely backward in the pre-colonial days. They did have little chance to get education due to the nature of their profession and economic backwardness. Education was confined mainly among the Brahmins and some other higher castes. There was a general perception among most of the Scheduled Caste communities that the education is a mater of the higher castes only. They have nothing to do with the school education. Attitude of the Scheduled Castes began to change only from the late nineteenth century. Immediately after the independence, the West Bengal Government showed its special interest to the educational development of the Scheduled Castes along with other backward communities through the reservation of seats in the educational institutes, by building hostels for them and providing book grants and scholarships. So there are some positive outcomes of these policies on the Scheduled Castes (including the Scheduled Caste migrants).

First and foremost noticeable development is the growth of literacy rates among the Scheduled Castes. Table 5.17 indicates that the rate of literacy among the Scheduled Castes of West Bengal has reached to 42.21% in 1991 from 13.58% of 1961. It is further increased to 59.09% in 2001. It is only one side of the coin. Other side is quite dark. If we compare the rate of illiteracy of the Scheduled Castes with others it would show that the share of the Scheduled Castes in the illiteracy is higher than their population percentage in the state. Table 5.18 shows that the Scheduled Castes are 22.79% of the total population of West Bengal while their share in the total illiteracy is 29.76%. It means the Scheduled Castes are far behind than the non-Scheduled people of the state.

Table 5.17: Literacy Rate of the Scheduled Caste Communities and the General Literacy Rate of West Bengal during 1961-1991.

Category	*1961*	*1971*	*1981*	*1991*	*2001*
SC	13.58	17.80	24.37	42.21	59.09
Others	29.58	33.20	48.64	57.69.	68.64

Source: Census, 1961, 1971, 1981, 1991,

Table 5.18: Rate of Illiteracy Among the Scheduled and Non-Scheduled People of West Bengal 2001

Category	*Population in lakh**	*%age in the total population*	*No. of the illiterates in lakh**	*%age of the total illiterates*
Scheduled Tribes	36.70	5.34	20.77	9.63
Scheduled Castes	156.69	22.79	68.18	29.76
Non-Scheduled people	494.26	71.87	130.74	60.61
Total	687.65	100.00	215.69	100.00

* Person above 7 years, Source: Census 2001

Second noticeable outcome of the policy of protective discrimination in the education sector is the increment of the participation of the Scheduled Caste students in the middle stage and in the high school stages. It is; however, much lower than the state average. At the same time discontinuity of education of the Scheduled Caste students in the higher secondary level is another major drawback in the process of their educational development. It can be properly understood from the Table 5.19. This table shows that the enrolment of the SC students in 1985-86 in the primary level was 1251444 but that in the higher secondary level was only 29382. Recent educational statistics of the state is also displaying the same phenomenon. Table 5.20 based on the sources of the Department of the Human Resource Development of the Government of India shows that in the primary level enrolment of the Scheduled Castes was satisfactory in West Bengal. But we notice gradual decline in the junior high and high school levels.

Table 5.19: Enrolment of Scheduled Caste Students in Different Stages in 1985-86

Educational Stage	*Boys*	*Girls*	*Total*
Primary Stage	788442	463002	1251444
Middle Stage	145442	65098	210540
High Scholl Stage	88842	22961	111803
Higher Secondary Stage	22440	6942	29382

Sources: Annapurna Sanyal, *Scheduled Caste and Scheduled Tribes in Indian Politics* (Calcutta: Minerva, 1991), p. 32.

Table 5.20: Enrolment of Scheduled Caste Students in Different Stages in 2003-04

Educational Level	*Total Student (lakhs)*	*Percentage of Scheduled Caste*	*Percentage of Scheduled Tribe*
Primary (1st-5th class)	103.28	28.22	5.94
Junior High	38.18	22.22	3.72
Madhyamik	14.99	19.83	3.28
Higher Secondary	7.36	15.74	2.10

Source: Sacchidananda Dutta Ray, *Paschim Bange Sikshaya Agragati: Parisankhan Alochana* (Kolkata: Seriban, 2008), p. 58.

Educational scenario of all Scheduled Caste communities is again unequal. In 1961 the rate of literacy among the following selected Scheduled Castes of West Bengal (as given in the table 5.21) was much lower than the state average. This rate in some cases was much lesser than the average literacy of the Scheduled Castes. Although the Rajbanshis, Namasudras, Poundras, Jhalo Malos and the Jelia Kaibartyas had higher literacy rate than the general rate of the SCs but the educational condition of the Bagdis, Doais, Binds, Tiyars, Gonrhis and the Keyots was really very much deplorable. Educational condition of these castes remained almost unchanged in comparison to the general educational rate of the state in subsequent census years. No Scheduled Caste community could uplift its educational level to the state average (57.69%) in 1991. Only the Namasudras and the Poundras have almost reached to the state average with 56% of literacy rate. Rest of the communities remain below 50%.

Table 5.21: Rate of Development of Literacy Rate among Certain Scheduled Caste Communities of West Bengal. 1961-1991 (In Percentage).

Caste	*1961*	*1971*	*1981*	*1991*
General	29.58	33.20	40.94	57.69
SC	13.58	17.80	24.37	42.21
Bagdi	8.74	10.79	13.96	30.02

Rajbanshi	14.75	17.56	24.65	40.72
Namasudra	21.03	26.86	36.87	56.18
Poundra	26.68	27.31	36.49	56.05
Jelia Kaibartya	17.95	20.47	30.18	49.31
Jhalo Malo	14.50	19.18	25.51	42.52
Doai	6.23	17.32	22.55	37.12
Bind	6.57	10.86	20.76	20.27
Keyot	13.81	16.56	23.21	41.76
Patni	16.19	18.93	25.44	49.40
Tiyar	8.06	20.40	25.33	45.16
Gonrhi	5.64	18.61	25.21	37.87

Source: Census, 1961, 1971, 1981, 1991,

Table 5.22: Literacy Rate among Sixteen Major Scheduled Caste Communities in West Bengal 2001 (In Percentage).

Sl No	*Name of the Caste*	*Male*	*Female*	*Total*
1	All Scheduled Castes	70.5	46.9	59.0
2	Rajbanshi	72.3	47.3	60.1
3	Namasudra	80.6	62.8	71.9
4	Bagdi	60.4	34.8	47.7
5	Pod/Poundra	83.5	59.9	72.1
6	Bauri	51.8	22.7	37.5
7	Chamar	58.6	34.1	47.0
8	Jalia Kaibartya	74.4	54.8	64.9
9	Hari	61.6	36.8	49.5
10	Dhoba	83.5	63.6	73.9
11	Sunri (excluding Saha)	92.7	71.4	82.5
12	Dom	58.9	32.6	46.0
13	Jhalo Malo	68.4	51.7	60.3
14	Lohar	61.1	31.3	46.5
15	Mal	51.9	26.8	39.6
16	Kaora	64.9	40.8	53.0
17	Tiyor	73.5	50.1	62.1
18	Non-Scheduled persons	80.46	66.08	73.56
19	State average	77.02	59.61	68.64

Source: Census 2001

However, in the census of 2001 we notice satisfactory progress in literacy rate of certain Scheduled Castes. The Namasudras (71.9%), Pods (72.1%), Sunris (82.5%), Dhobas (73.9%), have crossed the state average (68.64%). The Sunris and the Dhobas are more advanced than the Non-Scheduled communities (73.56%). The Rajbanshis, the Jelia Kaibartyas and the Jhalo Malos have more than 60% literates. Rest of the Scheduled Caste communities have less than 60% literacy rate. Here the Scheduled Castes of 'East Bengal origins' are more advanced in terms of their literacy rate. Among them the Namasudras, Jelia Kaibartyas, and Jhalo Malos are very much significant. The Rajbanshis, the Poundras and the Sunris, who were distributed in both Bengal before the partition; have considerably developed their educational status in the post-partition period. So we may safely argue that the Scheduled Castes of East Bengal origin, inspite of their migration from the land of their forefathers; are more advanced. On the contrary the Bagdis, the Bauris, the Mals, the Doms, etc. i.e. the non-migrants; are far backward.

Table 5.23: Rate of Higher and Technical Education of the Scheduled Castes and Scheduled Tribes 2003-2004

	Total Students (thousands)	*Total Students (thousands)*	*Total %age of the State*	*Total %age of the State*
Educational level	*Scheduled Caste*	*Scheduled Tribe*	*Scheduled Caste*	*Scheduled Tribe*
1. PhD, D.Sc.D.Phil.	0.06	0.00	9.48	0.00
2. M.A.	4.60	0.73	12.64	2.10
3.M. Sc.	1.65	0.25	11.83	1.78
4. M.Com.	0.65	0.13	10.08	2.03
5. B.A./B.A.(Honours)	55.44	7.35	16.05	2.13
6.B.Sc/B.Sc(Honours)	11.02	1.39	10.42	1.31
7. B.Com/B.com(Honours)	10.75	1.45	8.37	1.13
8. B.E/B.Sc(Eng)/B.arch	0.36	0.01	0.82	0.02
9. Medical (Allopath, Homeopathy, Ayurvedic) Nursing, Pharma Degree	0.55	0.02	13.95	0.38

10. B.Ed /B.T.	1.34	0.24	16.11	2.93
11. Another Service (Like Law) Degree	1.48	0.35	22.92	5.43
(a) Total: 1st to 11th	87.89	11.92	12.58	1.71
12. Polytechnic	1.73	0.16	28.39	2.66
13. Teacher Training School.	0.88	0.23	16.09	4.20
14. Technical, Industrial, Art and Craft School.	1.91	0.89	15.02	7.00
(b). (12)+(13)+(14)	4.53	1.28	18.60	5.28
(a) + (b)	92.42	13.20	12.78	3.51

Source : Sacchidananda Dutta Ray, *Paschim Bange Sikshaya Agragati : Parisankhan Alochana* (Kolkata, Seriban, 2008).

Rate of higher education of the Scheduled Caste communities is beyond level that was expected. It may be clarified from the point that a portion of the seats, reserved for the Scheduled Caste student in the engineering colleges of West Bengal; used to be remained vacant every year. However, in non-technical education, reserved quota never remained vacant. Again, all Scheduled Caste communities have no equal progress in higher education. Here, we find considerable progress of the Rajbanshis, Namasudras, Poundras, Jhalo Malos and Jelia Kaibartyas. Other Scheduled Castes of West Bengal are still beyond the level in case of higher education.

5.5.2. Economic Status

Like the education, economic development of the Scheduled Castes has been a priority sector for both the West Bengal and the Union Government. Maximum emphasis has been given to the land rights. There are total three phases in the land reform policy in West Bengal after the independence. After the adoptation of *Land Acquisition Act (1953),* a large number of *jotedars* lost their lands in excess to the limit of seventy-five bighas. *Khas* (vested) land had been distributed to the landless cultivators. In case of South Bengal, the *jotedars* were mostly of non-Scheduled Caste/Scheduled Tribe communities. But in North Bengal victim *jotedars* were mostly of the Koch-Rajbanshis (agriculturist SCs). So there was a strong voice for the distribution of the vested land to the Koch-Rajbanshis in North Bengal.

In 1955 the Siliguri Zonal Kshatriya Samity (SZKS), an organization of the Rajbanshis, resolved that

'in the law made for acquisition re-distribution of lands the necessary provision is required to be made by the Govt. of West Bengal so that the lands acquired from Rajbanshi-Kshatriya Jotedars of Bengal are distributed among the native cultivators of the locality who mostly belong to the Rajbanshi-Kshatriya community and who are actually landless since long past.[66]

Similar demands were also raised by other Scheduled Caste organizations of North Bengal.

Second phase of land reforms was undertaken in West Bengal with the coming of the United Front (UF) Government in 1967. The UF Government, during 1967-70; had vested one million acre of land. It had broken the backbone of social domination of the landed aristocrats (*jotedars*) of West Bengal.[67] Moreover it became a policy of the state to give preferences to the Scheduled Castes and Scheduled Tribes in possessing the vested land.[68] But the problem of land alienation and distribution of surplus land to the land less peasantry was not solved.

However, third phase of land reforms called 'Operation Barga' under the LF Government was successful in vesting family land and recording 1.2 million of sharecroppers within three years (1978-81).[69] According to the official sources, 428179.95 hector vested land has been distributed among 2605432 beneficiaries. In North Bengal, 170081.80 hector vested land was distributed among 671841 beneficiaries out of which 301498 are Scheduled Castes and 144184 are Scheduled Tribes.[70]

Table 5.24.: Scheduled Castes and Scheduled Tribes Families of Some Districts of West Bengal Benefited by the Operation Barga (31.12.85).

District/State	*Total Figure*	*Scheduled Caste*	*Scheduled Tribes*
West Bengal	1346757	401617	162662
Bankura	99952	28260	11896
Burdwan	109325	36290	14535
Midnapur	297296	51572	31762

Darjeeling	12831	4139	3028
Jalpaiguri	55792	25769	12841
Cooch Behar	74420	44507	770
24 Parganas	167888	57899	9672
West Dinajpur	96431	26534	28699
Malda	75453	19056	18993

Sources: Department of SC and ST Welfare, Government of West Bengal.

The land reform policy has its positive impact on the 'Scheduled people' of the State. Landless peasantry now got the taste of land ownership and earning livelihood from their own land instead of living by merely as wage earner. But the scenario of engagement of the Scheduled Castes in the primary sector of economy has not changed considerably. In 1971, 81% of the Scheduled Caste workers were engaged in the primary sector which reduced to 72.39% after 20 years i.e. in 1991. One may not be puzzled to see the highest concentration of the SC workers in agricultural sector mainly as labourer. Unsurprisingly the census of 1991 has recorded 2054552 and 1372616 persons as agricultural labourer and agriculturists respectively.

Table 5.25: Categories of SC Main Workers of West Bengal 1991.

Working Sector	*Total*	*Male*	*Female*
Cultivators	1372616	1289350	83266
Agrl. Labourer	2054552	1633528	421024
Livestock, forestry etc.	144970	126641	18329
Mining & Quarrying	44422	40896	3526
Household Industry	161964	107422	54542
Other than Household Industry	361696	318033	43663
Construction	75843	72593	3250
Trade & Commerce	283743	260951	22792
Transport, Storage, etc.	174534	172180	2354
Other Services	321839	245799	76040
Marginal workers	361023	64998	296025
%	2.25	0.78	3.82
Non-Workers	10723409	3994441	6728968
%	66.69	47.97	86.78

Sources: Cultural Research Institute, *Short Note on the Scheduled Castes of West Bengal*, (Kolkata: Government of West Bengal, 2005), p. 59.

But all Scheduled communities of West Bengal are not engaged in agricultural works. The fishermen of West Bengal are the 'sons of the water'. Whole economic status of the fishermen Scheduled Castes of West Bengal is very much deplorable. Majority of them are 'internal capture fishers' who are dependent to the whims of the nature. 'Capture fishing' as a profession hardly fulfills minimum needs of the fishermen throughout the year. Still they are engaged in this profession, as they do not have any other sector to be engaged in. In North Bengal, fishing is now a seasonal profession because of shortage of water and scarcity of fish in the river system of North Bengal. In rest of the year, the traditional fishermen of North Bengal earn their livelihood from other sources particularly by rickshaw pulling (*rickshawala*), retailing vegetables (*sabjiwala*), breaking stones and as agricultural labouers.

In case of Sundarbans and the coastal belt of Digha, condition of the fishermen Scheduled Castes have no different feature. They are engaged in marine fishing as small shareholders as they do not have sufficient capital. Modern technology, essential for modern fishing industry, requires huge capital, which are generally being supplied by the non-Scheduled Caste traders and fish farmers. The traditional fishermen are working in the advanced mechanized fishing boats as labourer or as very small shareholders of the total earning in marine fishing. The children of the traditional fishermen, instead of going to the schools; are engaged in min (seed of bagda) collection in Sundarban area what is a risky job. It frequently appears in the media reports that crocodiles, tigers and poisonous snakes are causing death of the socio-economically marginalized fishermen. The womenfolk of the fishermen lost their traditional jobs of net knitting and basket making and are trying to earn livelihood as maid servants in the urban and suburban area, and as *bidi* binders and seasonal agricultural labourer in the rural area.

So it appears that occupational mobility becomes a common phenomenon among the Scheduled Castes (both the refugees and the hosts) in West Bengal. Many of their traditional occupations were no more viable for survival after their migration to West Bengal. So they were compelled to take up new occupation(s). Practically they turned to wage earner.

However, occupational mobility was always not been downward. Rather upward mobility is noticeable among some castes. Percentage of the Scheduled Caste workers in the secondary and the tertiary sectors has been increased from 7.53% and 11.47% of 1971 to 12.00% and 15.61% in 1991 respectively. But there are wide variations in progress among the Scheduled Caste communities of West Bengal. Our field survey in certain districts of West Bengal is also very much identical with this phenomenon. In my survey I have noticed that in Cooch Behar and Murshidabad the migrants East Bengali Scheduled Castes have made them capable of engaging in the secondary sectors including white colour jobs. But in case of Midnapur district, the condition of the migrant Scheduled Castes is no way satisfactory. It is due to the fact that the persons interviewed in Midnapur were mostly camp refugees whereas the person of Cooch Behar and Murshidabad were non-campers. So we may conclude that the non-campers, inspite of not getting assistance from the Government and other agencies, were more successful in rehabilitation in West Bengal. The camp refugees as we discussed in the last chapter were the worst victims of the partition.

5.6. Contested Identity of the Migrant Scheduled Castes in Different States of India

Although most of the Scheduled Caste communities of colonial Bengal have retained their Scheduled Status in postcolonial West Bengal but many of them after their migration to India have been deprived from the opportunity of Scheduled Caste status. We can get an idea about the communities which got Scheduled Caste status in Northeast India from the table 5.26. It shows that the Namasudras, Jhalo Malos or Malos, Jelia Kaibartyas, Bhuimalis, Pantis and the Bagdis have been enlisted as Scheduled Castes among the Scheduled Caste communities of East Bengali origin in Northeast India.

Assam, being the largest states of the 'seven sisters'; has received largest number of East Bengali Scheduled Caste refugees. Here almost all the Scheduled Castes refugees of East Pakistan have been granted Scheduled Caste status by the Government. Here the Namasudras, Jhalos and the Bhuimalis have significant concentration. The Namasudras constitutes 30.4% of the total Scheduled Caste population of this state. The Kaibartya caste is although largest Scheduled Caste community of Assam but most of them are indigenous people of Assam, not the migrants from East Bengal or East Pakistan. They have been settled here since the time immemorial along with indigenous Scheduled Caste communities like the Brittial Banias, Patnis, Sutradhars, and Hiras. The Scheduled Castes of East Bengal origin have main concentration in Cachar, Karimganj, Marigaon, Hailakandi, Bongaigaon, Nagaon, Nalbari and Barpeta districts. The East Bengali Scheduled Castes of Assam are mostly concentrated in the rural areas. According to 2001 Census, 85% of the Scheduled Castes are living in rural areas.

Table 5.26: Scheduled Caste Communities of Northeastern States of India.

Arunachal Pradesh, Assam, Meghalaya and Mizoram	*Manipur*	*Tripura*
1. Bansphor	1. Dhupi, Dhobi	1. Bagdi, 2. Bhuimali, 3. Bhunar,
2. Bhuimali, Mali	2. Lois	4. Chamar, Muchi, 5. Dandasi,
3. Brittial Bania, Bania	3. Muchi, Ravidas	6. Dhenuar 7. Dhoba, 8. Dum,
4. Dhupi, Dhobi	4. Namasudra	9. Ghasi, 10. Gour, 11. Gur,
5. Dugla, Dholi	5. Patni	12. Jalia Kaibartyya, 13. Kahar,
6. Hira, 7. Jalkeot	6. Sutradhar	14. Kalindi, 15. Kan, 16. Kanda,
8. Jhalo, Malo,	7. Yaithibi.	17. Kanugh, 18. Keot, 19. Khadit,
9. Kaibartya, Jaliya		20. Kharia, 21. Koch,22. Koir,
10. Lalbegi, 11. Mahar		23. Kol, 24. Kora, 25. Kotal,
12. Mehtar, Bhangi		26. Mahisyadas, 27. Mali,
13. Muchi, Rishi		28. Mehtor, 29. Musahar,
14. Namasudra		30. Namasudra, 31. Patni, 32. Sabar,
I5. Patni, 16. Sutradhar.		33. Dhulhi, Sabdakar, Badyakar
		34. Natta, Nat

Table 5.27: Scheduled Caste Population of Assam 2001.

Sl No	*Name of the Major Scheduled Caste*	*Total Population*	*Proportion to the total SC population*
1	All Scheduled Castes	825,949	100%
2	Bansphor	14,760	0.8
3	Bhuimali	57,974	3.2
4	Brittial Bania	47,974	2.6
5	Dhupi	49,929	2.7
6	Dugla	6,364	0.3
7	Hira	55,106	3.0
8	Jalkeot	23,511	1.3
9	Jhalo	77,533	4.2
10	Kaibartya	581,559	31.8
11	Lalbegi	552	0.0
12	Mahara	1,725	0.1
13	Mehtar	12,715	0.7
14	Muchi	70,954	3.9
15	Namasudra	555,621	30.4
16	Patni	151,992	8.3
17	Sutradhar	62,032	3.4

Source: Census of India 2001

The total population of Tripura was estimated 3,199,203 in the census of 2001 of which 555,724 persons are Scheduled Castes i.e. 17.4% of the total population of the state. Here the Namasudras are 35.7% of the total Scheduled Caste population who have been mainly migrated from the districts of East Bengal. The Scheduled Caste communities like the Jalia Kaibartyas, Dhobas and the Malis have also migrated in large scale in Tripura from East Bengal. Although the Mahisyadas is a Scheduled Caste community in Tripura but they were not recognized as Scheduled Caste in colonial Bengal.

The Scheduled Castes of Tripura are mainly concentrated in West Tripura district having its common border with present Bangladesh. More than half of the total Scheduled Caste populations (53.2%) of the state are living here. Most of the Scheduled Castes of Tripura are rural dwellers. In the urban areas the percentage of the Namasudras, Dhobas, Jelia Kaibartyas, and the Mahishyadas are less than 20%.

Table 5.28: Scheduled Caste population of Tripura 2001.

Sl No	*Name of the Major Scheduled Caste*	*Total Population*	*Proportion to the total SC population*
1	All Scheduled Castes	555,724	100%
2	Namasudra	198,423	35.7
3	Mahisyadas	129,588	23.3
4	Jalia Kaibartya	90,476	16.3
5	Dhoba	45,378	8.2
6	Mali	44,643	8.0
7	Chamar	11,275	2.0
8	Patni	5,703	1.0

Source: Census of India, 2001

Table 5.29: Scheduled Caste Population of Meghalaya, 2001.

Sl No	*Name of the Major Scheduled Caste*	*Total Population*	*Proportion to the total SC population*
1	All Scheduled Castes	11,139	100%
2	Namasudra	2,754	24.7
3	Muchi	2,037	18.3
4	Jhalo	1,469	13.2
5	Mehtar	726	6.5
6	Bhuimali	410	3.7
7	Brittial Bania	349	3.1
8	Bansphor	325	2.9
9	Sutradhar	300	2.7
10	Dhupi	188	1.7
11	Kaibartya	113	1.0

Source: Census of India, 2001.

The Scheduled Castes of Meghalaya are mainly concentrated in West Garo Hills (66.8%) and East Khasi Hills (20.9%). Here we notice that the Namasudras, Jhalos(Jhalo Malos or Malos of West Bengal), Sutradhars, Bhuimalis, Dhupi and Kaibartyas have been recognized as Scheduled Castes among the Scheduled Castes of East Bengal. Here the Scheduled Castes of East Bengali origins are basically rural dwellers.

In other states of Northeast India, the Scheduled Castes of East Bengali origin have very less concentration. Although 60,037 persons have been identified as Scheduled Castes in Manipur in 2001 but Scheduled Castes of East Bengali origin are less than 10%. Here 3,312 persons are Namasudras and 3335 persons are Patnis. Most of the Patnis again are of Northeast Indian origin.

In Arunachal Pradesh, 6188 persons have been identified as Scheduled Castes in 2001 out of which 1334 are Namasudras 1327 are Kaibartyas and 137 are Bhuimalis. 54 are Jhalo Malos. Rests of the Scheduled Castes of this state are basically of non-Bengali origin.

In Mizoram, figure of the Scheduled Castes has been estimated as 272 in 2001. Of the total Scheduled Caste population, Namasudra have return with the highest population (38), followed by Patni (28), Bhuimali (19), Dhupi (12), Hira (11), Muchi (10). The rest of the Scheduled Castes have less than 10 persons each.

Table 5.30 A: Scheduled Caste Communities of Bihar and Orissa.

Bihar	*Orissa*
1. Bantar, 2. Bauri, 3. Bhogta 4. Bhuiya, 5 Bhumij, 6. Charmarkar Rabidas, 7. Chaupal, 8.Dabgar 9.Dhobi, Rajak, 10. Dom, Dhangad, Bansphor, Dharikar, Dharkar, Dornra 11. Dusadh, Dhari, Dharhi ,12. Ghasi, 13. Halalkhor, 14. Hari, Mehtar, Bhangi 15. Kanjar, 16. Kurariar, 17. Lalbegi, 18. Mushar, 19. Nat, 20. Pan, Sawasi, Poor,	1.Adi-Andhra ,2.Amant, Amat, Dandachhatra Majhi, 3.Audhelia, 4.Badaik, 5.Bagheti, Baghuti, 6.Bajikar, 7.Bari, 8.Bariki, 9.Basor, Burud,10.Bauri, 11.Bauti, 12.Bavuri, 13.Bedia or Bejia , 14.Beldar,15.Bhata, 16.Bhoi,17.Chachati, 18. Chakali, 19.Chamar, Muchi, Satnami, Ravidas, 20.Chandala, 21.Chandhai Maru, 22.Dandasi, 23.Dewar, Dhibara, Keuta, Kaibarta, 24.Dhanwar, 25.Dhoba, Dhobi, 26.Dom, Dombo, Duria Dom , 27.Dosadha, 28.Ganda, 29.Ghantaragada Ghantra, 30.Ghasi, Ghasia, 31.Ghogia, 32.Ghusuria, 33.Godagali, 34.Godari, 35.Godra,36.Gokha, 37.Gorait, Korait 38.Haddi, Hadi, Hari, 39.Irika, 40.Jaggali, 41.Kandra, 42.Karua, 43.Katia, 44.Kela, 45.Khadala, 46.Kodalo, Khodalo, 47.Kori,

21. Pasi, 22. Rajwar, 23. Turi.	48.Kummari, 49.Kurunga, 50.Laban, 51.Laheri, 52.Madari, 53.Madiga, 54.Mahuria, 55.Mala, Jhala, Malo, 56.Mang, 57.Mangan, 58.Mehra, Mahar, 59.Mehter, Bhangi, 60.Mewar, 61.Mundapotta, 62.Musahar , 63.Nagarchi, 64.Namasudra, 65.Paidi, 66.Painda, 67.Pamidi, 68.Pan, 69.Panchama,70.Panika, 71.Panka, 72.Pantanti, 73.Pap, 74.Pasi , 75.Patial, 76.Rajna,77.Relli ,78.Sabakhia, 79.Samasi, 80.Sanei, 81.Sapari 82.Sauntia, Santia, 83.Sidhria, 84.Sinduria, 85.Siyal, Khajuria , 86.Tamadia, 87.Tamudia, 88.Tanla, 89. 91.Turi, 92.Ujia, 93 Valmiki, 94.Mangali 95.Mirgan

Table 5.30 B: Scheduled Caste Communities of Uttaranchal and Uttar Pradesh.

Uttaranchal	*Uttar Pradesh*
1. Agaria, 2. Badhik, 3. Badi, 4. Baheliya, 5.Baiga, 6. Baiswar, 7. Bajaniya, 8. Bajgi, 9. Balhar, 10. Balai, 11. Balmiki 12. Bangali, 13. Banmanus, 14. Bansphor, 15. Barwar, 16. Basor, 17. Bawariya, 18. Beldar, 19. Beriya, 20. Bhantu, 21. Bhuiya, 22. Bhuyiar, 23. Boria, 24. Chamar, Dhusia, Jhusia, Jatava, 25. Chero, 26. Dabgar, 27. Dhangar, 28. Dhanuk, 29. Dharkar, 30. Dhobi, 31. Dom, 32. Domar, 33. Dusadh, 34. Dharmi, 3S. Dhariya, 36. Gond, 37. Gwai, 38. Habura, 39. Hari, 40. Hela, 41. Kalabaz, 42. Kanjar, 43. Kapariya, 44. Karwai, 45. Kharaita, 46. Kharwar (excluding Vanwasi),	1. Agariya, 2. Badhik, 3. Badi, 4. Bahelia, 5. Baiga 6. Baiswar, 7. Bajaniya, 8. Bajgi, 9. Balahar, 10. Ballli, 11. Balmiki, 12. Bangali, 13. Banmanus, 14. Bansphor, 15 Barwar, 16. Basor, 17. Bawariya, 18. Beldar, 19. Beriya, 20. Bhantu, 21. Bhuiya, 22. Bhuyiar, 23. Boira, 24. Chamar, Dhusia, Jhusia, Jatava, 25. Chero , 26. Dabgar, 27. Dhangar, 28. Dhanuk, 29. Dharkar, 30. Dhobi, 31. Dom, 32. Domar, 33. Busadh, 34. Gharamj, 35. Ghasiya, 36. Gond I [excluding Mehrajganj, Sidharth Nagar, Basti Gorakhpur, Deoria, Mau, Azamgarh, Jonpur, Balia, Gazipur,Varanasi, Mirzapur and Sonbhadra, 37. Gual, 38. Habura, 39. Hari, 40. Hela, 41. Kalabaz , 42. Kanjar, 43. Kapariya, 44. Karwal, 45. Khairaha 46. Kharwar (excluding Benbansi), 47. Khatik, 48. Khorot, 49. Kol, 50. Kori , 51. Korwa, 52. Lalbegi, 53. Majhwar, 54. Mazhabi, 55. Musahar, 56. Nat, 57. Pankha, 58. Parahiya, 59. Pasitarmali, 60. Patari 61. Rawat, 62. Saharya, 63.Sanaurhiya, 64. Sansiya, 65. Shilpkar, 66. Turaiha.

47. Khatik, 48. Kharot,
49.Kol, 50. Kori, 51. Korwa,
52. Laibegi

Although the Scheduled Caste communities of East Bengal have migrated in large scale in Uttar Pradesh, Uttaranchal, Madhya Pradesh, Orissa and Bihar but they have mostly been deprived from the Scheduled Caste status. Table 5.30 A and 5.30B show that the Namasudras and the Jhalo Malos have been granted Scheduled Caste status in Orissa only. In other states as mentioned above the Scheduled Castes migrants of Bengal (including the Namasudras and the Jhalo Malos) do not have any Scheduled status. Here they are being treated as the people of 'general category.' This type of identification has deprived large number of Scheduled Castes of East Bengal origin from the basic rights of Scheduled status as enshrined in the Constitution of India. However, in Uttaranchal these unrecognized Scheduled Castes people have raised their voice for Scheduled Caste recognition what not yet materialized.

NOTES AND REFERENCES

1. Hiranmoy Bandyopadhyay, *Udvastu* (Calcutta: Shisu Sahitya Samsad, 1970), 48.
2. *Star of India,* May 12, 1947,
3. Anasuya Basu Ray Chaudhury, Politics of Rehabilitation: Struggle of the Scheduled Refugees in West Bengal, in *Voice of Dalit (Vol. 3, No. 1, Jan-June)* 2010, p.65.
4. *Ibid.*
5. Resignation letter of Mr. Jogendra Nath Mondal dated 8th October, 1950. See Appendix.
6. *Ibid.*
7. *Ibid.*
8. *Ibid.*
9. Anasuya Basu Ray Chaudhury, *Politics of Rehabilitation*, p. 66.
10. State Bureau of Statistics, Government of West Bengal, *Report on the Sample Survey for Estimating the Socio-economic Characteristics of displaced persons migrating from Eastern Pakistan to the state of West Bengal* (Calcutta, 1951), p. 19.

11. *Ibid*, p. 20.
12. State Statistical Bureau, Government of West Bengal, *Rehabilitation of Refugees: A Statistical Survey* (Calcutta, 1955).
13. Hiranmoy Bandyopadhyay, *Udvastu,* p. 49; also see the map. 5.1.
14. Swapan K. Biswas, *Colonization and Rehabilitations in Andaman and Nicobar Islands* (Delhi: Abhijeet Publications, 2009), p. 78.
15. *Ibid.*
16. *Ibid*, 79.
17. Nitish Biswas, *Nainitaler Pathe Pathe* (Kolkata: Aiktan Gabeshana Samsad, 2002), p.30.
18. *Ibid.*, p. 105.
19. Saibal Kumar Gupta, *Dandakaranya: A Survey of Rehabilitation,* edited by Alok Kumar Ghosh (Calcutta: Bibhasha, 1999), p. 4.
20. *Ibid.*
21. *Ibid.*, p. 5.
22. *Ibid.,* p. 17.
23. Alok Kumar Gosh, From Caste to Class: The Dalit Experience of Partition in Bengal, in Biswajit Chatterjee and Debi Chatterjee (eds.): *Dalit Lives and Dalit Vision in Eastern India* (Kolkata: Centre fro Rural Resources, 2007), p. 13.
24. Saibal Kumar Gupta, *Dandakaranya: A survey of Rehabilitation*, p. 17.
25. K. Maudood Elahi, Refugees in Dandakaranya, *International Migration Review,* Vol. 15, No. 1/2, *Refugees Today (Spring - Summer,* 1981), pp. 219-225.
26. Saibal Kumar Gupta, *Dandakaranya: A survey of Rehabilitation,* pp.17-38.
27. *Ibid.*, p. 37.
28. Memorandum, submitted by Mr. Raiharan Barai, General Secretary of the Udvastu Unnayanshil Samity on 22nd March 1979 to the Enquiry Committee headed by Shri Prasannabhai Mehta.
29. Alok K. Ghosh, *From Caste to Class,* p. 13.
30. *Ibid.*
31. Jagadish Chandra Mondal, *Marichjhapi: Naisabder Antarale* (Kolkata: Sujan Publications, 2002), p. 49.
32. *Ibid.*, p. 49.

33. *Memorandum.*
34. *Anandbazar Patrika 26th April,* 1978.
35. *Ibid.*
36. Niranjan Haldar, *Marichjhapi* (Calcutta, 1986), p.36.
37. Ross Mallick, Refugee Resettlement in Forest Reserves: West Bengal Policy Reversal and the Marichjhapi Massacre, *The Journal of Asian Studies,* Vol. 58, No. 1 (Feb., 1999), p.107.
38. *Ibid.*
39. Mrityunjoy Pramanik, *Banglabibhagottar Udvastu Itihas Charchar Prekshite Marichjhapi,* unpublished M.Phil. Dissertation, (Kolkata, Jadavpur University, 2010), p.57.
40. Jagadish Chandra Mondal, *Marichjhapi*, pp.54-55.
41. *Ibid.*p.59.
42. *Dandakaranya theke phire asha udbastuder prati Mukhhyamantrir abedan,* a leaflet, published by the Government of West Bengal. For details see Madhumay Pal (ed.): *Marichjhapi: Chhinna Desh, Chhinna Itihas* (Kolkata: Gangchil, 2009).
43. *Ibid.*
44. Jagadish Chandra Mondal, *Marichjhapi*, p. 55.
45. Mrityunjoy Pramanik,*Banglabibhagottar Udvastu Itihas Charchar Prekshite Marichjhapi,* p. 61.
46. *Ibid.*, p. 61.
47. *Ibid.*
48. Jagadish Chandra Mandal, *Marichjhapi*, p.51.
49. *Memorandum.*
50. Mrityunjoy Pramanik: *Banglabibhagottar Udvastu Itihas Charchar Prekshite Marichjhapi*, p.62.
51. Memorandum
52. *Ibid.*
53. Ross Mallick, *Refugee Resettlement in Forest Reserves*, p. 108.
54. Niranjan Halder, *Marichjhapi*, p. 40.
55. *Memorandum,* also *see* Jagadish Chandra Mondal, *Marichjhapi*, p. 59.
56. Madhumay Paul (ed.): *Marichjhapi: Chhinna Desh, Chhinna Itihas*, p. 272.
57. Published in the *Kalantar* from 25th to 28th February 1979. Also *see* Jagadish Chandra Mondal, *Marichjhapi*, p. 56.

58. Amiya Kumar Samanta, Marichjhapi, in Madhumay Paul (ed.), *Marichjhapi: Chhinna Desh, Chhinna Itihas* (Kolkata: Gangchil, 2009),p. 245.
59. Ross Mallick, Refugee Resettlement in Forest Reserves, p. 111.
60. Ashim Mukherjee, Fishermen, in *Frontier,* January 10, 1981, Vol. 13, no, 20,p.3.
61. Hiranmoy Bandyopadhyay: *Udvastu,* p. 49.
61. The fishermen refugees of camps of Nadia and 24 Parganas were given rehabilitation in the riverbed of the Bhagirathi at Kanchrapara.
62. For more details *see* Rup Kumar Barman,*Fisheries and Fishermen* (Delhi: Abhijeet Publications, 2008).
63. *Bhagirathi* 1.1(8th May, 1969), p.5.
64. *Bhagirathi* 1.3 (8th July, 1969), p.4.
65. *Constitution of the Paschim Banga Matsyajibi Samity* (Calcutta, Paschim Banga Matsyajibi Samity, 1969).
66. Proceedings of the First Annual Conference of the Siliguri Zonal Kshatriya Samity, dated 8th April, 1955; also *see*: *Contested Regionalism: A New Look on History, Cultural Change and Regionalism of North Bengal and Lower Assam* (Delhi: Abjiheet Publications, 2007).
67. D. Bandyopadhyay, Land Reforms in West Bengal: Remembering Harekrishna Konar and Benoy Choudhury, *EPW XXXV, no.21 and 21*(7th May 2000), p. 1796.
68. Annapurna Sanyal, *Scheduled Caste and Scheduled Tribes in Indian Politics* (Calcutta: Minerva, 1991), p. 25.
69. D. Bandyopadhyay, Land Reforms in West Bengal, p. 1797.
70. Dept. of SC and ST Welfare. Govt. of West Bengal, *Hataman Jara Tulechhe Shir* (Bengali) (Calcutta, 1987.), p. 7; Dinesh Dakua, *Kamtapuri Andolon Ekti Jana Bichhinna Andolan,* (Calcutta, National Book Agency Pvt. Ltd, 2003), pp. 30-31.

6

Partition of Bengal and Struggle for Existence of the Non-Migrant Scheduled Castes: The Rajbanshis of North Bengal

Partition of Bengal in 1947 was appeared as a serious challenge to both India and Pakistan. It not only brought significant changes in the social and economic lives of the 'forced migrants' but also radically changed the entire socio-economic and political structure of pre-partition Bengal. So a significant number of non-immigrant (pre-settled) Scheduled Castes of West Bengal, i.e. the hosts; could not escape from the curse of partition. In post-partition India and East Pakistan, they not only lost the position of their bargaining power but also threatened due to excessive migration of the people in the 'Scheduled Caste concentrated districts of West Bengal'. It created socioeconomic and political tensions among the non-migrant (local) Scheduled Castes. This type of impact of partition has been evidently noticed in case of North Bengal. Here the Rajbanshis (largest Scheduled Caste community of West Bengal) are struggling for existence with their strangulated sociopolitical life. Along with other developments in post-colonial North Bengal, this aspect of partition of Bengal has created such a complex situation that the host people of that region have repeatedly raised their voice against the consequences of partition of Bengal. So they have been clamouring for autonomy as the means of recovery of their grievances. In this chapter I'll highlight this aspect of partition of Bengal in somewhat objective outlook.

6.1. Post-Partition Rajbanshi Identity in India

The Rajbanshis of North Bengal, an agriculturalist and largest Scheduled Caste community of undivided Bengal; once organized themselves under the banner of their social and political organization called Rajbanshi Kshatriya Samity (founded in 1910). In the chapter two I have critically analyzed the nature of their social movement. It appears that in the late colonial Bengal, the Rajbanshis had developed a kind of social integrity through the social reform movement which popularly conceptualized as *kshatriyaization* and led to the growth of self consciousness and formation of a social identity. At the same time, they placed them in the politics of Bengal as a strong political force. But in postcolonial India, caste identity of the Rajbanshis became a matter of confusion due to the partition and large scale presence of the Rajbanshis in Bihar, Assam, Meghalaya and other states of Northeast India. After the partition of Bengal, former Kshatriya Samity with its head quarter at Rangpur (East Pakistan) lost its social influence over the scattered Rajbanshi population of India. So the local committees (*mandals*) of the former Kshatriya Samity began to reorganize in different parts of North Bengal in order to face the challenges of the new political situation. A new branch of the Kshatriya Samity was founded on 8th November, 1962 at Dinhata (Cooch Behar) called Rajbanshi Kshatriya Samity which emerged as a central organization of the Rajbanshis of North Bengal and Assam.[1] This organization had deep sympathy to the socioeconomic and cultural development of the Rajbanshis including the formation of a linguistic state for them.[2] But the Bangiya Rajbanshi Kshatriya Samity, centered in Calcutta, was another parallel organization of the Rajbanshis of West Bengal.[3] Its main purpose were to (i) develop educational status of the Rajbanshis (ii) to change social customs in accordance with the new situation (iii) achieve political rights, (iv) arrange vocational training, etc.[4] So it seems that the Rajbanshis of West Bengal lost their social and political homogeneity what they achieved under the colonial rule.

Condition of the Rajbanshis of Assam was more crucial just immediately after the independence. Although the Koches and the Rajbanshis have been categorized as Scheduled Castes (SC) in West Bengal and in Meghalaya Koches have been recognized as Scheduled Tribe (ST) but they do not have any fixed status in Assam. On the recommendations of the Kaka Kalelkar Commission (1953-55) the Koch-Rajbanshis of Assam were declared as OBC (Other Backward Castes) in 1953 but the Rajbanshis of Goalpara district were granted a new status called MOBC (Most Other Backward Caste).[5] So there is no common status of the Rajbanshis in postcolonial India.

However, the postcolonial concept of 'Rajbanshi' (Koch-Rajbanshi) means indigenous people, those who adopted Rajbanshi/Kamtapuri dialect/language as their lingua franca; including the Rajbanshis, Koches, Paliyas, native Muslims (Nashya Shaikhs) and other tribal and non-tribal people of North Bengal and Northeast India. So the sociopolitical organizations founded by the Koch-Rajbanshis like the Uttar Khanda Dal (UKD 1969), Uttarbanga Tapashili Jati O Adibashi Sangathan (UTJAS 1979), Koch-Rajbongshi International (KRI 1984), Bharatiya Kamta Rajya Parishad (BKRP 1986), Kamtapur Peoples' Party (1995), and Greater Cooch Behar People's Association (GCBPA, 1998) have categorically classified the Rajbanshis/Kamtapuri of postcolonial period as a composition of 'all Rajbanshis, Koch, Mech, etc., listed as Scheduled Castes and Tribes in the Constitution (SC and ST) Order of 1950; local Muslims and bonafide refugees entering in the region.'[6] So 'Rajbanshi identity' obviously is a greater connotation in postcolonial India than the 'Rajbanshi caste' of colonial period. It is now a 'cultural community' than a 'caste community'. So in postcolonial India the Rajbanshis of North Bengal began to reorganize themselves on the cultural ground rather than caste identity.

6.2. Demographic Impact of Partition on the Rajbanshis of North Bengal

Immediate effect of the partition of Bengal in 1947, so far

been noticed in case of North Bengal; is the rapid changes in the demographic composition. The host people of the region apparently received a threat from the flow of large number of refugees. Merger of Cooch Behar State to India in 1949 and its incorporation to West Bengal as a district in 1950 had also produced similar changes in Cooch Behar.

Table 6.1: Comparative Table of Population Growth Rates in West Bengal and North Bengal (in %).

Census	*West Bengal*	*North Bengal*
1951-61	32.80%	40.49%
1961-71	26.87%	33.01%
1971-81	23.17%	27.63%
1981-91	24.55%	27.61%
1991-2001	17.84%	22.43%

Source: Census of India, 1951, 1961, 1971, 1981, 1981, 1991 and 2001.

It is, however, very difficult to determine the exact figure of the refugees who got shelter in North Bengal. But we can get some idea about the migration of the Rajbanshis and other communities to North Bengal from East Pakistan from the population growth rate of the districts of North Bengal. The Rajbanshi population in West Bengal was increased 61.90% during the period between 1951 and 1961, 66.83% during 1971-1981 and 25.70 % during 1981-1991. At the same time average population growth rate of North Bengal had remained always higher than that of West Bengal average in each decadal census (see table 6.1). This phenomenon clearly indicates a large-scale cross border and inter-state migration to North Bengal.

Table 6.2: Distribution of the Rajbanshi Population in Postcolonial North Bengal (% to Total Population).

District	*1951*	*1961*	*1971*	*1981*	*1991*
Darjeeling	3%	3.5%	3.06%	3.6%	7.44%
Jalpaiguri	32.68%	35.19%	32.03%	29%	23.42%
Cooch Behar	47%	46%	46.84%	40.96%	39.86%

West Dinajpur	12%	10%	13.13%	21.16%	15.65%
Malda	3.84%	4.28%	4.94%	4.79%	4.29%

Sources: Computed from the Census of India, 1951, 1961, 1971, 1981, 1991 and 2001.

Huge migration of the East Bengalese had a negative impact on the concentration of the Rajbanshis in the districts of North Bengal. Inspite of migration of the Rajbanshis from the districts of East Bengal to present North Bengal, percentage of the Rajbanshis in the total population is in decreasing order. Table 6.2 indicates that the population of the Rajbanshis in Cooch Behar district was 47% in 1951 which decreased to 39.86% in 1991 where the Scheduled Castes have largest percentage even in 2001. Condition of Jalpaiguri district is more critical where the percentage of the Rajbanshis has been decreased from 32.68% (of 1951) to 23.42% in 1991. However, in other districts of North Bengal, percentage of the Rajbanshis shows a little increase. But at the same time number of the non-Rajbanshi Scheduled Castes population is now significant in the North Bengal districts (table 6.3) which is directly linked with the competition within the Scheduled Caste category.

Table 6.3: Distribution of Scheduled Caste and Rajbanshi Population in North Bengal Districts, 2001.

State/District	*Total SC*	*Rajbanshi*	*Koch*	*Non Koch-Rajbanshi SCs*	*Total population*
West Bengal	18452555	3386617	12727	15053211	80221171
North Bengal	4413239	2688580	12287	1712372	14721977
Darjeeling	258881	129904	199	128778	1605900
Jalpaiguri	1248577	811567	472	436518	3403204
Cooch Behar	1242374	972803	1251	268320	2478242
Uttar Dinajpur	676582	405140	1687	269755	2441824
Dakshin Dinajpur	432660	224988	3454	204218	1502647
Malda	554165	144158	5224	404783	3290160

Source: Computed from the Census of India, 2001.

6.3. Voices Against the Consequences of the Partition of Bengal

Decrement in the population percentile has its direct impact on the socio-cultural and political prominence of the local people. The pre-settlers now become subordinate to new settlers since the new comers have gradually established their domination in all aspects of society including politics, economy and culture of North Bengal. So the socio-political associations formed by the Rajbanshis in postcolonial North Bengal and Assam had categorically raised the question of rights of the indigenous people (*deshi*) and proposed to form a separate state in North Bengal. Even these organizations publicly expressed their hatred against the new settlers (immigrants or *bhatia*). Here we may cite the example of the Siliguri Zonal Rajbanshi Kshatriya Samity (SZKS), the Kamtapur Rajjya Sangram Parishad (KRSP founded in 1967), the Uttar Khanda Dal (UKD) etc. In a memorandum submitted to the Prime Minister of India, in 1981 the UKD categorically expressed that

> 'immediate effects of the partition, as is now well known, was the huge influx of refugees from the then East Pakistan. West Bengal had to throw its border open and its arms of welcome wide to receive the East Pakistan refugees as they were known as one nation, viz. the Bengalese, during the pre-partitioned societies. Hence, North Bengal which happened, because of a chance of historical circumstances, to be part of West Bengal could not also raise its voice of objection and had been forced by the command of history to fall in lie with West Bengal in its endeavour to accommodate the refugees. As a result North Bengal had to live with a chunk of people alien to its customs, language and culture'.[7]

The Uttar Banga Tapashili Jati O Adibashi Sangathan (North Bengal Scheduled Castes and Scheduled Tribes Association or UTJAS), Bharatiya Koch Rajbongshi Kshatriya Mahasabha

(BKRKM), Koch-Rajbongshi International (KRI) and Bharatiya Kamta Rajjya Parishad (BKRP) have also raised similar voice. It means the partition of Bengal and the migration of the refugees as an essential by-product of the partition; has developed a negative attitude among the host people.

The UKD had also identified the process of subordination of the indigenous people of North Bengal due to the partition of Bengal. The UKD had highlighted that

> with the passage of time the refugees driven by the dire necessity of survival began to corner every possible means of earning money and in the process pushing the local inhabitants to backward places. These activities of the refugees were supported and backed by the government and the business community at Calcutta who felt it obligatory to render all possible help to the refuges partly because of their own feelings of kinship with the refugees and partly because of hulla-ballus raised by the Calcutta-based news papers. This process of business activities had acted as catalytic agents in economic fields which had rooted out most of the indigenous people from all towns and had taken away all business from them. This so happened because the Calcutta centered business community stood at the back of the refugees and the Calcutta based government tried to look to the interests of the refugees at the cost of and with sheer neglect of the local people. As a result ------the indigenous population of the area irrespective of the caste, creeds and religion, have become hewers of wood and drawers of water to the refugees who are now lording it over original people so to speak.[8]

Thus it appears that the pre-settled communities of North Bengal were deprived due to the migration of the East Bengalese to this region. In order to legitimize and popularize its arguments, the UKD categorically raised the question of distinct but endangered culture of the Koch-Rajbanshis. It stated that the people inhabiting this area have a distinct culture based on distinct language which is not any way inferior to any other culture of India if not superior to some of them in some respects.[9]

The UKD had also frequently talked against the negative attitude of the immigrant East Bengalese to the language and culture of the Rajbanshis. Thus it further says

> 'the language spoken by the people residing in this vast area with slight variation from place to place dose not bear any distinct name of its own though it has got a vast treasure of literature dating back from the nineteenth century. It is not a local dialect of the Bengali language.....The Bengalese, learned and illiterate, derisively called our language the Bahe Bhasa by which they display their own ignorance and a show of haughtiness and expression of hate complex to the local, as Bahe is only a word to address an esteemed person or an unknown personality......[10]

Shri Kalindra Nath Barman, one of the founder leaders of the UKD; had published a small monograph titled '*Ekti Birat Giggasa : Ora Bahe Na Bangali*?' in 1970 for drawing wide attention of intellectual community.[11] In that work he categorically raised the strangulated condition of the Rajbanshis of North Bengal and appealed to the educated section of that community together with other marginalized communities of that region to come forward for upward development through active political participation and collective action.

Thus the UKD, together with the consequences of the partition of Bengal of 1947 and other grounds of socioeconomic deprivation, had demanded a separate state comprising five districts of North Bengal, namely Cooch Behar, Jalpaiguri, Darjeeling, West Dinajpur and Malda within the framework of the Indian Constitution for the overall development of North Bengal along with the protection of endangered culture, economic development and establishment of political domination of the pre-settled communities. In a 34 points memorandum, submitted to the Government of West Bengal in 1977, it had also demanded an academy for the Kamtapuri language, 90% reservation of jobs for the Scheduled Castes and Scheduled Tribes of North Bengal (Scheduled Castes 50% and Scheduled Tribes 40%).[12] Being induced by the *Bideshi-Kheda* (expulsion of the foreigners) aspect of the Assam movement the UKD raised the *Bhatia-Khedao* (expulsion of the immigrants) slogan.[13]

The UKD began to organize conferences, meetings and strikes in different districts of North Bengal through peaceful democratic means for materializing its demands. But in the election it could not get significant achievement. So it appears that the demands of the UKD did not have mass support.

However, in the 1980s we find the Uttar Banga Tapashili Jati O Adibashi Sangathan (UTJAS) in the position of leadership of the Rajbanshis and other indigenous communities of North Bengal. The UTJAS stood for the socioeconomic development of the Scheduled Castes and the Scheduled Tribes of North Bengal and to fight against the discriminations committed against them.[14] Even it demanded 60% reservation of seats for the Scheduled Castes and Scheduled Tribes in the educational institutions and government jobs of North Bengal.[15] Like the UKD, the UTJAS was instrumental against the influx of refugees from erstwhile East Pakistan. UTJAS always propagated that 'the refugees those who entered into North Bengal after 1971 should not be given political rights.' It relentlessly criticized the land reform policies of the LF Government.[16] Regarding the question of possession and distribution of *khas* (vested) land, several clashes broke out between the UTJAS supporters and the Left party supporters in the 1980s particularly in Tufanganj subdivision of Cooch Behar district. Police arrested several members of the UTJAS. Even some UTJAS supporters were injured and one UTJAS activist named Naren Das was died due to the police firing on 11th April, 1980 at Tufanganj.[17]

The UTJAS organized a *Gana Anasan Satyagraha* (mass hunger Satyagraha) from 1st March to 8th July, 1980, as a protest of Tufanganj incident. The Bharatiya Tapashili Parishad, a Scheduled Caste /Scheduled Tribe organization centered in Calcutta; had supported the UTJAS movement. It categorically stated that 'the recent movement which is going on under the banner of North Bengal SC/ST Association is not a movement of disintegration rather it is a movement of economic development of downtrodden people.'[18] The UTJAS had also got active support from the Bangiya Rajbanshi Kshatriya Samity.[19] The LF Government of West Bengal, however, viewed the whole incident of Tufanganj as a separatist movement (*bichhinatabadi andolon*) driven by the UTJAS, an organization which wants to drive out the refugees from North Bengal.[20]

While the UKD and the UTJAS were engaged in mobilizing the Scheduled Caste and Scheduled Tribes of North Bengal, one sociopolitical organization called the Bharatiya Koch-Rajbongshi Kshatriya Mahasabha (BKRKM), was born in Assam in 1984 under the leadership of Dr. Purna Narayan Sinha (ex M.P. from Tezpur) for overall development of the Koch-Rajbanshi community. It expressed that

> 'the Koch-Rajbongshis are indigenous people of Eastern and Northeastern India, highly backward in social, political, educational and economic affairs although they have Scheduled Caste status in West Bengal and Tripura. But in other states they do not have Scheduled status. So all Koch-Rajbanshis of India should stand united and make efforts to secure equal social, political and economic status as one class'.[21]

It again stated that the survival of the Koch-Rajbanshis of North Bengal and Lower Assam is being threatened due to 'illegal immigration of aliens into their country.' So this organization demanded to the Central Government 'to detect the foreigners and deport them from India by gearing up intensive action so that culture, economy and national security of this part of India could be protected from illegal inroads from a foreign country like Bangladesh'.[22]

In the second conference held at Burirhat, Dinhata in 1986 the BKRKM was renamed as the Koch-Rajbongshi International (KRI). The KRI had chosen its executive members from different states and countries including Nepal, Bangladesh and Bhutan. It was strongly supported by the UKD, Kamta Rajjya Parishad, Chilarai Sangha, All Assam Koch-Rajbanshi Kshatriya Sammelan (Assam) and the Rajbanshi Bhasha Prachar Samity (Nepal).[23]

The KRI had deep concern for the cultural-linguistic identity of the Koch-Rajbanshis. It also demanded

(i) the reservation of 80% jobs for the Koch-Rajbanshis in North Bengal,

(ii) formation of a state in North Bengal or at least Union Territory status should be given to the erstwhile Cooch Behar State along with the areas specified by the UKD,

(iii) formation of a military regiment in the name of Chilarai,

(iv) the Koch-Rajbanshis of Assam and Meghalaya should be declared as Scheduled Tribe(ST),

(v) the Kamrupi-Kamtapuri culture should be protected from further degradation,

The KRI, like other political organization of the Rajbanshis, had similar voice in regards to the refugee issue and migration or infiltration from Bangladesh. It resolves that 'due to the heavy influx of people from outside North Bengal the Koch-Rajbongshis are being threatened with total extinction inspite of their past heritage and martial glory and that no protection is being given to them by the Government. This Conference (KRI) therefore demand to the Government to take such measure by which it will be possible to safeguard the ethnic identity of the Koch-Rajbongshis of the erstwhile Cooch Behar State taking 1951 as the base year for migration from other states, provided that no year need be applied in case of Koch Rajbongshis'.[24]

The question of illegal migration is no doubt a legitimate one. But the extraordinary demand of identifying the post-1951 non-Koch-Rajbanshi immigrants as alien is something ambiguous.

Like the KRI, another political organization operated from Lower Assam (Gauripur) called Bharatiya Kamta Rajjya Parishad (BKRP) under the leadership of B.K.Barua began to mobilize the linguistic and cultural feelings of the Koch-Rajbanshis including the formation of a separate state in North Bengal. In order to materialized the demands, the BKRP in its mass meting held on 6th August 1986 resolved that ----'in view of the fact that independence has no meaning for the poor and neglected people of Kamtapur, no Kamtapuri will take part in any official or non-official functions in the celebration of 'Independence Day'—all the programmes shall be boycotted.' However, in practice this organization did not have mass support.

Although this kind of movement for the formation of a separate state could not get major success in the 1980s but the 1990s is witness of organized movements in North Bengal particularly after the formation of the Kamtapur People's Party (KPP) in 1995. The KPP is determined to create a separate state (Kamtapur) and recognition of the Kamtapuri/Rajbanshi language. It has few other objectives which have already been raised by the former organizations of the Koch-Rajbanshis. The KPP is said to have supported by a militant organization called KLO (Kamtapur Liberation Organization). According to the Government reports 'the KLO is a militant organization which adopted the policy of murder of the left political leaders and abduction. It has its link with other militant organizations of Northeast India like the ULFA'.[25] The KPP has active support from the All Kamtapur Student Union (AKSU) and the AKRASU (All Koch-Rajbanshi Student Union) although the KPP itself is suffering from factionalism.

But the formation of the Greater Cooch Behar Peoples Association (GCBPA) in 1998 had again revived the anti-immigrant feelings of the local Rajbanshis of Cooch Behar, Jalpaiguri and lower Assam. Its main objectives are to form a separate state in Sub-Himalayan Bengal and Lower Assam particularly comprising with territories of erstwhile Koch kingdom of sixteenth-seventeenth century; to maintain the cultural heritage of Cooch Behar, and all round development of people of Cooch Behar.[26]

The GCBPA categorically raised the question of merger of Cooch Behar State to India in 1949 and its transition to a district of West Bengal in 1950. To the GCBPA, the transition of Cooch Behar State to district of West Bengal is invalid and hence Cooch Behar should be declared as a 'separate state' within the constitution of India with the territories formerly belonged to the Koch kingdom. The GCBPA had submitted several memorandums to the Central Government describing the legitimacy of its demands. The GCBPA has undertaken several programs for arousing the sentiment of the local people of Cooch Behar and other parts of North Bengal and Lower Assam in favour of their movement.[27]

6.5. Observation

Partition of Bengal and migration of the East Bengalese including the Scheduled Castes had deep impacts on the society and economy of both sides of Bengal. Huge migration of people from East Pakistan to North Bengal had radically changed the demographic, political and economic structure of the land. Like Tripura population concentration of majority community of colonial period was suddenly reversed. Here the Rajbanshis who had significant concentration in Cooch and Jalpaiguri district began to be marginalized in politics and economy. So like northeast India a trend has developed here among the Rajbanshis against the consequences of partition of Bengal of 1947. So certain sociopolitical organizations formed by the Rajbanshis have raised the question of their cultural identity with a separate state within the basic structure of the Indian Constitution as the means of solution of their grievances.

NOTES AND REFERENCES

1. Upendra Nath Barman, *Uttar Banglar Sekal O Amar Jiban Smriti,* (Jalpaiguri, 1382, BS), p. 49.
2. Siliguri Anchalik (Zonal) Kshatriya Samity in its First Annual Conference held on 8th April 1955, supported the formation of linguistic state in India and emphasized on the continuity of reservations policy for the Rajbanshis and implementation of reservations in the semi-government organizations. *Resolutions passed in the First Annual Conference of the Siliguri Anchalik (zonal) Kshatriya Samity* held at Haidarpara, Dist. Jalpaiguri.
3. Bangiya Rajbanshi Kshatriya Samity was founded in 1943 in

Calcutta and got registration in 1944. *Annual Report of the Bangiya Rajbanshi Kshatriya Samity* (Calcutta, 1986), p. 4.

4. Naresh Chandra Sarkar (ed.) *Mukur 2.1*(6 January, 1990), p. 1.
5. P.S.Datta, Movement for Scheduled Status in a Poly-ethnic Society: The Case of the Koch-Rajbongshis of Assam, *Journal of North East India Council for Social Science Research II.11* (1978), p.31.
6. Maynaguri Declaration of the Bharatiya Kamta Rajya Parishad, Circular No.KRP/dated 8th August 1986.
7. Memorandum, submitted by Panchanan Mallick to the Prime Minister of India dated 24th August, 1980.
8. *Ibid.*
9. *Ibid.*
10. *Ibid.*
11. Kalindra Nath Barman, *Ekti Birat Giggasa: Ora Bahe Na Bangali,* (Siliguri: Panchanan Asram, 1377 B.S.).
12. *Paribartan* 3.4(16th August, 1980), p.26.
13. *Ibid.*, pp.28-29.
14. Memorandum dated 11.08.1980 submitted by Prabhat Sen Eshor, Secretary, UTJAS, to the Prime Minister of India.
15. *The Statesman*, 30th October 1986.
16. Dhirendra Nath Das, *Regional Movement: Ethnicity and Politics* (New Delhi: Abhijeet Publications, 2005), pp.91-95.
17. Letter of Sri Prasenjit Barman, M.P. (Rajjya Sabha) dated 15th April 1980 to the Prime Minister of India; also memorandum submitted by UTJAS dated 11.08.1980 to the Prime Minister of India.
18. Letter of the Secretary of the Bharatiya Tapashili Parishad to Prasenjit Barman, M.P. dated 28.06.80 no 491, /1(4)/ICSC/80.
19. Letter of the Secretary Bangiya Rajbanshi Kshatriya Samity, to the Chief Minister of West Bengal, dated 16.08.80.
20. *Paribartan* (7-13 May 1980), p.75.
21. Minute of Proceedings of the BKRKM held at Halakura, Dhubri on 16-17 February 1984.
22. *Ibid.*
23. Minute of Proceedings of the KRI, 1986.
24. *Ibid.*
25. *The Statesman*, 9th May 2000.

26. Letter of the Secretary GCBPA dated 25.09.2002 to the District Magistrate, Cooch Behar; Memorandum submitted by the GCBPA to the Home Minister of India, dated 6th December, 2000; Memorandum submitted by the GCBPA to the President of India, dated 5.04.2001.
27. Souvenir of the GCBPA, published by the Block Committee of the GCBPA, dated 21.11.2004.

Conclusion

Birth of independent India and Pakistan from the garb of colonial India in 1947 through the partition had generated the forces of 'forced migration' of the minorities from both the newly born countries. The minorities were shocked by seeing the horrified and tensed situation. In case of East Pakistan the Hindus of upper, middle and lower class background began to migrate to India mainly to West Bengal. So rehabilitation of the forced migrants was a complicated task for the Government of West Bengal. It was also a great problem for those people who lost everything due to the partition. Here the Scheduled Castes of East Bengal were worst sufferer since they were mostly very poor and backward in terms of their possession of capital good, earning and social status.

It has been noticed in the present study that the colonial policy of social classification, growth of self awareness in the late nineteenth and the early twentieth century had generated a trend of social reform movement among the Scheduled Caste communities of Bengal. Social reformers of these communities had adopted two specific strategies for their upward mobility—— (i) elimination of certain cultural practices which were considered 'unclean' by the upper castes; and (ii) adoption of respectable social practices and ritual from the upper caste Hindus including holding *paita* (scared thread). Emphasis on the spread of education and acquiring government jobs had contributed to the social, economic and political development of these marginal people. But adoption of certain rituals from the upper castes such as prohibition of widow remarriage and maintaining distance from the unreformed lower castes had strengthened caste prejudices in colonial Bengal. Inspite of limitations this kind of social movement had structurally integrated certain lower caste communities of colonial Bengal. They were successful to develop a kind of feeling of respectable (!) caste identity. So the 'caste' as a social institution secured more legitimate social ground.

Social reform movement of the Scheduled Castes got a new dimension with the beginning of electoral politics in Bengal. After the adoption of the *Government of India Act, 1919* and the *Government of India Act, 1935* caste-based social movements of the Scheduled Castes of Bengal were transformed into a political movement. They now placed them as an inseparable part of provincial level electoral politics of Bengal. Emerging sociopolitical 'elite leaders' of the Scheduled Caste communities were also successful to place the Scheduled Castes of Bengal as a 'bargaining power' in between the nationalist and the communal political trends. So the National Congress, All India Muslim League, Krishak Praja Party and provincial level other political forces had tried their best to mobilize the Scheduled Castes of Bengal in their favour during the period between 1937 and 1945. But in the election of 1946 Scheduled Castes of Bengal began to join the Congress-led nationalist politics and the communist-led class politics. So on the eve of independence of India, they lost their own political identity when they merged themselves to the Congress-led political decision i.e. support to the partition of Bengal. Thus with the partition of India the Scheduled Castes of Bengal lost their position of bargaining power in politics. They along with the upper caste Hindus and other minority communities now were forced to migrate to West Bengal and other states of India from East Bengal.

Forces of 'forced migration' from East Pakistan were generated for several reasons. Generalized violence and a sense of insecurity were major factors of forced migration of the minorities. Communal violence was created mainly due to the persecution of the minorities for their economic location and communal membership. Although a small section of the urban and educated people of the minority communities had migrated to India as 'voluntary migrants' especially with the 'option of transfer' but most of the migrants were 'forced migrants'. They were scattered in different states of India and tried to settle in the new land by their own efforts. However, huge flow of the minorities including the Scheduled Castes was started since the beginning of 1950. Although the Scheduled Castes were the active partner of East Pakistan Government immediately after the partition, they too felt insecure. I have also noticed that the Scheduled Castes of East Pakistan were also migrated to India for their vulnerable economic condition. Economically they received sever challenges with the beginning of fresh competition in their traditional occupations, i.e. the Muslims working force gradually began to enter into the professions hitherto monopolized by the Scheduled Caste workers.

Although in 1948 the United Nations Organization had adopted the Universal Declaration of Human Rights and formed the 'United Nations' High Commission for Refugees' what provided the legal regime for refugee rehabilitation but India inspite of being an independent state could not take bold steps in this regard. The measures taken by the West Bengal and the Union Governments were unplanned in nature since they did neither have any previous experience nor had capability of proper rehabilitation of the refugees. Again we notice discriminatory treatment regarding the rehabilitation. The 'upper caste middle class Hindus' were allowed to stay in such lands of urban and the semi-urban areas of West Bengal which were forcibly acquired popularly called squatters' colonies. The lower Castes on the other hand were encouraged to move towards the remote areas. Fortunes of the agriculturist refugees were again full with diversity. The agriculturist families who took shelter in 24 Parganas, Nadia and Burdwan got more suitable agricultural land whereas the land allotted to the refugees in

Bankura, Birbhum, Midnapur and Jalpaiguri were infertile and almost unsuitable for survival.

Condition of the refugees in Assam and other states of Northeast India was no way better than the refugees who took shelter in West Bengal. However, in case of Tripura the refugees and the voluntary migrants had outnumbered the local people. So in long run a sense of deprivation had developed among the hosts. It was stimulated by the determined attitude of the refugees for survival by any cost. As a consequence, a section of the youths of Northeast India had raised the question of rights of the 'sons-of the soil'. The refugees were branded as foreigner (*bideshi*) and received violent antagonism of the locals. It further generated the forces of re-migration of the refugees towards West Bengal.

In this study I have observed that the experience of the Scheduled Castes as forced migrants especially as 'refugees' and their resettlement in India is something different that the non-Scheduled Caste refugees. Since the Scheduled Castes were not equipped with advanced knowledge other than their traditional profession they did not have any other option but to continue with the same profession in new land. So the Scheduled Caste refugees (except some higher educated persons) were forced to move towards rural and backward areas including forest, riverbed, foothill and hilly land because of their occupational background. Even the West Bengal and the Union Governments had consciously adopted the policy of rehabilitation of the Scheduled Caste refugees in the deep forest, hilly land and islands of remote location. They were sent to infertile tracts of Orissa, Madhya Pradesh and Chhattisgarh; foothill but fertile jungle tract of the Terrai of Uttaranchal; hilly and forest but fertile land of Andaman and Nicobar Islands; and certain other states of India. However, all the settlement sites were not suitable for survival of the refugees. So many refugees left the settlement sites. But when the Dandakaranya-returned refugees entered to Marichjhapi Island of 24 Parganas District in 1978 for resettlement the Government of West Bengal had raised the question of 'animal right', i.e. probable impact of human habitation in the ecology of Sundarban. Here the protection of tiger (animal right) got more priority than the 'human right' (of the refugees) for which the government had adopted the policy of forcible eviction of the refugees. So the atrocity on the Scheduled Castes in Marichjhapi is an ugly episode of history of postcolonial forced migration from East Pakistan and Bangladesh.

Partition of Bengal in 1947 has also generated a tensed situation in a certain part of West Bengal particularly among the host Scheduled Castes. This phenomenon has been clearly noticed in our filed survey carried out in the districts of North Bengal especially among the Rajbanshi Scheduled Castes. The Rajbanshis who were majority in certain districts of North Bengal in pre-partition days gradually lost their prominence in the post partition days due to the huge migration of people from East Pakistan what radically changed the entire socio-economic and political structure of the land. So along with other postcolonial developments in North Bengal the question of huge migration of people from East Bengal has been frequently raised by the sociopolitical organizations of the Rajbanshis. So it contributed to the growth of regionalism in North Bengal.

Inspite of facing atrocities and receiving discriminatory treatment from the Governments and the host society, the Scheduled Castes forced migrants of East Pakistan in long run have placed them as an essential part of West Bengal society. In West Bengal, they are enjoying the reservation facility as enshrined in the constitution of India. It is a noticeable fact that the Scheduled Castes of East Bengal origin are more advanced in West Bengal in terms of their literacy rate and in their presence in the government jobs. Although in other states of India all the Scheduled Caste communities of East Bengal origin have not granted the 'scheduled facilities' but they have successfully developed picturesque villages in the forest lands, riverbeds, or in the place of impregnable geography at the cost of hardship as a means of survival. 'It is a kind victory of history over geography.'

Appendices

APPENDIX 1

FULL TEXT OF THE THIRD JUNE PLAN.

Introduction

1. On February 20th, 1947, His Majesty's Government announced their intention of transferring power in British India to Indian hands by June 1948. His Majesty's Government had hoped that it would be possible for the major parties to cooperate in the working-out of the Cabinet Mission Plan of May 16th, 1946 and evolve for India a Constitution acceptable to all concerned. This hope has not been fulfilled.
2. The majority of the representatives of the Provinces of Madras, Bombay, the United Provinces, Bihar, Central Provinces and Berar, Assam, Orissa and the North-West Frontier Province, and the representatives of Delhi, Ajmer-Merwara and Coorg have already made progress in the task of evolving a new Constitution. On the other hand, the Muslim League Party, including in it a majority of the representatives of Bengal, the Punjab and Sind as

also the representatives of British Baluchistan, has decided not to participate in the Constituent Assembly.

3. It has always been the desire of His Majesty's Government that power should be transferred in accordance with the wishes of the Indian people themselves. This task would have been greatly facilitated if there had been agreement among the Indian political parties. In the absence of such agreement, the task of devising a method by which the wishes of the Indian people can be ascertained has devolved upon His Majesty's Government. After full consultation with political leaders in India His Majesty's Government have decided to adopt for this purpose the plan set out below. His Majesty's Government wishes to make it clear that they have no intention of attempting to frame any ultimate Constitution for India; this is a matter for the Indian themselves. Nor is there anything in this plan to preclude negotiations between communities for a united India.

The Issues to be Decided

4. It is not the intention of His Majesty's Government to interrupt the work of the existing Constituent Assembly. Now that provision is made for certain Provinces specified below, His Majesty's Government trust that, as a consequence of this announcement, the Muslim League representatives of these Provinces, a majority of whose representatives are already participating in it, will now take their due share in its labours. At the same time, it is clear that any Constitution framed by this Assembly cannot apply to those parts of the country which are unwilling to accept it. His Majesty's Government are satisfied that the procedure outlined below embodied the best political method of ascertaining the wishes of the people of such areas on the issue whether their Constitution is to be framed:

a) in the existing Constituent Assembly, or

b)in a new and separate Constituent Assembly consisting of the representatives of those areas which decide not to participate in the existing Constituent Assembly.

When this has been done, it will be possible to determine the authority or authorities to whom power should be transferred.

Bengal and the Punjab

5. The Provincial Legislative Assembly of Bengal and the Punjab (excluding the European members) will, therefore, each be asked to meet in two parts, one representing the Muslim majority districts and the other the rest of the Province. For the purpose of determining the population of districts, the 1941 census figures will be taken as authoritative. The Muslim majority districts in these two Provinces are set out in the appendix to this Announcement.
6. The members of the two parts of each Legislative Assembly sitting separately will be empowered to vote whether or not the Province should be partitioned. If a simple majority of either part decides in favour of partition, division will take place and arrangements will be made accordingly.
7. Before the question as to the partition is decided, it is desirable that the representative of each part should know in advance which Constituent Assembly the Province as a whole would join in the event of the two parts subsequently deciding to remain united. Therefore, if any member of either Legislative Assembly so demands, three shall be held a meeting of all members of the Legislative Assembly (other than Europeans) at which a decision will be taken on the issue as to which Constituent Assembly the Province as a whole would join if it were decided by the two parts to remain united.
8. In the event of partition being decided upon, each part of the Legislative Assembly will, on behalf of the areas they represent, decide which of the alternatives in paragraph 4 above to adopt.

9. For the immediate purpose of deciding on the issue of partition, the members of the Legislative Assemblies of Bengal and the Punjab will sit in two parts according to Muslim majority districts (as laid down in the appendix) and non-Muslim majority districts. This is only a preliminary step of a purely temporary nature as it is evident that for the purposes of a final partition of these Provinces a detailed investigation of boundary questions will be needed; and, as soon as, decision involving partition has been taken for either Province, a Boundary Commission will be set up by the Governor-General, the membership and terms of reference of which will be settled in consultations with those concerned. It will be instructed to demarcate the boundaries of the two parts of the Punjab on the basis of ascertaining the contiguous majority areas of Muslims and non-Muslims. It will also be instructed to take into account other factors. Similar instructions will be given to the Bengal Boundary Commission. Until the report of a Boundary Commission has been put into effect, the provisional boundaries indicated in the appendix will be used.

Sind

10. The Legislative Assembly of Sind (excluding the European members) will at a special meeting also take its own decision on the alternatives in paragraph 4 above.

North West Frontier Province

11. The position of the North-West Frontier Province is exceptional. Two of the three representatives of this Province are already participating in the existing Constituent Assembly. But it is clear, in view of its geographical situation, and other considerations, that if the, whole or any part of the Punjab decides not to join the existing Constituent Assembly, it will be necessary to give the North-West Frontier Province an opportunity to reconsider its position. Accordingly, in such an event,

a referendum will be made to the electors of the present Legislative Assembly in the North-West Frontier Province to choose which of the alternatives mentioned in paragraph 4 above they wish to adopt. The referendum will be held under the aegis of the Governor-General and in consultation with the Provincial Government.

British Baluchistan

12. British Baluchistan has elected a member, but he has not taken his seat in the existing Constituent Assembly. In view of its geographical situation this Province will also be given an opportunity to reconsider its position and to choose which of the alternatives in paragraph 4 above to adopt. His Excellency the Governor-General is examining how this can most appropriately be done.

Assam

13. Though Assam is predominantly a non-Muslim Province, the district of Sylhet which is contiguous to Bengal is predominantly Muslim. There has been a demand that, in the event of the partition of Bengal, Sylhet should be amalgamated with the Muslim part of Bengal. Accordingly, if it is decided that Bengal should be partitioned, a referendum will be held in Sylhet district under the aegis of the Governor-General and in consultation with the Assam Provincial Government to decide whether the district of Sylhet should continue to form part of the Assam Province or should be amalgamated with the new Province of Eastern Bengal, if that Province agrees. If the referendum results in favour of amalgamation with Eastern Bengal, a Boundary Commission with term of reference similar to those for the Punjab and Bengal will be set up to demarcate the Muslim majority areas of Sylhet district and contiguous Muslim majority areas of adjoining districts, which will then be transferred to Eastern Bengal. The rest of the Assam Province will be in any case continue

to participate in the proceedings of the existing Constituent Assembly.

Representation in Constituent Assembly

14. If it is decided that Bengal and the Punjab should be partitioned, it will be necessary to hold fresh elections to choose their representatives on the scale of one for every million of population according to the principle contained in the Cabinet Mission's Plan of May 16th, 1946. Similar elections will also have to be held for Sylhet in the event of it being decided that this district should form part of East Bengal. The Number of representatives to which each area would be entitled is as follows :

Province	*General*	*Muslims*	*Sikhs*	*Total*
Sylhet District	1	2	nil	3
West Bengal	15	4	nil	19
East Bengal	12	29	nil	41
West Punjab	3	12	2	17
East Punjab	6	4	2	12

15. In accordance with the mandates given to them, the representative of the various areas will either join the existing Constituent Assembly or form the new Constituent Assembly.

Administrative Matters

16. Negotiations will have to be initiated as soon as possible on the administrative consequences of any partition that may have been decided upon :

a) Between the representatives of the respective successor authorities about all subjects now dealt with by the Central Government, including Defence, Finance and Communications.

b) Between different successor authorities and His Majesty's Government for treaties in regard to matters arising out of the transfer of power.

c) In the case of Provinces that may be partitioned, as to the administration of all provincial subjects such as the division of assets and liabilities, the police and other services, the High Courts, Provincial Institutions, etc.

The Tribes of the North West Frontier

17. Agreements with tribes of the North-West Frontier of India will have to be negotiated by the appropriate successor authorities.

The States

18. His Majesty's Government wish to make it clear that the decision announced above relate only to British India and that their policy towards Indian States contained in the Cabinet Mission Memorandum of 12th May 1946 remained unchanged.

Necessary for Speed

19. In order that the successor authorities may have time to prepare themselves to take over power, it is important that all the above process should be completed as quickly as possible. To avoid delay, the different Provinces or parts of Provinces will proceed independently as far as practicable within the conditions of this Plan. The existing Constituent Assembly and the new Constituent Assembly (if formed) will proceed to frame Constitutions for their respective territories: they will of course be free to frame their own rules.

Immediate Transfer of Power

20. The major political parties have repeatedly emphasized their desire that there should be the earliest possible transfer of power in India. With this desire His Majesty's Government are in full sympathy, and they are willing

to anticipate the date of June, 1948, for the handling over of power by the setting up of an independent Indian Government or Governments at an even earlier date. Accordingly, as the most expeditious, and indeed the only practicable way of meeting this desire, His Majesty's Government propose to introduce legislation during the current session for the transfer of power this year on a Dominion States basis to one or two successor authorities according to the decisions taken as a result of this announcement. This will be without prejudice to the right of the Indian Constituent Assemblies to decide in due course whether or not the part of India in respect of which they have authority will remain within the British Commonwealth.

Further Announcement by the Governor General

21. His Excellency the Governor-General will from time to time make such further announcements as may be necessary in regard to procedure or any other matters for carrying out the above arrangements.

APPENDIX

The Muslim majority districts of the Punjab and Bengal according to 1941 census.

1. The Punjab:

Lahore Division--Gujranwala, Gurudaspur, Lahore, Sheikhpura, Sialkot

Rawalpindi Division---Attock, Gujrat, Jhelum, Mianwali, Rawalpindi, Shahpur.

Multan Division---Dera Ghazi Khan, Jhang, Lyallpur, Montgomery, Multan, Muzaffargarh.

2. Bengal:

Chittagong Division--- Chittagong, Noakhali, Tippera.

Dacca Division---Bakherganj, Dacca, Faridpur, Mymnesingh.

Rajshahi Division---Bogra, Dinajpur, Malda, Pabna, Rajshahi, Rangpur.

Presidency Division---Jessore, Murshidabad, Nadia.

The Viceroy's House
New Delhi.

APPENDIX 2

THE INDIAN INDEPENDENCE ACT, 1947.

An Act to make provision for the setting up in India of two independent Dominions, to substitute other provisions for certain provisions of the Government of India Act, 1935, which apply outside those Dominions, and to provide for other matters consequential on or connected with the setting up of those Dominions, (18th July 1947).

Be it enacted by the King's most Excellent Majesty, by and with the advice and consent of the Lords Spiritual and Temporal, and Commons, in this present Parliament assembled, and by the authority of the same, as follows:

The New Dominions

1. (1) As from the fifteenth day of August, nineteen hundred and forty-seven, two independent Dominions shall be set up in India, to be known respectively as India and Pakistan.

(2) The said Dominions are hereafter in this Act referred to as 'the new Dominions' and the said fifteenth day of August is hereafter in this Act referred to as 'the appointed day'.

Territories of the New Dominions

2.(1) Subject to the provisions of subsections (3) and (4) of this section, the territories of India shall be the territories under the sovereignty of his Majesty which, immediately before the appointed day, were included in British India except the territories which, under subsection (2) of this section, are to be the territories of Pakistan.

(2) Subject to the provisions of subsection (3) and (4) of this section, the territories of Pakistan shall be —

(a) the territories which, on the appointed day, are included in the Provinces of East Bengal and West Punjab, as constituted under the two following sections;

(b) the territories which, at the date of the passing of this Act. Are included in the Province of Sind and the Chief Commissioner's Province of British Beluchistan; and

(c) if, whether before or after the passing of this Act but before the appointed day, the Governor-General declares that the majority of the valid votes cast in the referendum which, at the date of the passing of this Act, is being or has recently been held in that behalf under his authority in the North-West Frontier Province are in favour of representatives of that Province taking part in the Constituent Assembly of Pakistan, the territories which, at the date of the passing of this Act, are included in that Province.

(3) Nothing in this section shall prevent any area being at any time included or excluded from either of the new Dominions, so, however, that---

(a) no area forming part of the territories specified in subsection (1) or, as the case may be, subsection (2), of this section shall be included in either Dominion without the consent of that Dominion; and

(b) no area which forms part of the territories specified in the said subsection (1) or, as the case may be, the said subsection (2), or which has after the appointed day been included in either Dominion, shall be excluded from that Dominion without the consent of that Dominion.

(4) Without prejudice to the generality of the provisions of subsection (3) of this section, nothing in this section shall be construed as preventing the accession of Indian States to either of the new Dominions.

Bengal and Assam

3.(1) As from the appointed day----

(a) the Province of Bengal, as constituted under the Government of India Act, 1935, shall cease to exist; and

(b) there shall be constituted in lieu thereof two new Provinces, to be known respectively as East Bengal and West Bengal.

(2) If, whether before or after the passing of this Act, but before the appointed day, the Governor-General declares that the majority of the valid votes cast in the referendum which, at the date of the passing of this Act, is being or has recently been held in that behalf under his authority in the District of Sylhet are in favour of that District forming part of the new Province of East Bengal, in accordance with the provisions of subsection (3) of this section, form part of the new Province of East Bengal.

(3) The boundaries of the new Provinces aforesaid and, in the event mentioned in subsection (2) of this section, the boundaries after the appointed day of the Province of Assam, shall be such as may be determined, whether before or after the appointed day, by the award of a boundary commission appointed or to be appointed by the Governor-General in that behalf, but until the boundaries are so determined---

(a) the Bengal Districts specified in the First Schedule to this Act, together with, in the event mentioned in subsection (2) of this section, the Assam District of Sylhet, shall be treated as the territories which are to be comprised in the new Province of East Bengal.

(b) the remainder of the territories comprised at the date of passing of this Act in the Province of Bengal shall be treated as the territories which are to be comprised in the new Province of West Bengal; and

(c) in the event mentioned in subsection (2) of this section, the District of Sylhet shall be excluded from the Province of Assam.

(4) In this section, the expression 'award' means, in relation to a boundary commission, the decision of the Chairman of that commission contained in this report to the Governor-General at the conclusion of the commission's proceedings.

Short Title

This Act may be cited as the Indian Independence Act, 1947.

Schedules

First Schedule

Bengal Districts provisionally included in the new Province of East Bengal

In the Chittagong Division----- the districts of Chittagong, Noakhali and Tippera.

In the Dacca Division---- the districts of Bakarganj, Dacca, Faridpur and Mymensingh.

In the Presidency Division----- the districts of Jessore, Murshidabad and Nadia.

In the Rajshahi Division------ the districts of Bogra, Dinajpur, Malda, Pabna, Rajshahi and Rangpur.

Second Schedule

District provisionally included in the new Province of West Punjab

In the Lahore Division----- the districts of Gujranwala, Gurudaspur, Lahore, Sheikhupura and Sialkot.

In the Rawalpindi Division------the districts of Attock, Gujrat, Jhelum, Mianwali, Rawalpindi and Shahpur.

In the Multan Division-----the districts of Dera Ghazi Khan, Jhang, Lyallpur, Montgomery, Multan and Muzaffargarh.

APPENDIX 3

LETTER OF RESIGNATION OF JOGENDRA NATH MANDAL, MINISTER FOR LAW AND LABOUR, GOVERNMENT OF PAKISTAN, ADDRESSED TO LIAQUAT ALI KHAN, PRIME MINISTER OF PAKISTAN (DATED 8TH OCTOBER 1950)

My dear Prime Minister,

It is with a heavy heart and a sense of utter frustration at the failure of my lifelong mission to uplift the backward Hindu masses of East Bengal that I feel compelled to tender resignation of my membership of your cabinet. It is proper that I should set forth in detail the reasons which have prompted me to take this decision at this important juncture of the Indo-Pakistani subcontinent.

1. Before I narrate the remote and immediate causes of my resignation, it may be useful to give a short background of the important events that have taken place during the period of my co-operation with the League. Having been approached by a few prominent League leaders of Bengal in February 1943, I agreed to work with them in the Bengal Legislative Assembly. After the fall of the Fazlul Haq ministry in March 1943, with a party of 21 Scheduled Caste M. L. A.s I agreed to cooperated with Khwaja Nazimudding, the then leader of the Muslim League Parliamentary Party who formed the Cabinet in April 1943. Our co-operation was conditional on certain specific terms, such as the inclusion of three Scheduled Caste Ministers in the Cabinet, sanctioning of a sum of Rupees five Lakhs as annual recurring grant for the education of the Scheduled Castes, and the unqualified application of the communal ration rules in the matter of appointment of Government services.
2. Apart from these terms, the principal objectives that prompted me to work in co-operation with the Muslim League was, first that the economic interests of the

Muslims in Bengal were generally identical with those of the Scheduled Castes. Muslims were mostly cultivators and labourers, and so were members of the Scheduled Castes. One section of Muslims were fishermen, so was a section of the Scheduled Castes as well, and secondly that the Scheduled Castes and the Muslims were both educationally backward. I was persuaded that my co-operation with the League and its Ministry would lead to the undertaking on a wide scale of legislative and administrative measures which, while promoting the mutual welfare of the vast bulk of Bengal's population, and undermining the foundations of vested interest and privilege, were further the cause of communal peace and harmony. It may be mentioned here that Khwaja Nazimuddin took three Scheduled Caste Ministers in his cabinet and appointed three Parliamentary Secretaries from amongst the members of my community.

Suhrawardy Ministry

3. After the general elections held in March 1946 Mr. H. S. Suhrawardy became the leader of the League Parliamentary Party in March 1946 and formed the League Ministry in April 1946. I was the only Scheduled Caste member returned on the federation ticket. I was included in Mr. Surhawardy's Cabinet. The 16th day of August of that year was observed in Calcutta as 'The Direct Action Day' by the Muslim League. It resulted, as you know, in a holocaust. Hindus demanded my resignation from the League Ministry. My life was in peril. I began to receive threatening letters almost every day. But I remained steadfast to my policy. Moreover, I issued an appeal through our journal 'Jagaran' to the Scheduled Caste people to keep themselves aloof from the bloody feud between the Congress and the Muslim League even at the risk of my life. I cannot but gratefully acknowledge the fact that I was saved from the wrath of infuriated Hindu mobs by my Caste Hindu neighbours. The Calcutta carnage was followed by the 'Noakhali

Riot' in October 1946. There, Hindus including Scheduled Castes were killed and hundreds were converted to Islam. Hindu women were raped and abducted. Members of my community also suffered loss of life and property. Immediately after these happenings, I visited Tipperah and Feni and saw some riot-affected areas. The terrible sufferings of Hindus overwhelmed me with grief, but still I continued the policy of co-operation with the Muslim League. Immediately after the massive Calcutta Killing, a no-confidence motion was moved against the Suhrawardy Ministry. It was only due to my efforts that the support of four Anglo-Indian members and of four Scheduled Caste members of the Assembly who had hitherto been with the Congress could be secured, but for which the Ministry would have been defeated.

4. In October 1946, most unexpectedly came to me through Mr. Suhrawardy the offer of a seat in the Interim Government of India. After a good deal of hesitation and being given only one hour's time to take my final decision, I consented to accept the offer subject to the condition only that I should be permitted to resign if my leader Dr. B. R. Ambedkar disapproved of my action. Fortunately, however, I received his approval in a telegram sent from London. Before I left for Delhi to take over as Law member, I persuaded Mr. Suhrawardy, the then Chief Minister of Bengal, to agree to take two ministers in his Cabinet in my place and to appoint two parliamentary Secretaries from the Scheduled Caste Federation Group.
5. I joined the Interim Government on November 1, 1946. After about a month when I paid a visit to Calcutta, Mr. Suhrawardy apprised me of the communal tension in some parts of East Bengal, especially in Gopalganj Sub-division, where the Namasudras were in majority, being very high. He requested me to visit those areas and address meetings of Muslims and Namasudras. The fact was that Namasudras in those areas had made

preparations for retaliation. I addressed about a dozen of largely attended meetings. The result was that Namasudras gave up the idea of retaliation. Thus an inevitable dangerous communal disturbance was averted.

6. After a few months, the British Government made their June 3 Statement (1947) embodying certain proposals for the partition of India. The whole country, especially the entire non-Muslim India, was startled. For the sake of truth I must admit that I had always considered the demand of Pakistan by the Muslim League as a bargaining counter. Although I honestly felt that in the context of India as a whole Muslims had legitimacy cause for grievance against upper class Hindu chauvinism, I held the view very strongly indeed that the creation of Pakistan would never solve the communal problem. On the contrary, it would aggravate communal hatred and bitterness. Besides, I maintained that it would not ameliorate the condition of Muslims in Pakistan. The incvitable result of the partition of the country would be to prolong, if not perpetuate, the poverty, illiteracy and miserable condition of the toiling masses of both the States. I further apprehended that Pakistan might turn to be one of the most backward and undeveloped countries of the South East Asia.

Lahore Resolution

7. I must make it clear that I had thought that an attempt would be made, as is being done at present, to develop Pakistan as a purely 'Islamic' State based on the Shariat and the injunctions and formulae of Islam. I presumed that it would be set up in all essential after the pattern contemplated in the Muslim League resolution adopted at Lahore on March 23, 1940. That resolution stated inter alia that (I) "geographically contiguous areas are demarcated into regions which should be constituted with such territorial readjustments as may be necessary, that the areas in which the Muslims are numerically in majority as in the north-western and eastern zones

of India, should be grouped to constitute independent States in which the Constituent units shall be autonomous and sovereign" and (II) "adequate, effective and mandatory safeguard should be specifically provided in the Constitution for minorities in these units and in these regions for the protection of their religious, cultural, political, administrative and other rights and interests in consultation with them". Implicitly in this formula were (a) that North Western and Eastern Muslim zones should be constituted into two independent States, (b) that the constituent units of these States should be autonomous and sovereign, (c) that minorities' guarantee should be in respect of rights as well as of interest and extend to every sphere of their lives, and (d) that Constitutional provisions should be made in these regards in consultation with the minorities themselves. I was fortified in my faith in this resolution and the professions of the League Leadership by the statement Qaid-e-Azam Mohammed Ali Jinnah was pleased to make on the 11th August 1947 as the President of the Constituent Assembly giving solemn assurance of equal treatment for Hindus and Muslims alike and calling upon them to remember that they were all Pakistanis. There was then no question of dividing the people on the basis of religion into full-fledged Muslim citizens and zimmies being under the perpetual custody of the Islamic State and its Muslims citizens. Every one of these pledges is being flagrantly violated apparently to your knowledge and with your approval in complete disregard of the Qaid-e-Azam's wishes and sentiments and to the detriment and humiliation of the of the minorities.

Partition of Bengal

8. It may also be mentioned in this connection that I was opposed to the partition of Bengal. In launching a campaign in this regard I had to face not only tremendous resistance from all quarters but also unspeakable abuse, insult and dishonour. With great regret,

I recollect those days when 32 crores of Hindus of this Indo-Pakistan Sub-continent turned their back against me and dubbed me as the enemy of Hindus and Hinduism, but I remained undaunted and unmoved in my loyalty to Pakistan. It is a matter of gratitude that my appeal to 7 million Scheduled Caste people of Pakistan evoked a ready and enthusiastic response from them. They lent me their unstinted support sympathy and encouragement.

9. After the establishment of Pakistan on August 14, 1947 you formed the Pakistan Cabinet, in which I was included and Khwaja Nazimuddin formed a provisional Cabinet for East Bengal. On August 10, I had spoken to Khwaja Nazimuddin at Karachi and requested him to take 2 Scheduled Caste Ministers in the East Bengal Cabinet. He promised to do the same sometime later. What happened subsequently in this regard was a record of unpleasant and disappointing negotiation with you, Khwaja Nazimuddin and Mr. Nurul Amin, the present Chief Minister of East Bengal. When I realized that Khwaja Nazimudding was avoiding the issue on this or that excuse, I became almost impatient and exasperated. I further discussed the matter with the President of the Pakistan Muslim League and its East Bengal Branch. Ultimately, I brought the matter to your notice. You were pleased to discuss the subject with Khwaja Nazimuddin in my presence at your residence. Khwaja Nazimuddin agreed to take one Scheduled Caste Minister on his return to Dacca. As I had already become septic about the assurance of Khwaja Nazimuddin, I wanted to be definite about the time-frame. I insisted that he must act in this regard with a month, failing which I should be at liberty to resign. Both you and Khwaja Nazimuddin agreed to the condition. But alas! You did not perhaps mean what you said, Khwaja Nazimuddin did not keep his promise. After Mr. Nurul Amin had became the Chief Minister of East Bengal, I again took up the matter with him. He also followed the same old familiar tactics of evasion. When I again called your

attention to this matter prior to your visit to Dacca, in 1949you were pleased to assure me that Minority Ministers would be appointed in East Bengal, and you asked 2/3 names from me for consideration. In stat deference to your wish, I sent you a note stating the Federation Group in the East Bengal Assembly and suggesting three names. When I made enquires as to what had happened on your return from Dacca, you appeared to be very cold and only remarked: "Let Nurul Amin return from Delhi". After a few days I again passed the matter. But you avoided the issue. I was then forced to come to the conclusion that neither you not Mr. Nurul Amin had any intention to take any Scheduled Caste Minister in the East Bengal Cabinet. Apart from this, I was noticing that Mr. Nurul Amin and some League leaders of East Bengal were trying to create disruption among the Members of the Scheduled Caste Federation. It appeared to me that my leadership and widespread popularity were considered ominous. My outspokenness, vigilance and sincere efforts to safeguard the interests of the minorities of Pakistan, in general, and of the Scheduled Caste, in particular, were considered a matter on annoyance to the East Bengal Government and few League leaders. Undaunted, I took my firm stand to safeguard the interests of the mionorities of Pakistan.

Anti-Hindu Policy

10. When the question of partition of Bengal arose, the Scheduled Caste people were alarmed at the anticipated dangerous result of partition. Representation on their behalf were made to Mr. Suharwardy, the then Chief Minister of Bengal who was pleased to issue a statement to the press declaring that none of the rights and privileges hitherto enjoyed by the Scheduled Caste People would be curtailed after partition and that they would not only continue to enjoy the existing rights and privileges but also receive additional advantages. This

assurance was given by Mr. Suharwardy not only in his personal capacity but also in his capacity as the Chief Minister of the League Ministry. To my utter regret it is to be stated that after partition particularly after the death of Qaid-e-Azam, the Scheduled Castes have not received a fair deal in any matter. You will recollect that from time to time I brought the grievance of the Scheduled Castes to your notice. I explained to you on several occasions the nature of inefficient administration in East Bengal. I made serious charges against the police administration. I brought to your incidents of barbarous atrocities perpetrated by the police on frivolous grounds. I did not hesitate to bring to your notice the anti-Hindu policy pursued by the East Bengal Government especially the police administration and a section of Muslim League leaders.

Some Incidents

11. The first incident that shocked me took place at a village called Digharkul near Gopalganj where on the false complaint of a Muslim brutal atrocities were committed on the local Namasudras. The fact was that a Muslim who was going in a boat attempted to throw his net to catch fish. A Namasudra who was already there for the same purpose opposed the throwing of the net in his front. This was followed by some alternation and the Muslim got annoyed and went to the nearby Muslim village and made a false complaint that he and a woman in his boat had been assaulted by the Namasudras. At that time, the S.D.O. of Gopalganj was passing in a boat through the canal, who without making any enquiry accepted the complaint as true and sent armed police to the spot to punish the Namasudras. The armed police came and the local Muslims also joined them. They not only raided some houses of the Namasudras but merciless beat both men and women, destroyed their properties and took away valuables. The merciless beating of a pregnant women resulted in

abortion on the spot. This brutal action on the part of the local authority created panic over a large area.

12. The second incidence of police oppression took place in early part of 1949 under P. S. Gournadi in the district of Barisal. Here a quarrel took place between two groups of members of a Union Board. One group which was in the good books of the police conspired against the opponents on the plea of their being Communists. On the information of a threat of attack on the Police Station, the O. C., Gournadi requisitioned armed forces from the headquarters. The Police, helped by the armed forces, then raided a large number of houses in the area, took away valuable properties, even from the house of absentee-owners who were never in politics, far less in the Communist Party. A large number of persons over a wide area were arrested. Teachers and students of many High English Schools were Communist suspects and unnecessarily harassed. This area being very near to my native village, I was informed of the incident. I wrote to the District Magistrate and the S. P. for an enquiry. A section of the local people also prayed for an enquiry by the S. D.O. But no enquiry was held. Even my letters to the District authorities were not acknowledged. I then brought this matter to the notice of the highest Authority in Pakistan, including yourself but to no avail.

Women for Military

13. The atrocities perpetrated by the police and the military on the innocent Hindus, especially the Scheduled Castes of Habibgarh in the District of Sylhet deserve description. Innocent men and women were brutally tortured, some women ravished, their houses raided and properties looted by the police and the local Muslims. Military pickets were posted in the area. The military not only oppressed these people and took away stuff forcibly from Hindu houses, but also forced Hindus to sent their women-folk at night to the camp to satisfy the carnal desires

of the military. This fact also I brought to your notice. You assured me of a report on the matter, but unfortunately no report was forthcoming.

14. Then occurred the incident at the Nachole in the District of Rajshahi where in the name of suppression of Communists not only the police but also the local Muslims in collaboration with the police oppressed the Hindus and looted their properties. The Santhals then crossed the border and came over to West Bengal. They narrated the stories of atrocities wantonly committed by the Muslims and the police.

15. An instance of callous and cold-blooded brutally is furnished by the incident that took place on December 20, 1949 in Kalshira under P. S. Mollarhat in the District of Khulna. What happened was that late at night four constables raided the house of one Joydeb brahma in village Kalshira in search of some alleged Communist. At the scent of the police, half a dozen of young men some of whom might have been Communist, escaped from the house. The police constable entered into the house and assaulted the wife of Joydeb Brahma whose cry attracted her husband and a few companions who escaped from the house. They became desperate, re-entered the house, found 4 constables with one gun only. That perhaps might have encouraged the young men who struck a blow on an armed constable who dies on the spot. The young men then attacked another constable when the other two ran away and raised alarm which attracted some neighbouring people who came to their rescue. As the incident took place before sunrise when it was dark, the assailants fled with the dead body before the villagers could come. The S. P. of Khulna with a contingent of military and armed police appeared on the scene in the afternoon of the following day. In the meantime, the assailants fled and the intelligent neighbours also fled away. But the bulk of the villagers remained in their houses as they were absolutely innocent and failed to realize the consequence of the happening.

Subsequently, the S. P., the military and armed police began to beat mercilessly the innocents of the entire village, encouraged the neighbouring Muslims to take away their properties. A number of persons were killed and men and women were forcibly converted. Household deities were broken and places of worship desecrated and destroyed. Several women were raped by the police, military and local Muslims. Thus a veritable hell was let loose not only in the village of Kalshira which is 1½ miles in length with a large population, but also in a number of neighbouring Namasudra village. The village Kalshira was never suspected by the authority to be a place of Communist activities. Another village called Jhalardanga, which was at a distance of 3 miles from Kalshira, was known to be a centre of Communist activities. This village was raided by a large contingent of police on that day for hunt of the alleged Communists, a number of whom fled away and took shelter in the aforesaid house of village Kalshira which was considered to be a safe place for them.

16. I visited Kalshira and one or two neighbouring villages on the 28th February 1950. The S. P., Khulna and some of the prominent League leaders of the district were with me. When I came to the village Kalshira I found the place desolate and in ruins. I was told in the presence of S. P. that there were 3.50 homesteads in this village, of these, only three had been spared and the rest had been demolished. Country boats and heads of cattle belonging to the Namasudras had been all taken away. I reported those facts to the Chief Minister, Chief Secretary and Inspector of General of Police of East Bengal and to you.

17. It may be mentioned in this connection that the news of this incident was published in West Bengal Press and this created some unrest among the Hindus there. A number of sufferers of Klashira, both men and women, homeless and destitute had also come to Calcutta and narrated the stories of their sufferings which resulted

in some communal disturbances in West Bengal in the last part of January.

Causes of the February Disturbance

18. It must be noted that stories of a few incidents of communal disturbance that took place in West Bengal as a part of repercussion of the incidents at Kalshira were published in exaggerated form in the East Bengal press. In the second week of February 1950 when the Budget Session of the East Bengal Assembly commenced, the Congress Members sought permission to move two adjournment motions to discuss the situation created at Kalshira and Nachole. But the motions were disallowed. The Congress members walked out of the Assembly in protest, this action of the Hindu members of the Assembly annoyed and enraged not only the Ministers but also the Muslim leaders and officials of the Province. This was perhaps one of the principal reasons for Dacca and East Bengal riots in February 1950.

19. It is significant that on February 10, 1950 at about 10 o'clock in the morning a woman was painted with red to show that her breast was cut off in Calcutta riot, and was taken round the East Bengal Secretariat at Dacca. Immediately the Government servants of the Secretariat struck work and came out in procession raising slogans of revenge against the Hindus. The procession began to swell as it passed over a distance of more than a mile. It ended in a meeting at Victoria Park at about 12 o'clock in the noon where violent speeches against the Hindus were delivered by several speakers, including officials. The fun of the whole show was that while the employees of the Secretariat went out of procession, the Chief Secretary of the East Bengal Government was holding a conference with his West Bengal counterpart in the same building to find out ways and means to stop communal disturbances in the two Bengal.

Officials Helped Looters

20. The riot started at about 1 p. m. simultaneously all over the city. Arson, looting of Hindu shops and houses and killing of Hindus, wherever they were found, commenced in full swing in all parts of the city. I got evidence even from the Muslims that arson and looting were committed even in the presence of high police officials. Jewellery shops belonging to the Hindus were looted in the presence of police officers. They not only did not attempt to stop loot, but also helped the looters with advice and direction. Unfortunately for me, I reached Dacca at 5 o'clock in the afternoon on the same day, in February 10, 1950. To my utter dismay, I had occasion to see and know things from close quarters. What I saw and learnt from firsthand information was simply staggering and heart-rending.

Background of the Riot

21. The reasons for the Dacca riot were mainly five :

(i) To punish the Hindus for the daring action of their representatives in the Assembly in their expression of protest by walking out of the Assembly when two adjournment motions on Kalshira and Nachole affairs were disallowed.

(ii) Dissension and differences between the Suhrawardy Group and the Nazimuddin Group in the Parliamentary Party were becoming acute.

(iii) Apprehension of launching of a movement for re-union of East and West Bengal by both Hindu and Muslim leaders made the East Bengal Ministry and the Muslim League nervous. They wanted to prevent such a move. They thought that any large-scale communal riot6 in East Bengal was sure to produce reactions in West Bengal where Muslims might be killed. The result of such riots in both East and West Bengal, it was believed, would prevent any movement for re-union of Bengal.

(iv) Feeling of antagonism between the Bengali Muslims and non-Bengali Muslims in East Bengal was gaining ground. This could only be prevented by creating hatred between Hindus and Muslims of East Bengal. The language question was also connected with it and

(v) The consequences of non-devaluation and the Indo-Pakistan trade deadlock to the economy of East Bengal were being felt most acutely first in urban and rural areas and the Muslim League members and officials wanted to divert the attention of the Muslim masses from the impending economic breakdown by some sort of Jihad against Hindus.

Staggering Details – nearly 10,000 Killed

22. During my nine days' stay at Dacca, I visited most of the riot affected areas of the city and suburbs. I visited Mirpur also under P. S. Tejgaon. The news of the killing of hundreds of innocent Hindus in trains, on railway lines between Dacca and Narayanganj, and of Dacca and Chittagong gave me the rudest shock. On the second day of Dacca riot, I met the Chief Minister of East Bengal and requested him to issue immediate instructions to the District authorities to take all precautionary measures to prevent spreading of the riot in district towns and rural areas. On the 20th February 1950m I reached Barisal town and was astounded to know of the happenings in Barisal. In the district town, a number of Hindu houses were burnt and a large number of Hindus killed. I visited almost all riot-affected areas in the District. I was simply puzzled to find the havoc wrought by the Muslim rioters even at places like Kasipur, Madhabpasha and Lakutia which were within a radius of six miles from the District town and were connected with motorable roads. At the Madhabpasha Zamindar's house, about 200 people were killed and 40 injured. A place, called Muladi, witnessed a dreadful hell. At Muladi Bandar alone, the number killed would total more than three hundred, as were reported to me by the local Muslims including some officers. I visited

Muladi village also, where I found skeletons of dead bodies at some places. I found dogs and vultures eating corpses on the river-side. I got the information there that after the whole-scale killing of all adult males, all the young girls were distributed among the ringleaders of the miscreants. At a place called Kaibartakhali under P.S. Rajapur, 63 persons were killed. Hindu houses within a stone's throw distance from the said thana office were looted, burnt and inmates killed. All Hindu shops of Babuganj Bazar were looted and then burnt and a large number of Hindus were killed. From detailed information received, the conservative estimate of casualties was placed at 2,500 killed in the District of Barisal alone. Total casualties of Dacca and East Bengal riot were estimated to be in the neighbourhood of 10,000killed. The lamentation of women and children who had lost their all including near and dear ones melted my heart. I only asked myself "What was coming to Pakistan in the name of Islam".

No Earnest Desire to Implement Delhi Pact

23. The large scale exodus of Hindus from Bengal commenced in the latter part of March. It appeared that within a short time all the Hindus would migrate to India. A war cry was raised in India. The situation became extremely critical. A national calamity appeared to be inevitable. The apprehended disaster, however, was avoided by the Delhi Agreement of April 8. With a view to reviving the already lost morale of the panicky Hindus, I undertook an extensive tour of East Bengal. I visited a number of places of the district of Dacca, Barisal, Faridpur, Khulna and Jessore. I addressed dozens of largely attended meetings and asked the Hindus to take courage and not to leave their ancestral hearths and homes. I had this expectation that the East Bengal Government and Muslim League leaders would implement the terms of the Delhi Agreement. But with the lapse of time, I began to realize that neither the

East Bengal Government nor the Muslim League leaders were really earnest in the matter of implementation of the Delhi Agreement. The East Bengal Government was not only ready to set up a machinery as envisaged in the Delhi Agreement, but also was not willing to take effective steps for the purpose. A number of Hindus who returned to native village immediately after the Delhi Agreement were not given possession of their homes and lands which were occupied in the meantime by the Muslims.

24. My suspicion about the intention of League leaders was confirmed when I read editorial comments by Moulana Akram Khan, the President of the Provincial Muslim League in the "Baisak" issue of a monthly journal called 'Mohammadi'. In commenting on the first radio-broadcast of Dr. A. M. Malik, Minister for Minority Affairs of Pakistan, from Dacca Radio Station, wherein, he said, "Even Prophet Mohammed had given religious freedom to the Jews in Arabia", Moulana Akram Khan said, "Dr. Malik would have done well had he not made any reference in his speech to the Jews of Arabia. It is true that the Jews in Arabia had been given religious freedom by Prophet Mohammed; but it was the first chapter of the history. The last chapter contains the definite direction of prophet Mohammed which runs as follows : "Drive away all the Jews out of Arabia". Even despite this editorial comment of a person who held a very high position in the political, social and spiritual life of the Muslim community, I entertained some expectation that the Nurul Amin Ministry might not be so insincere. But that expectation of mine was totally shattered when Mr. Nurul Amin selected D. N. Barari as a Minister to represent the minorities in terms of the Delhi Agreement which clearly states that to restore confidence in the minds of the minorities one of their representatives will be taken in the Ministry of East Bengal and West Bengal Government.

Nurul Amin Government's Insincerity

25. In one of my public statement, I expressed the view that the appointment of D. N. Barari as a Minister representing the minorities not only did not help restore any confidence, but, on the contrary, destroyed all expectations illusions, if there was any in the minds of the minorities about the sincerity of Mr. Nurul Amin's Government. My own reaction was that Mr. Nurul Amin's government was no only insincere but also wanted to defeat the principal objectives of the Delhi Agreement. I again repeat that D. N. Barari does not represent anybody except himself. He was returned to the Bengal Legislature Assembly on the Congress ticket with the money and organization of the Congress. He opposed the Scheduled Caste Federation candidates. Some time after his election, he betrayed the Congress and joined the Federation. When he was appointed a Minister he had ceased to be a member of the Federation too. I know that East Bengal Hindus agree with me that by antecedents, character and intellectual attainments Barari is not qualified to hold the position of a Minister as envisaged in the Delhi Agreement.

26. I recommended three names to Mr. Nurul Amin for this office. One of the persons I recommended was an M.A., L.L.B., Advocate, Dacca High Court. He was Minister for more than 4 years in the first Fazlul Haq Ministry in Bengal. He was chairman of the Coal Mines Stowing Board, Calcutta, for about 6 years. He was the senior Vice-President of the Scheduled Caste Federation. My second nominee was B.A., L.L.B. he was a member of the Legislative Council for 7 years in the pre-reform regime. I would like to know what earthly reasons there might be for Mr. Nurul Amin in not selecting any of these two gentlemen and appointing instead a person whose appointment as Minister I strongly objected to for very rightly considerations. Without any fear of contradiction I can say that this action of Mr.

Nurul Amin in selecting Barari as a Minister in terms of the Delhi Agreement is conclusive proof that the East Bengal Government was neither serious nor sincere in its professions about the terms of the Delhi Agreement whose main purpose is to create such conditions as would enable the Hindus to continue to live in East Bengal with a sense of security to their life, property, honour and religion.

Government Plan to Squeeze out Hindus

27. I would like to reiterate in this connection my firm conviction that East Bengal Government is still following the well-planned policy of squeezing Hindus out of the Province. In my discussion with you on more than one occasion, I gave expression to this view of mine. I must say that this policy of driving out Hindus from Pakistan has succeeded completely in West Pakistan and is nearing completion in East Pakistan too. The appointment of D. N. Barari as a Minister and the East Bengal government's unceremonious objection to my recommendation in this regard strictly conform to name of what they call an Islamic State. Pakistan has not given the Hindus entire satisfaction and a full sense of security. They now want to get rid of the Hindu intelligentsia so that the political, economic and social life of Pakistan may not in any way be influenced by them.

Evasive Tactics to Shelve Joint Electorate

28. I have failed to understand why the question of electorate has not yet been decided. It is now three years that the minority sub-committee has been appointed. It sat on three occasions. The question of having joint or separation electorate came up for consideration at a meeting of the Committee held in December last when all the representatives of recognized minorities in Pakistan expressed their view in support of Joint Electorate with reservation of seats for backward minorities. We, on

behalf of the Scheduled Castes, demanded joint electorate with reservation of seats for Scheduled Castes. This matter again came up for consideration at a meeting called in August last. But without any discussion whatsoever on this point, the meeting was adjourned sine die. It is not difficult to understand what the motive is behind this kind of evasive tactics in regard to such a vital matter on the part of Pakistan's rulers.

Dismal Future for Hindus

29. Coming now to the present condition and the future of Hindus in East Bengal as a result of the Delhi Agreement, I should say that the present condition is not only unsatisfactory but absolutely hopeless and that the future completely dark and dismal. Confidence of Hindus in East Bengal has not been restored in the least. The Agreement is treated as a mere scrap of paper alike by the East Bengal government and the Muslim League. That a pretty large number of Hindus migrants, mostly Scheduled Caste cultivators are returning to East Bengal is no indication that confidence has been restored. It only indicates that their stay and rehabilitation in West Bengal or elsewhere in the Indian Union have not been possible. The sufferings of refugee life are compelling them to go back to their homes. Besides, many of them are going to bring movable articles and settle or dispose of immovable properties. That no serious communal disturbance has recently taken place in East Bengal is not to be attributed to the Delhi Agreement. It could not simply continue even if there were no Agreement or Pact.

30. It must be admitted that the Delhi Pact was not an end in itself. It was intended that such conditions would be created as might effectively help resolve so many disputes and conflict existing between India and Pakistan. But during this period of six months after the Agreement, no dispute or conflict has really been resolved. On the contrary, communal propaganda and anti-India propaganda

by Pakistan both at home and abroad are continuing in full swing. The observance of Kashmir Day by the Muslim League all over Pakistan is an eloquent proof of communal anti-India propaganda by Pakistan. The recent speech of the governor of Punjab (Pak) saying that Pakistan needed a strong Army for the security of Indian Muslims has betrayed the real attitude of Pakistan towards India. It will only increase the tension between the two countries.

What is Happening in East Bengal Today

31. What is today the condition in East Bengal? About fifty lakhs of Hindus have left since the partition of the country. Apart from the East Bengal riot of last February, the reasons for such a large scale exodus of Hindus are many. The boycott by the Muslims of Hindu Lawyers, medical practitioners, shop-keepers, traders and merchants has compelled Hindus to migrate to West Bengal in search of their means of livelihood. Wholesales requisition of Hindu houses even without following due process of law in many and non-payment of any rent whatsoever to the owners have compelled them to seek for Indian shelter. Payment of rent to Hindu landlords was stopped long before. Besides, the Ansars against whom I received complaints all over are a standing menace to the safety and security of Hindus. Interference in matters of education and methods adopted by the Education Authority for Islamisation frightened the teaching staff of Secondary Schools and Colleges out of their old familiar moorings. They have left East Bengal. As a result, most of the educational institutions have been closed. I have received information that sometime ago the Educational Authority issued circular in Secondary Schools enjoying compulsory participation of teachers and students of all communities in relation from the Holy Koran before the school work commenced. Another circular requires headmasters of schools to name the different blocks of the premises

after 12 distinguished Muslims, such as Jinnah, Iqbal, Liaquat ali, Nazimuddin etc. Only very recently in an educational conference held at Dacca, the President disclosed that out of 1,500 High English Schools in East Bengal, only 500 were working. Owing to the migration of Medical Practitioners there is hardly any means of proper treatment of patients. Almost all the priests who used to worship the household deities at Hindu houses have left. Important places of worship have been abandoned. The result is that the Hindus of East Bengal have got now hardly any means to follow religious pursuits and performance of social ceremonies like marriage where the services of a priest are essential Artisans who made images of gods and goddesses have also left. Hindu Presidents of Union Boards have been replaced by Muslims by coercive measures with the active help and connivance of the police and Circle Officers. Hindu headmasters and Secretaries of Schools have been replaced by Muslims. The life of the few Hindu government servants has been made extremely miserable as many of them have either been superseded by junior Muslims or dismissed without sufficient or any cause. Only very recently a Hindu Public Prosecutor of Chittagong was arbitrarily removed from service as has been made clear in a statement made by Srijukata Nelie Sengupta against whom at least no change of anti-Muslim bias prejudice or malice can be leveled.

Hindus Virtually Outlawed

32. Commission of thefts and dacoities even with murder is going on as before. Thana offices seldom record half the complaints made by the Hindus. That the abduction and rape of Hindu girls have been reduced to a certain extent is due only to the fact that there is no Caste Hindu girl between the ages of 12 and 30 living in East Bengal at present. The few depressed class girls who live in rural areas with their parents are not even spared by Muslim goondas. I have received information

about a number of incidents of rape of Scheduled Caste Girls by Muslims. Full payment is seldom made by Muslims buyers for the price of jute and other agricultural commodities sold by Hindus in market places. As a matter of fact, there is no operation of law, justice or fair-play in Pakistan, so far as Hindus are concerned.

Forced Conversions in West Pakistan

33. Leaving aside the question of East Pakistan let me now refer to West Pakistan, especially Sind. The West Punjab had after partition about a lakh of Scheduled Castes people. It may be noted that a large number of them were converted to Islam. Only 4 out of a dozen Scheduled Castes girls abducted by Muslims have yet been recovered in spite of repeated petitions to the Authority. Names of those girls with names of their abductors were supplied to the government. The last reply recently given by the Officer-in-Charge of recovery of abducted girls said that "his function was to recover Hindu girls and 'Achhuts' (Scheduled Castes) were not Hindus". The condition of the small number of Hindus that are still living in Sind and Karachi, the capital of Pakistan, is simply deplorable. I have got a list of 363 Hindu temple and gurdwars of Karachi and Sind (which is by no means an exhaustive list) which are still possession of Muslims. Some of the temples have been converted into cobbler's shops, slaughter houses and hotels. None of the Hindus has got back possession of their landed properties which were taken away from them without any notice and distributed amongst refugees and local Muslims. I personally know that 200 to 300 Hindus were declared non-evacuees by the custodian a pretty long time ago. But up till now properties have no been restored to any one of them. Even the possession of Karachi Pinjirapole has not been restored to the trustees, although it was declared non-evacuees property sometime ago. In Karachi I had received petitions from many unfortunate fathers and husbands of abducted

Hindu girls, mostly Scheduled Castes. I drew the attention of the 2nd Provisional government to this fact. There was little or no effect. To my extreme regret I received information that a large number of Scheduled Castes who are still living in Sind have been forcibly converted to Islam.

Pakistan 'Accursed' for Hindus

34. Now this being in brief the overall picture of Pakistan so far as the Hindus are concerned, I shall not be unjustified in stating that Hindus of Pakistan have to all intents and purposes been rendered "Stateless" in their own houses. The have no other fault than that they profess the Hindu religion. Declarations are being repeatedly made by Muslim League leaders that Pakistan is and shall be an Islamic state. Islam is being offered as the sovereign remedy for all earthly evils. In the matchless dialectics of capitalism and socialism you present the exhilarating democratic synthesis of Islam equally and fraternity. In that grand setting of the Shariat Muslims alone are rulers while Hindus and other minorities are zimmies who are entitled to protection at price, and you know more than anybody else Mr. Prime Minister, what that price is. After anxious and prolonged struggle I have come to the conclusion that Pakistan is no place for Hindus to live in and that their future is darkened by the ominous shadow of conversion or liquidation. The bulk of the upper class Hindus and politically conscious scheduled castes have left East Bengal. Those Hindus who will continue to stay accursed in Pakistan will, I am afraid, by gradual stages and in a planned manner be either converted to Islam or completely exterminated. It is really amazing that a man of your education, culture and experience should be an exponent of a doctrine fraught with so great a danger to humanity and subversive of all principles of equality and good sense. I may tall you and your fellow workers that Hindus will not allow themselves, whatever the treat or

temptation, to be treated as Zimmies in the land of their birth. Today they may, as indeed many of them have already done, abandon their hearths and homes in sorrow but in panic. Tomorrow they strive for their rightful place in the economy of life. Who knows what is in the womb of the future ? when I am convinced that my continuance in office in the Pakistan Central Government is not of any help to Hindus I should not with a clear conscience, create the false impression in the minds of the Hindus of Pakistan and peoples abroad that Hindus can live therer with honour and with a sense of security in respect of their life, property and religion. This is about Hindus.

No Civil Liberty Even For Muslims

35. And what about the Muslims who are outside the charmed circle of the League rulers and their corrupt and inefficient bureaucracy? There is hardly anything called civil liberty in Pakistan. Witness for example, the fate of Khan Abdul Ghaffar Khan than whom a more devout Muslim had not walked this earth for many years and of his gallant patriotic brother Dr. Khan Sahib. A large number of erstwhile League leaders of the Northwest and also of the Eastern belt of Pakistan are in detention without trial. Mr. Suhrawardy to whom is due in a large measure the League's triumph in Bengal is for practical purpose a Pakistani prisoner who has to move under permit and open his lips under orders. Mr. Fazlul Haq, that dearly loved grand old man of Bengal, who was the author of that now famous Lahore resolution, is ploughing his lonely furrow in the precincts of the Dacca High Court of Judicature, and the so called Islamic planning is as ruthless as it is complete. About the East Bengal Muslims in general, the less said the better. They were promised of autonomous and sovereign units of the independent State. What have they got instead? East Bengal has been transformed into a colony of the western belt of Pakistan, although it

contained a population which is larger than that of all the units of Pakistan put together. It is a pale ineffective adjunct of Karachi doing the latter's bidding and carrying out its orders. East Bengal Muslims in their enthusiasm wanted bread and they have by the mysterious working of the Islamic State and the Shariat got stone instead from the arid deserts of Sind and the Punjab.

My Own Sad and Bitter Experience

36. Leaving aside the overall picture of Pakistan and the callous and cruel injustice done to others, my own personal experience is no less sad, bitter, and revealing. You used your position as the Prime Minister and leader of the Parliamentary Party to ask me to issue a statement, which I did on the 8th September last. You know that I was not willing to make a statement containing untruths and half truths, which were worse that untruths. It was not possible for me to reject your request so long as I was there working as a Minister with you and under your leadership. But I can no longer afford to carry this load of false pretensions and untruth on my conscience and I have decided to offer my resignation as your Minister, which I am hereby placing in your hands and which, I hope, you will accept without delay. You are of course at liberty to dispense with that office or dispose of it in such a manner as may suit adequately and effectively the objectives of your Islamic State.

Yours sincerely,

Sd./-J.N. Mandal

8th October 1950

APPENDIX 4

CASTE-WISE DISTRIBUTION OF THE SCHEDULED CASTE POPULATION IN WEST BENGAL (1961-2001).

Caste	*1961*	*1971*	*1981*	*1991*	*2001*
All Scheduled Castes	6890314	8816028	12000768	16080611	18452555
Bagdi	10968851	1291127	1831565	2354609	2740385
Bahelia	1263	2189	4602	7921	5124
Baiti	8269	7410	10034	14691	12408
Banter	435	637	2086	5452	753
Bauri	501269	624077	732205	950692	1091022
Beldar	1795	1682	1829	4727	4213
Bhokta	987	333	13807	16425	15478
Bhuimali	39181	45059	47521	678887	81103
Bhuiya	53329	58453	93411	120377	127199
Bind	22924	20772	34028	45067	51828
Chamar	396591	507759	711024	924547	995756
Chaupal	523	655	2515	8312	6375
Dabgar	72	93	460	1599	140
Damai(Nepali)	11486	11553	18842	23367	17387
Dhoba	154791	191063	251737	339555	369808
Doai	14191	4770	8054	10232	5089
Dom	151818	174367	231595	283691	316337
Doshad	25835	32072	39284	55005	62258
Ghasi	11941	16494	17411	21670	15881
Gonrhi	13859	12153	14832	2389	1437
Halalkhor	326	479	1348	2389	1437
Hari	125880	161357	267465	360736	390619
Jalia Kaibarta	117384	204679	318344	442783	409303
Jhalo Malo	68757	89918	150557	220306	293714
Kadar	5610	7400	9782	15657	25350
Kami(Nepali)	26148	31590	42493	56212	49704
Kandra	25430	42294	65183	80131	92364
Kanjhar	1417	1219	1067	1849	279
Kaorah	117929	145442	180912	249400	263731

Karenga	11332	12388	21129	27016	33563
Kaur	2394	5841	20860	23670	11384
Keyot	23174	24397	45282	60704	74078
Khaira	67913	63513	77605	89970	111967
Khatik	2716	1425	4862	12577	9050
Koch	3522	17257	9714	14844	12727
Konai	43101	59223	71423	90023	108795
Konwar	3895	1469	2841	5486	4779
Kotal	7700	15537	19310	22606	25052
Kurariar	772	164	1416	1555	837
Lalbegi	845	1384	1179	136	561
Lohar	83545	103033	151609	219798	279582
Mahar	6760	12221	17706	23630	28419
Mal	117704	158419	204775	230638	273641
Mallah	12366	21596	38103	49415	51501
Musahar	13058	12426	17628	22804	22332
Namasudra	729057	980524	1692233	2581549	3212393
Not	899	74	3376	3880	178
Nuniya	17561	21531	41531	48971	56888
Palia	73997	100571	116719	133806	130817
Pan	3370	3690	9328	15319	23032
Pasi	13881	20478	21367	28378	25460
Patni	6288	12781	22466	29515	30429
Pod	875525	975352	1536197	1985243	2216513
Rajbanshi	1201717	1353919	2258760	2839481	3386617
Rajwar	41133	53168	85374	110176	99562
Sarki(Nepali)	5232	5337	11292	16909	11111
Sunri(Except Saha)	106870	166418	152331	329770	31753
Tiyar	39633	79786	82106	159499	195340
Turi	19048	23190	28443	39908	38738

Source: Population census in India (1961-2001 Years).

APPENDIX 5

DISTRIBUTION OF THE SCHEDULED CASTES IN DIFFERENT DISTRICTS OF WEST BENGAL 2001.

Country /State/ District	*Types*	*Person*	*Male*	*Female*
INDIA	Total	166635700	86088760	80546940
	Rural	133010878	68603342	64407536
	Urban	33624822	17485418	16139404
WEST BENGAL	Total	18452555	9469659	8982896
	Rural	15524925	7950837	7574088
	Urban	2927630	1518822	1408808
Darjeeling	Total	258881	132858	126023
	Rural	207422	106352	101070
	Urban	51459	26506	24953
Jalpaiguri	Total	1248577	642828	605749
	Rural	1124404	578943	545461
	Urban	124173	63885	60288
Koch Bihar	Total	1242374	636446	605928
	Rural	1197449	613853	583596
	Urban	44925	22593	22332
Uttar Dinajpur	Total	676582	348693	327889
	Rural	623649	320785	302864
	Urban	52933	27908	25025
Dakshin Dinajpur	Total	432660	222063	210597
	Rural	397599	204008	193591
	Urban	35061	18055	17006
Maldah	Total	554165	284726	269439
	Rural	518987	266759	252228
	Urban	35178	17967	17211
Murshidabad	Total	703786	360734	343052
	Rural	610729	313445	297284
	Urban	93057	47289	45768
Birbhum	Total	889894	456719	433175
	Rural	830700	426868	403832
	Urban	59194	29851	29343

Barddhaman	Total	1860754	954951	905803
	Rural	1384945	707681	677264
	Urban	475809	247270	228539
Nadia	Total	1365985	700622	665363
	Rural	1128190	579378	548812
	Urban	237795	121244	116551
24 Parganas(N)	Total	1840397	949294	891103
	Rural	1208661	622536	586125
	Urban	631736	326758	304978
Hugli	Total	1188881	601232	587649
	Rural	981740	493762	487978
	Urban	207141	107470	99671
Bankura	Total	997408	506868	490540
	Rural	943745	479898	463847
	Urban	53663	26970	26693
Puruliya	Total	463956	237724	226232
	Rural	408706	209575	199131
	Urban	55250	28149	27101
Medinipur	Total	1576337	801964	774373
	Rural	1453133	739229	713904
	Urban	123204	62735	60469
Haora	Total	658707	335761	322946
	Rural	465837	235172	230665
	Urban	192870	100589	92281
Kolkata	Total	274835	150866	123969
	Rural	0	0	0
	Urban	274835	150866	123969
24 Parganas (S)	Total	2218376	1145310	1073066
	Rural	2039029	1052593	986436
	Urban	179347	92717	86630

APPENDIX 6

PERCENTAGE TO THE TOTAL POPULATION OF THE SCHEDULED CASTES OF WEST BENGAL 1991 AND 2001.

Country/State/ District	*Total person 1991*	*Male 1991*	*Female 1991*	*Total person 2001*	*Male 2001*	*Female 2001*
India	16.48	16.53	16.44	16.20	16.18	16.22
Rural	18.04	18.16	17.91	17.91	17.98	17.85
Urban	11.99	11.92	12.07	11.75	11.61	11.91
West Bengal	23.62	23.45	23.81	23.02	22.84	23.21
Rural	27.56	27.59	27.53	26.88	26.85	26.92
Urban	13.23	12.99	13.51	13.05	12.82	13.32
Darjiling	16.15	16.12	16.18	16.09	15.99	16.19
Rural	18.14	18.24	18.03	19.05	19.11	18.99
Urban	11.59	11.43	11.77	9.89	9.67	10.13
Jalpaiguri	36.99	37.10	36.87	36.71	36.71	36.71
Rural	39.33	39.52	39.11	40.24	40.28	40.19
Urban	25.06	24.82	25.32	20.46	20.35	20.58
Koch Bihar	51.76	51.71	51.80	50.11	50.03	50.20
Rural	54.51	54.47	54.55	53.14	53.04	53.23
Urban	19.25	18.83	19.69	19.91	19.67	20.16
N Dinajpur	29.04	29.04	29.04	27.71	27.68	27.74
Rural	31.19	31.23	31.14	29.04	29.05	29.03
Urban	15.09	15.20	14.95	17.98	17.95	18.01
S Dinajpur	28.98	29.06	28.90	28.78	28.83	28.74
Rural	31.11	31.21	31.01	30.44	30.46	30.41
Urban	15.13	15.09	15.17	17.81	17.96	17.66
Maldah	18.12	18.18	18.06	16.84	16.85	16.83
Rural	18.46	18.53	18.38	17.02	17.04	17.00
Urban	13.74	13.62	13.86	14.60	14.52	14.69
Murshidabad	13.40	13.44	13.35	12.00	12.00	11.99
Rural	13.01	13.06	12.95	11.90	11.90	11.89
Urban	16.74	16.75	16.73	12.70	12.72	12.68
Birbhum	30.68	30.72	30.63	29.51	29.53	29.49
Rural	31.34	31.44	31.24	30.13	30.19	30.07

Urban	23.96	23.53	24.41	22.91	22.52	23.31
Barddhaman	27.44	27.05	27.89	26.98	26.61	27.39
Rural	32.11	31.92	32.32	31.85	31.60	32.11
Urban	18.80	18.47	19.20	18.68	18.33	19.08
Nadia	29.01	29.11	28.91	29.66	29.60	29.73
Rural	30.87	30.94	30.80	31.12	31.02	31.22
Urban	22.66	22.76	22.55	24.28	24.29	24.26
24 Pargans(N)	21.49	21.35	21.64	20.60	20.46	20.74
Rural	30.63	30.76	30.50	29.60	29.61	29.59
Urban	12.78	12.66	12.91	13.02	12.88	13.18
Hugli	24.12	23.76	24.50	23.58	23.22	23.96
Rural	29.14	28.93	29.37	29.27	29.05	29.50
Urban	13.02	12.86	13.20	12.27	12.08	12.49
Bankura	31.37	31.24	31.51	31.24	30.98	31.51
Rural	31.97	31.86	32.08	31.91	31.67	32.17
Urban	24.75	24.41	25.12	22.81	22.37	23.27
Puruliya	19.35	19.41	19.29	18.29	18.31	18.27
Rural	19.14	19.26	19.01	17.92	17.99	17.84
Urban	21.37	20.82	21.99	21.63	21.16	22.14
Medinipur	16.34	16.28	16.41	16.40	16.31	16.50
Rural	16.64	16.62	16.66	16.84	16.77	16.92
Urban	13.64	13.29	14.03	12.52	12.34	12.72
Haora	15.79	15.35	16.29	15.42	14.98	15.90
Rural	22.08	21.91	22.26	21.96	21.71	22.23
Urban	9.40	9.09	9.77	8.96	8.68	9.29
Kolkata	6.45	6.53	6.34	6.01	6.03	5.98
Rural	-	-	-	-	-	-
Urban	6.45	6.53	6.34	6.01	6.03	5.98
24 Parganas(S)	34.45	34.42	34.49	32.12	32.13	32.11
Rural	37.04	37.13	36.95	35.03	35.12	34.94
Urban	17.55	17.27	17.87	16.51	16.33	16.71

Bibliography

Bengali

Adhikary, Hari Kishor: *Rajbanshi Kulapradip*, 1314, B.S.

Bandyopadhyay, Hiranmoy: *Udvastu*, Calcutta, Sahitya Samsad, 1970.

Bandyopadhyay, Sandip: *Deshbhag: Smriti ar Sattwa*, Kolkata, Progressive Publishers, 1999.

Barma, Panchanan: *Raysaheb Panchanan Rachanbali*, edited and compiled by Ramendranath Adhikary, Cooch Behar, 1398, B.S.

Barman, Kalindra Nath: *Ekti Birat Giggasa: Ora Bahe Na Bangali?*, Siliguri, Panchanan Ashram, 1377, B.S.

Barman, Rup Kumar: Adwaita Katha Sahitye Samajchitra: Bahu Kaunik Dristite, in Susanta Haldar (ed): *Bhasaman-5*, Kolkata, Adwaita Malla Barman Educational and Cultural Society, 2003, pp.104-115.

————:Jati Parichiti Gathan, Uttaran O Elite Netritya, in *Itihas Anusandhan 18*, Kolkata, West Bengal History Council, 2004.

————: Malo Samajer Atmachetana O Adwaita Malla Barman,

in Susanta Haldar (ed): *Bhasaman-8*, Kolkata, Adwaita Malla Barman Educational and Cultural Society, 2006, pp.34-39.

————: Jaldushan O Matsyajibi, in Susanta Haldar (ed): *Bhasaman*-6, Kolkata, Adwaita Malla Barman Educational and Cultural Society, 2004, pp 22-28.

Barman, Upendra Nath: *Sekaler Uttar Bangla O Amar Jiban Smriti*, Jalpaiguri, 1985.

————: *Rajbanshi Kshatriya Jatir Itihas*, 4th edn, Jalpaiguri, 1401 B.S.

Basu, Dakshinaranjan (comp. and ed.): *Chhere Asha Gram*, Calcutta, Jignasa, 1975.

Basu, Nirmal Kumar: *Satchallisher Diary*, edited by Abhik Kumar Dey, Kolkata, Punascha, 2009.

Biswas, Nitish: *Nainitaler Pathe Pathe*, Kolkata, Aiktan Gabeshana Samsad, 2002.

Chakraborti, Tridib, Ray Mandal, Nirupama and Ghosal, Poulami (compiled and edited): *Dhvangsa O Nirnam: Bangiya Udvastu Samajer Svakathitha Bibaran*, Kolkata, Seriban, 2007.

Dakua, Dinesh: *Kamtapuri Andolan Ekti Jana Bichhinna Andolan*, Calcutta, National Book Agency Pvt. Ltd, 2003.

Das, Brajanath Das: *Jhalla Malla Kshatriya Itihas*, Dacca, date not found.

Das Ray, Sashi Bhusan : *Jyoty*, Dacca, date not found.

Dutta, Debabratta: *Vijagarh Ekti Udvastu Upanibesh*, Kolkata, Progressive Publishers, 2001.

Dutta, Harsha (ed): *Bish Sataker Bangali Jiban o Samskriti*, Kolkata, Pustak Bipani.

Dutta Ray, Sacchidananda: *Paschim Bange Sikshaya Agragati: Parisankhan Alochna,* Kolkata, Seriban, 2008.

Halder, Niranjan: *Marichjhapi*, Calcutta, 1986.

Kavya Bhusan, Maniram: *Rajvanshi Kshatriya Dipak*, 1318, B.S.

————: *Paundra Kshatriya Kula Dipana*, 1319, B.S.

Kundu, Tridip Santapa : Bangali nari jibane deshbhager prabhab, in Chattopadhyay, Goutam (ed.), *Itihas Anusandhan*, Vol. 13,Kolkata,Farma K.L.M.Pvt. Ltd., 1999, pp.589-599.

————: Bardhakye Bastuchyuti: Bangalay desbhagjanita durbhoger ekti dik, in Chattopadhyay, Goutam (ed.): *Itihas Anusandhan, vol. 15*, Kolkata, Farma K.L.M.Pvt. Ltd., 2001, pp.392-397.

————: Chhinnamul Chhelebela: Bangalay deshbhagjanita paristhitir ekti dik, in Chattopadhyay, Goutam (ed.), *Itihas Anusandhan, Vol.14,* Kolkata, Farma K.L.M.Pvt. Ltd., 2000, pp. 296-293.

Malla Barman, Adwaita : *Titas Ekti Nadir Nam* , in *Adwaita Malla Barman Rachana Sangraha,* edited by Achintya Biswas, Kolkata, Deys Publishing, 2000, also *A River Called Titas*, an English translation by Kalpana Bardhan, New York, Penguin Books, 1992.

Malla Barman, Dharmachand: *Sanschipta Jhalla Malla Kshatriya Tatta*, Dacca, 1923.

Malla Barman, Mahendra Nath: *Dwitiya Varna Kshatriya*, Mymensingh, 1914.

————: *Sanschipta Kshatriya Tatta*, Dacca, 1923.

Malla Barman, Mahim Chandra: *Jhalla Malla Parichaya*, Mymensingh, 1331, B.S.

Mandal, Jagadish Chandra: *Marichjhapi: Naisabder Antarale*, Kolkata, Sujan Publications, 2002.

Mondal, Sibendra Narayan: *Rajbanshi Kshatriya Jatir Sanschipta Itihas*, Gauripur, India Press, 1972.

Pal, Madhumay(ed); *Marichjhapi: Chinnadesh, Chhinna Itihas*, Kolkata, Gangchil, 2009.

Phukan, Haliram Dhekial: *Assam Buranji,* edited by Jatindra Mahun Bhattacharjee, Guwahati, Mokshada Pustakalay, 1369, B.S.

Pramanik, Mrityunjoy: *Banglabibhagottar Udvastu Itihas Charchar Prekshite Marichjhapi,* Unpublished M.Phil. Dissertation, Jadavpur University, 2010.

Sarkar, Naresh Chandra (ed.): *Mukur 2.1*(6 January, 1990).

Singha, Kshetra Nath Singha: *Roy Saheb Panchanan Barmar Jibani Ba Rangpur Kshatriya Samitir Itihas*, Rangpur, 1940.

Sanskrit

Brihaddharmma Purana, edited by Panchanan Tarkaratna, 2nd ed., Calcutta, Bangabasi Electro-machine Press, 1314 B.S.

English

Alavi, Hamza: Misreading Partition Road Signs, *Economic and Political Weekly* (November 2-9, 2002), pp. 4515-4523.

Albiruni, A.H.: *Makers of Pakistan and Modern Muslim India*, Lahore, Muhammad Ashraf, 1950.

Ansari, Sarah: *Life after Partition: Migration, Community and Strife in Sindh, 1947–1962*, Oxford University Press, 2005.

Bagchi, Jasodhara and Dasgupta, Subhoranjan (eds): *The Trauma and the Triumph: Gender and Partition in Eastern India*, Kolkata, Stree, 2003.

Bahadur, Lal: *Struggle for Pakistan: Tragedy of the Triumph of the Muslim Communalism in India 1906-1947*, New Delhi, Sterling, 1988.

Bakshi, S.R.: *Congress, Muslim League, and Partition of India*, New Delhi, Deep & Deep Publications, 1990.

Bandyopadhyay, D.: Land Reforms in West Bengal: Remembering Harekrishna Konar and Benoy Choudhury, *EPW*, XXXV, no.21 and 21(7th May 2000).

————: Tebhaga Movement in Bengal: A Retrospect, *EPW*, Vol.36 No 1 (October 13-19, 2001).

Bandyopadhyay, Sandip: 'Partition and the Forgotten People', *Frontier*, 2-8 August 1997.

————: The Riddles of Partition: Memories of Bengali Hindus' in Ranabir Samaddar (ed.): *Reflections on Partition in the East*, Delhi, Vikas Publishing House, 1997.

————: Million Seeking Refuge: The Refugee Question in West Bengal, 1971, in Pradip Kumar Bose (ed.): *Refugees in West Bengal: Institutional Processes and Contested Identities*,

Kolkata, Mahanirban Calcutta Research Group, 2000, pp. 32-48.

Bandyopadhyay, Sekhar: 'Changing Borders, Shifting Loyalties: Religion, Caste and the Partition of Bengal in 1947', *Asian Studies Institute (1999).*

————: *Caste, Culture and Hegemony: Social Domination in Colonial Bengal*, New Delhi, Sage Publications, 2004.

————: *Caste, Protest and Identity in Colonial Bengal: The Namasudras of Bengal 1872-1947*, Surrey, Curzon Press, 1997.

Banerjee, Dilip: *Election Recorder*, Calcutta, Book Front Publication Forum, 1990.

Banerjee, Sudeshna: "Displacement within Displacement: The Crisis of Old Age in the Refugee Colonies of Calcutta", *Studies in History,* 19, 2, n.s. (2003).

Barman, Rup Kumar: Contested Ethnicity and Regional Assertion: A Study from Contemporary North Bengal, *Journal of History,* Vols. 22&23 (2004-05/2005-06), pp. 99-119.

————: Caste Identity Formation: Mobility and Elite Leadership, in B.K.Saha (ed): *Wealth and Welfare*, Kolkata, Academic Enterprise, 2005, pp.53-64.

————: Dalit Refugees or Refugee Dalits? Post-Partitioned Dalit Lives in Eastern India, in *Dalit Lives and Dalit Visions in Eastern India,* Kolkata, Centre for Rural Resources, 2007, pp. 112-119.

————: *From Tribalism to State: Reflections on the Emergence of the Koch Kingdom*, Delhi, Abhijeet Publications, 2007.

————: *Contested Regionalism: A New Look on History, Cultural Change and Regionalism of North Bengal and Lower Assam*, Delhi, Abhijeet Publications, 2007.

————: Caste and Class Awareness among the Fishermen of Bengal, *Voice of Dalit, Vol.1 No.1 (Jan-July), 2008,* 67-90.

————: *Fisheries and Fishermen: A Socio-economic History of Fisheries and Fishermen of Colonial Bengal and Postcolonial West Bengal*, Delhi, Abhijeet Publications, 2008.

————: Partition of Bengal And Struggle For Existence of The Scheduled Castes: Impact of The Partition (1947) On the Rajbanshis of North Bengal, *Voice of Dalit, Volume 2 Issue 2 (July-Dec 2009),* pp 141-163.

————: Caste Violence in India, *Voice of Dalit, Vol. 3, No 2 (July-December, 2010).*

Basu Ray Chaudhury, Anasua: Nostalgia of 'Desh', Memories of Partition", *Economic and Political Weekly* (December 25, 2004).

————: Politics of Rehabilitation: Struggle of the Scheduled Castes Refugees in West Bengal, in *Voice of Dalit (Vol. 3, No1 Jan-June) 2010.*

Basu Roy Chowdhury, Sabyasachi: Exiled to the Andamans: The Refugees from East Pakistan, in Pradip Kumar Bose(ed): *Refugees in West Bengal: Institutional Processes and Contested Identities*, Kolkata, Mahanirban Calcutta Research Group, 2000, pp.130-141.

Bharadwaj, Prasant, Khwaja, Asim and Mian, Atif: 'The Big March: Migratory Flows after the Petition of India' *EPW (August 30)2008*, pp.39-49.

Bhasin, Avtar Singh: *Some Called it Partition Some Freedom* Delhi, Siba Exim Pvt. Ltd, 1998.

Biswas, Swapan: *Colonization and Rehabilitations in Andaman and Nicobar Island*, Delhi, Abhijeet Publications, 2009.

Bose, Chhonda: Migration in the Andaman and Nicobar Islands during 1951-1991 from East Bengal: Trend and Flow, in Biswajit Chatterjee and Debi Chatterjee (eds): *Dalit Lives and Dalit Vision in Eastern India*, Kolkata , Centre for Rural Resource on behalf of the Centre for Ambedkar Studies of Jadavpur University, 2007, pp.94-106.

Bose, Pablo: Dilemmas of Diaspora: Partition, Refugees, and the Politics of "Home"', *Refugee*, Vol. 23, No.1, Issue *Dilemmas of Diaspora,* Internet edition.

Bose, Pradip Kumar (ed.): *Refugees in West Bengal: Institutional Processes and Contested Identities*, Kolkata, Mahanirban Calcutta Research Group, 2000.

Batabyal, Rakesh: *Communalism in Bengal: From Famine to Noakhali 1943-1947*, New Delhi, Sage Publications, 2005.

Butalia, Urvashi: Community, State and Gender: On women Agency during partition, *EPW*, (24th April, 1993).

————: *The Other Side of Silence: Voices from the Partition of India*, New Delhi, Penguin Books, 1998.

Chakraborti, Prafulla K.: *The Marginal Men: The Refugees and the Left Political Syndrome in West Bengal*, Kalyani, Lumiere Books, 1990.

Chakraborty, Dipesh: 'Remembered villages: Representations of Hindu-Bengali memories in the aftermath of the partition', South Asia: *Journal of South Asian Studies, 18:2,* 109-129; also published, in D.A. Low and Howard Brasted (eds): *Freedom, Trauma, Continuities: Northern India and Independence*, New Delhi, Sage, 1998.

Chakravartty, Gargi: *Coming Out of Partition: Refugee Women of Bengal*, New Delhi, Bluejay Books, 2005.

Chatterjee, Biswajit and Chatterjee, Debi (eds.): *Dalit Lives and Dalit Vision in Eastern India*, Kolkata, Centre for Rural Resource on behalf of the Centre for Ambedkar Studies of Jadavpur University, 2007.

Chatterjee, Debi: *Ideas and Movements in Caste in India: Ancient to Modern Times*, Delhi, Abhijeet Publications, 2010.

Chatterjee, Nilanjana: Midnight's Unwanted Children: East Bengali Refugees and the Politics of Rehabilitation. Unpublished Ph.D. dissertation, Brown University, 1992.

Chatterjee, Nilanjana: The East Bengal Refugees: A Lesson in Survival, in Sukanta Chaudhuri (ed.): *Calcutta: The Living City*, Calcutta, Oxford University, Press, 1994.

Chatterjee, Partha: *Bengal 1920-1947: The Land Question*, Calcutta, KP Bagchi and Company, 1984.

Chatterji, Joya: *Bengal Divided: Hindu communalism and partitions 1932-1947*, Cambridge University Press, 1994, First paperback Indian edition, New Delhi, Foundation Books, 1996.

————: "The Fashioning of a Frontier: The Radcliffe Line and the Bengal's Border Landscape, 1947-52", *Modern Asian Studies*, vol. 33, no. 1 (1999), pp. 185-242.

————: "Right or Charity? The Debate over Relief and Rehabilitation in West Bengal" in Suvir Kaul (ed): *The Partitions of Memories: The Afterlife of the Division of India*, Delhi, Permanent Black, 2001.

————: *The Spoils of Partition: Bengal and India 1947-1967*, Cambridge, Cambridge University Press, 2007.

Chatterji, Sunity Kumar: *Kirata Jana Kriti: The Indo-Mongoloids: Their Contribution to the History and Culture of India*, reprint edn. , Calcutta, The Asiatic Society, 1998.

————: *The Place of Assam in the History and Civilisation of India*, Gauhati, Gauhati University, 1970.

Chattopadhyay, Gautam: *Bengal Electoral Politics and Freedom Struggle 1862-1947,* Delhi, Indian Historical Studies, 1984.

Collins, L and Lapierre, D.: *Mountbatten and the Partition of India*, New Delhi, 1982.

Chaudhury, Pranati: *Refugees in West Bengal: A Study of the Growth and Distribution of Refugees Settlements within the CMD,* Occasional Paper 55, Calcutta, CSSS, 1983.

Das, Dhirendra Nath: *Regional Movement: Ethnicity and Politics*, Delhi, Abhijeet Publications, 2005.

Das, Manindra Nath: *Laws Relating to Partition* of *India*, 5th ed., Calcutta, Eastern Law House, 1999.

Das, M.N.: *Partition and Independence of India*, New Delhi, 1982.

Das, Samir: Refugee Crisis: Responses of the government of West Bengal, in Pradip Kumar Bose(ed.): *Refugees in West Bengal: Institutional Processes and Contested Identities*, Kolkata, Mahanirban Calcutta Research Group, 2000.

Das, Suranjan: *Communal Riots in Bengal, 1905-47,* Oxford University, South Asian Studies, 1991.

Das, Veena: *Critical Events: Moments in the Life of the Nation*, Delhi, Oxford University Press, 1994.

Dasgupta, Abhijit: The Politics of Agitation and Confession, Displaced Bengalis in West Bengal, in Ray, S.K.(ed.): *Refugee and Human Rights*, Jaipur, 2001.

Dasgupta, Saibal Kumar: *Dandakaranya: A Survey of Rehabilitation of Saibal Kumar Gupta*, edited by Alok Kumar Ghosh, Kolkata, Bibhasha, 1999.

Dasgupta, Subhendu, Making of a Refugee History: A Review, in Biswajit Chatterjee and Debi Chatterjee (eds), *Dalit Lives and Dalit Visions in Eastern India*, Kolkata, Centre for Rural Resources, 2007.

De, Soumitra: *Nationalism and Separatism in Bengal: A Study of India's Partition*, New Delhi, Vikas and Har Anand Publications, 1992.

Deb, Arun Deb: The UCRC: Its role in establishing the Rights of Refugee Squatters in Calcutta, in Pradip Kumar Bose(ed): *Refugees in West Bengal: Institutional Processes and Contested Identities*, Kolkata, Mahanirban Calcutta Research Group, 2000, pp.65-79.

Durani, F.K.: *The Meaning of Pakistan*, Lahore, Muhammad Asraf, 1944.

Datta, P.S.: Movement for Scheduled Status in a Poly-ethnic Society: The Case of the Koch-Rajbongshis of Assam, *Journal of North East India Council for Social Science Research II.11 (1978).*

Dirks, Nicholas B.: *Castes of Mind: Colonialism and the Making of Modern India*, Delhi, Permanent Black, 2001.

Donald L. Horowitz: *Ethnic Groups in Conflict*, Berkeley, University of California Press, 1985.

————————:*A Democratic South Africa? Constitutional Engineering in a Divided Society,* California University Press, 1991.

————————:*The Deadly Ethnic Riot,* California University Press, 2001.

Dutta, N.K.: *Origin and Growth of Caste in India (combined volume)*, Calcutta, Firma KLM Mukhopadhyay, Pvt. Ltd., 1969.

Elahi, K. Maudood: Refugees in Dandakaranya, *International*

Migration Review, Vol. 15, No. 1/2, *Refugees Today (Spring - Summer, 1981*), pp. 219-225.

Evera, Stephen Van: *Causes of War: Power and the Roots of Conflict*, Cornell, 1999.

Evera Stephen William Van (ed): *Nuclear Diplomacy and Crisis Management*, 1990.

————: *Soviet Military Policy*, 1989.

————: *The Star Wars Controversy*, 1986.

————: "Offense, Defense, and the Causes of War," *International Security,* Vol. 22, No. 4 (Spring 1998), pp. 5-43.

Fazila, Vazira and Zamindar, Yacoobali: *The Long Partition and the Making of Modern South Asia*, Columbia University Press, 2007.

Ferris, E.G. (ed): *Refugees and World Politics*, New York, Preager, 1985.

Gangopadhyay Bolan: Reintegrating the Displaced, Refracturing The Domestic: A Report on the experience of Uday Villa, in Pradip Kumar Bose(ed): *Refugees in West Bengal: Institutional Processes and Contested Identities*, Kolkata, Mahanirban Calcutta Research Group, 2000, pp.99-107.

Gilmartin, David: 'Partition, Pakistan, and South Asian History: In Search of a Narrative', *The Journal of Asian Studies, 57, 4. (November 1998),* 1068-1095.

Ghosh, Alok Kumar: Bengali Refugees at Dandakaranya: A Tragedy of Rehabilitation, Pradip Kumar Bose(ed): *Refugees in West Bengal: Institutional Processes and Contested Identities*, Kolkata, Mahanirban Calcutta Research Group, 2000, pp. 106-129.

————: The East Bengal Refugees: From Crisis to Identity, in Biswajit Chatterjee and Debi Chatterjee (eds.): *Dalit Lives and Dalit Vision in Eastern India*, Kolkata, Centre for Rural Resource on behalf of the Centre for Ambedkar Studies of Jadavpur University, 2007.

Ghosh, Alok Kumar Ghosh (ed.): *Dandakaranya: A Survey of Rehabilitation: Essays of Sri Saibal Kumar Gupta,* Calcutta, Bibhasha, 1999.

Ghosh, Papiya: *Muhajirs and the Nation: Bihar in the 1940s*, New Delhi, Routledge, 2010.

Ghosh, Papiya: *Partition and the South Asian Diaspora: Extending the Subcontinent*, New Delhi, Routledge, 2007.

————: Partition and South Asian Diaspora, in Omprakash Misra (ed): *Forced Migration in the South Asian Region: Displacement , Human Rights & Conflict Resolution*, New Delhi , Centre for Refugee Studies of Jadavpur University in Collaboration with Brookings Institution –SAIS Project Internal Displacement and Manak Publications Pvt. Ltd, 2004, pp.111-142.

Ghosh, D.K.and Ghosh, Sukla: *Legends of Origin of the Castes and Tribes of Eastern India,* Calcutta, Firm KLM, Pvt. Ltd., 2000.

Ghosh, Suniti Kumar: *The Tragic Partition of Bengal*, Allahabad, Indian Academy of Social Sciences, 2002.

Gupta, Amit Kumar (ed): *Myth and Reality: The Struggle for Freedom in India,* New Delhi, Monohar, 1987.

Gupta, P.S.: *Towards Freedom: Documents on the Movement for Independence in India, 1942-1944,* Delhi, Oxford University Press, 1997.

Halder, Dilip Kumar: Dalits are the worse victims of Partition: A Human Rights Question, in Biswajit Chatterjee and Debi Chatterjee: *Dalits Lives and Dalit Visions in Eastern India*, Kolkata, Center for Rural Resources, 2007.

————: *Atrocities on the Dalits Since the Partition of Bengal*, Delhi, Mittal, 2009.

Hasan, Mushirul: *India's Partition: Process, Strategy, and Mobilization*, Delhi, Oxford University Press, 1993.

————: *India Partitioned: The other face of freedom*, Delhi, New Lotus Collection, 1995.

Hutchins, F.G.: *India's Revolution, Gandhi and the Quit India Movement*, Cambridge M.A., Harvard University Press, 1973.

Jaffrelot, Christophe: *India's Silent Revolution: Rise of the Low Castes in North India Politics,* Delhi, Permanent Black, 2003.

Jalal, Ayesha: *The Sole spokesmen: Jinnah, The Muslim League and the Demand for Pakistan*, Cambridge University Press, 1985.

Kabir, Humayun: *Muslim Politics 1906-1942 and other essays*, Calcutta, Firma K.L. Mukhopadhyay, 1969.

Karma, A.J.: *The Prolonged Partition and Its Pogroms: Testimonies on Violence against Hindus in East Bengal 1946-64*, New Delhi, Voice of India, 2000.

Kaufmann, Chaim: Possible and Impossible Solutions to Ethnic Civil Wars, *International Security* 20:4 *(Spring 1996)*, 136-75.

————: Why Iraq Partitioned Itself, *Columbia International Affairs Online*, (September 2007).

————: An Assessment of the Partition of Cyprus, *International Studies Perspectives* 8:2 (May), 206-223.

————: "What Have We Learned About Ethnic Conflict? What Can We Do In Iraq?",*Harvard International Review* 28:4 (Winter), 44-50.

————: "Living Together after Ethnic Killing: in Theory, in History, and in Iraq Today," in Mia Bloom and Roy Licklider, eds., *Living Together after Ethnic Killing: Exploring the Chaim Kaufmann Argument* (Taylor and Francis, 2007).

————:"When All Else Fails: Ethnic Partitions and Population Transfers in the Twentieth Century," *International Security* 23:2 (Fall 1998.), 120-156.

Khan, Yasmin: *The Great Partition: the Making of India and Pakistan*, New Haven and London, Yale University Press, 2007.

Kishore, J. and Ray, P.C.: *The Pioneering Social Reformers of India*, New Delhi, Wisdom Publications, 2001.

Kudaisya, Ganesh: "Divided Landscapes, Fragmented Identities: East Bengal Refugees and their Rehabilitation in India 1947-79", in *Singapore Journal of Tropical Geography, Vol.17, No 1(1996)*, 24-49.

Kumar, Radha: The Troubled History of Partition, *Foreign Affairs v. 76 (Jan./Feb. 1997)*.

————: *The Troubled History of Partition*, in Prasenjit Duara (ed.), *Decolonization: Perspective from Now and Then*, New

York, Rutledge, 2004, pp. 162-170.

————: "Settling Partition Conflicts: Key Elements, Key Actors", in Michel Seymour (ed.), *The Future of the Nation State,* McGill-Queen's University Press, 2004.

————: "Ethnic Partitions and Peace Processes: Lessons Learnt, the Options Ahead" in Ghislaine Glasson Deschaumes and Rada Ivekovic (eds.), *Divided Countries, Separated Cities,* Oxford University Press India, 2003.

————: The Partition Debate: Colonialism Revisited or New Policies?, *The Brown Journal of International Affairs,* Winter/ Spring 2000.

Mahajan, Sucheta: *Independence and Partition: The Erosion of Colonial Power in India,* New Delhi, Sage, 2000.

Mallik, Hafiz: *Moslem Nationalism in India and Pakistan*, Washing DC, Public Affair Press, 1963.

Mallick, Ross: Refugee Resettlement in Forest Reserves: West Bengal Policy Reversal and the Marichjhapi Massacre, *The Journal of Asian Studies, Vol. 58, No. 1 (Feb., 1999),* pp. 104-125.

Martin, Montgomery: *The History, Antiquities, Topography and Statistics of Eastern India, 5 Vols. (1838),* reprint edn., Delhi, Cosmo Publications, 1976.

Mearsheimer, John: Shrink Bosnia to Save It," *New York Times*, March 31, 1993.

————: The Impossible Partition," *New York Times*, January 11, 2001.

Mearsheimer, John and Pape, Robert A. Pape: "The Answer: A Three-Way Partition Plan for Bosnia And How the U.S. Can Enforce It", *The New Republic*, June 14, 1993, pp. 22-28.

Mearsheimer, John J. and Evera, Stephen Van: When peace means War, *The New Republic,* December 18, 1995.

Mehata, Asoka and Patwardhan, Achhut: *The Communal Triangle in India*, Allahabad, Kitabstan, 1942.

Meherotra, S.R.: *Towards India's Freedom and Partition*, New Delhi, Vikas Publishing House Pvt. Ltd., 1979.

Menon, Ritu and Bhasin, Kamala: Recovery, Rapture, Resistance: Indian State and Abduction of Women during partition, *(EPW 24th April 1993).*

Menon, Ritu and Bhasin Kamala: *Borders and Boundaries: Women in India's Partition,* New Delhi, Kali for Women, 1998.

Misra, Omprakash (ed): *Forced Migration in the South Asian Regions: Displacement, Human Rights and Conflict Resolution,* New Delhi, Manak Publications Pvt. Ltd, 2004.

Misra, O.P. and Majumdar A.J. (eds.): *The Elsewhere People: Cross-border Migration, Refugee Protection and State Response,* New Delhi, Lancer's Books, 2003.

Moore, R.J.: *The Crisis of Indian Unity 1917-1940,* Oxford, 1974.

————: *Churchill, Cripps and India 1939-1945*, Oxford, Clarendon Press, 1979.

————: *Escape from Empire: The Attlee Government and the Indian Problem*, Oxford, Clarendon, 1983.

Mukherjee, Samar: Rehabilitation of the Bengali Refugees in S.K. Roy (ed.): *Refugees and Human Rights*, Jaipur, 2001.

Mukhopadhyay, Kali Prasad: *Partition, Bengal and After: the Great Tragedy of India*, New Delhi, Reference Press, 2007.

Qureshi, Ishtiaq Hussain: *The Muslim Community of Indo-Pakistan Subcontinent 610-1947,* Karachi, Ma'aref, 1977.

Pakrasi, Kant B.: *The Uprooted: a Sociological Study of the Refugees of West Bengal, India*, Calcutta, Editions Indians, 1971.

Palit, Chittabrata and Roy, Ujjal: *Bengal before and after the Partition (1947): The Changing Profile of a Province,* Kolkata, Corpus Research Institute, 2004.

Pandey, Gyanendra: The Prose of Otherness, in D. Arnold and D. Hardiman (eds.): *Subaltern Studies, vol. 4*, Delhi, OUP, 1994, pp. 188-221.

————: Memories of Partition, *Seminar, vol. 420,* August 1994.

————: *Remembering Partition, Violence, Nationalism and History in India*, Cambridge University Press, 2001.

————: India and Pakistan, 1947-2002', *Economic and Political Weekly*, March 16(2002).

————: Can a Muslim Be an Indian?' *Comparative Study of Society and History*, (2000)608-629.

Patil, V.T. and Trivedi, R.: *Refugee and Human Rights*, New Delhi, 2000.

Potter, D. C.: Manpower shortage and the end of colonialism: The Case of Indian Civil Service *(Modern Asian Studies 7(1973)* .pp.47-73.

Prasad, Rajendra: *India Divided*, 3rd edition, Bombay, Hind Kitab Ltd, 1947.

Rahman, S.: *Why Pakistan*, Lahore, Islamic Book Service, 1946.

Rizvi, Gowher: *Linlithgow and India: A study of British policy and the political impasse in India 1936-43* , London, Royal Historical Society, 1978.

Sinha, Dipankar: Adjustment and Transition in a Bengali Refugee Settlement: 1950-1999, in Pradip Kumar Bose(ed.): *Refugees in West Bengal: Institutional Processes and Contested Identities*, Kolkata, Mahanirban Calcutta Research Group, 2000, pp. 142-161.

Ray, Manas: Growing up refugee: On memory and locality, in Pradip Kumar Bose(ed.): *Refugees in West Bengal: Institutional Processes and Contested Identities,* Kolkata, Mahanirban Calcutta Research Group, 2000, pp.162-199.

Roy S.K. (ed.): *Refugee and Human Rights*, Jaipur, Rawat, 2001.

Samaddar, Ranabir Samaddar (ed.): *Partition Experience of the East: the Second Partition of Bengal*, Calcutta, Research Group and New Delhi, Vikas Publication House, 1997.

Samaddar, Ranabir: *Marginal Nation: Trans-border Migration from Bangladesh to West Bengal,* New Delhi, Thousand Oaks, London, Sage, 1999.

Sambans, Nicholas: Partition as a Solution to Ethnic War: An Empirical Critique of the Theoretical Literature, *World Politics 52 (July 2000)*, 437–83.

Sanyal, Annapurna: *Scheduled Caste and Scheduled Tribes in Indian Politics,* Calcutta, Minerva, 1991.

Sanyal, Charu Chandra: *The Rajbanshis of North Bengal*, Calcutta, The Asiatic Society, 1965.

Sanyal, Hites Ranjan: *Social Mobility in Bengal,* Calcutta, Papyrus, 1981.

Sayeed, Khalid Bin: *Pakistan: The Formative Phase 1857 – 1948*, Oxford University, 1968.

Sen, Asok and Banerjee, Alok: Calcutta Metropolitan District in the Urban Context of West Bengal (1951-81), Occasional Paper 60, Calcutta, CSSS, 1983.

Sen, P.K.: *Land and People of the Andaman*, Calcutta, The Post-Graduate Book Mart, 1955.

Sen, Sarbani: The legal regime for refugee relief and rehabilitation in West Bengal 1946-58, in Pradip Kumar Bose(ed): *Refugees in West Bengal: Institutional Processes and Contested Identities*, Kolkata, Mahanirban Calcutta Research Group, 2000. pp.49-64.

Sherwani, Latif Ahmed: *The Partition of India and Mountbatten*, Karachi, Council for Pakistan Studies, 1986.

Simon Epstein: District Officers in Decline: The Erosion of British Authority in the Bombay Country side *Modern Asian Studies 16(1982),* pp. 493-518.

Sinha, Dipankar: Foundation of Refugee Market: A Study in Self Reliance initiative, in Pradip Kumar Bose(ed):*Refugees in West Bengal: Institutional Processes and Contested Identities*, Kolkata, Mahanirban Calcutta Research Group, 2000, pp.80-97.

Sinha Ray, Kalyan: *Hari Buddha and the Namasudra Movement in Bengal*, in Biswajit Chatterjee and Debi Chatterjee (eds.): *Dalit Lives and Dalit Visions in Eastern India*, Kolkata, Centre for Rural Resources, 2007.

Sinha, Surajit: *Resettlement of the East Pakistan Refugees in Andaman Islands, Report on Survey of further possibility of Resettlement 1952,* Calcutta, West Bengal Government Press, 1955.

Singh, Anita Inder: *The Origins of the Partition of India 1936-1947*, Delhi, Oxford University Press, 1987.

Singh, Ekta: *Caste System in India: A Historical Perspective*, Delhi, Kalpaz Publications, 2005.

Singh, K.S.: *The Scheduled Castes*, revised edn. Calcutta, Oxford University Press and Anthropological Survey of India, 1999.

Talbot, Ian and Singh, Gurhapal: *The Partition of India*, New Delhi, Cambridge University Press, 2009.

Vasu, N.N.: *Social History of Kamarupa (3vols)*, reprint ed., New Delhi, Northern Book Center, 1972.

Venkateswar, D.: Ecological consequences of rehabilitation programmes in Andaman, in V. Sudarsan(ed.): *The Uprooted*, New Delhi, Gyan Publishing House, 1990.

Wise, James: *Notes on the Races, Castes, and Trades of Eastern Bengal*, Not Published, London, Harrison and Sons, 1883.

Yagati, Chinna Rao: *Dalit Studies: A Bibliographical Handbook*, New Delhi, Kanishka Publishers, Distributors, 2003.

Government Reports

Choudhuri, Harendra Narayan: *The Cooch Behar State and its Land Revenue Settlements,* Cooch Behar, The Cooch Behar State Press, 1903.

Government of West Bengal: *Report on the Sample Survey for Estimating the Socio-Economic Characteristics of displaces prisons migrating from Eastern Pakistan to the State of West Bengal*, Calcutta, State Statistical Bureau, 1951.

————: *Short Note on Scheduled Castes of West Bengal,* Kolkata, Cultural Research Institute, Backward Classes Welfare Department, 2005.

————: *Hataman Jara Tulechhe Shir*, Calcutta, Dept. of SC and ST Welfare, 1987.

————: *Rehabilitation of Refugees: A Statistical Survey 1955*, Calcutta, State Statistical Bureau, 1955.

Guha, B.S.(ed.): *Studies in Social Tension among the Refugees from East Pakistan*, Delhi, Department of Anthropology, Government of India, 1959.

Hunter, W.W.: *Statistical Account of Bengal, 20 vols.*, reprint edn., New Delhi, D.K. Publishing House, 1974.

Malik, Shahdeen: *Overview of Refugees, Stateless Persons and Internally Displaced Persons in Bangladesh*, in Regional Consultation on Refugee and Migratory Movements in South Asia, New Delhi, 12-14 November, 1996.

Mitra, A.K.: *The Tribes and Castes of West Bengal*, Alipore, West Bengal Government Press, 1953.

Sunder, D.: *Survey and Settlement of the Western Duars in the District of Jalpaiguri 1889-95*, Calcutta, Bengal Secretariat Press, 1895.

Newspaper/Periodicals/Magazines/Souvenirs

Anandabazar Patrika.

Bhagirathi

Constitution of the Paschim Banga Matsyajibi Samity, Calcutta, 1969

Frontier, January 10, 1981, Vol. 13, no, 20,

Paribartan (7-13 May 1980)

Souvenir of the GCBPA, published by the Block Committee of the GCBPA, dated 21.11.2004.

The Statesman.

Minutes/Proceedings/Memorandums/Letters

Annual Report of the Bangiya Rajbanshi Kshatriya Samity, 1986

Copy of Resolutions passed in the First Annual Conference of the Siliguri Anchalik (zonal) Kshatriya Samity in its First Annual Conference held at Haidarpara, Dist. Jalpaiguri.

Letter of Sri Prasenjit Barman, M.P. (Rajjya Sabha) dated 15th April 1980 to the Prime Minister of India.

Letter of the Secretary of the Bharatiya Tapashili Parishad to Prasenjit Barman, M.P. dated 28.06.80. No 491, /1(4)/ ICSC/80.

Letter of the Secretary Bangiya Rajbanshi Kshatriya Samity, to the Chief Minister of West Bengal, dated 16.08.80.

Letter of the Secretary GCBPA dated 25.09.2002 to the District Magistrate, Cooch Behar.

Memorandum dated 11.08.1980 submitted by Prabhat Sen Eshor, Secretary, UTJAS, to the Prime Minister of India.

Memorandum, submitted by Panchanan Mallik to the Prime Minister of India dated 24th August, 1980.

Memorandum submitted by the GCBPA to the Home Minister of India, dated 6th December, .2000.

Memorandum submitted by the GCBPA to the President of India, dated 5.04.2001.

Maynaguri Declaration of the Bharatiya Kamata Rajya Parishad, *Circular No.KRP/ dated 8th August 1986.*

Minute of Proceedings of the BKRKM held at Halakura, Dhubri on 16-17 February, 1984.

Webliography

http://www.banglapedia.org/httpdocs/HT/U_0020.HTM.

http://www.hreoc.gov.au/human_rights/immigration/asylum_seekers.html. Date of access 6th November, 2009.

Index

B